Song, Struggle, and Solidarity

Song, Struggle, and Solidarity

The New York City Labor Chorus in Its Twenty-fifth Year

Mark Abendroth

HAMILTON BOOKS
Lanham • Boulder • New York • London

Published by Hamilton Books
An imprint of The Rowman & Littlefield Publishing Group, Inc.
4501 Forbes Boulevard, Suite 200, Lanham, Maryland 20706
www.rowman.com

6 Tinworth Street, London SE11 5AL, United Kingdom

Copyright © 2020 The Rowman & Littlefield Publishing Group, Inc.

All rights reserved. No part of this book may be reproduced in any form or by any electronic or mechanical means, including information storage and retrieval systems, without written permission from the publisher, except by a reviewer who may quote passages in a review.

British Library Cataloguing in Publication Information Available

Library of Congress Cataloging-in-Publication Data

ISBN 978-0-7618-7184-2 (pbk)
ISBN 978-0-7618-7185-9 (electronic)

To members and leaders of the
New York City Labor Chorus—past, present, and future.
May you continue to sing your hearts out for generations to come.

Contents

Acknowledgments	ix
Introduction	1
1 A Brief History of Singing for Justice in the US Workplace	19
2 A History of the NYC Labor Chorus	41
3 Songs of the 25th-Anniversary Gala Concert	65
4 The 25th-Anniversary Year	85
5 Findings from Interviews	107
6 Final Discussion and Conclusions	131
Selected Bibliography	151
Index	157
About the Author	169

Acknowledgments

Many people helped me in developing and completing this book, and a brief mention is not enough for several. Family members, friends, and colleagues gave me helpful feedback and encouragement, and several members of the New York City Labor Chorus did the same in addition to volunteering their participation in an interview and in being named in my fieldnotes.

I must start with my parents, Sara and George. They have encouraged me from my youth onward to find my own path in life. Their loving guidance has nourished my curiosity and my joy of learning. My father read my chapter drafts, offering plenty of helpful feedback and then understanding when I explained what I could and could not consider changing. My mother decided to wait until the book is published, and I look forward to her response. I am forever grateful for their steadfast love. Also, I have been fortunate to have siblings, Paul Abendroth and Julie Weiss, in my life. They, too, have been wonderfully loving parents to their children.

Some friends helped in different ways. Chris Bystroff, a fellow tenor in the choir of the First Unitarian Universalist Society of Albany and fellow academic at another university, gave me valuable tips after reading the introduction. Chris also has brought his impressive musical talents, including composition, to the Justice Singers of the Capital Region, which I co-founded after leaving New York City for Albany. Close friends whom I have known a long time—Greg Brigham, Ken Kudrak, Brendan Obern, Loretta Koehler and her partner Steve Harvey—have continued to take interest in my general wellbeing and in my projects. Their caring support has helped to keep me going through some challenging times.

A few colleagues also have been truly supportive. Robert Darden and David Roediger, two researchers with giant contributions to the literature on music for social change, expressed enthusiasm for my project after reading chapter drafts. I also thank Brad Porfilio for his mentorship in our work a few years ago, when we co-edited a project with two volumes. Jelia Domingo, Dianne Ramdeholl, and Ajay Das, who are my colleagues at SUNY Empire State College (ESC) in New York City, have consistently encouraged and inspired me to keep advancing in my teaching and research while holding on to some measure of a work-life balance. I'm also grateful to ESC librarians for their patience with my interlibrary-loan requests and to librarians and staff at New York University's Tamiment Library and Robert F. Wagner Labor Archives for their help in locating documents and artifacts.

I thank Hamilton Books for believing in my project. Editors Holly Buchanan (now at Lexington Books) and Brooke Bures have been kind, patient, and very professional. I also thank Sam Brawand, an independent copy editor. Although I did not hire a copy editor in the end due to my limited budget, she suggested the title that I chose in the end.

It is hard to know where to start and end with the New York City Labor Chorus. I thank all who encouraged me in countless ways. The board of directors placed their trust in me to carry out the work successfully, and I hope that it meets their expectations. More chorus members than I imagined volunteered for the interview and for being named in my fieldnotes. Barbara Bailey and Jeff Vogel gave me documents and artifacts from their collections. Vogel also gave me detailed feedback on all my chapter drafts, and additional constructive criticism came from Terry Weissman, Bob Harris, and Rona Armillas. Brent Kramer helped me compile photos. Velma Hill encouraged me to attend the Great Labor Arts Exchange in 2016, and I hope to return many times. I thank director Jana Ballard, accompanist Dennis Nelson, and all members for making me want to become a better singer. It was truly an honor to sing with you all for six years!

I am grateful to all who gave me any combination of encouragement, suggestions, and indirect moral support. My work is better because of all these people, and any shortcoming is my responsibility.

I started with family and will end there. I thank my wife Liliana for being the love of my life and my best friend. I am blessed to have you in my life! Finally, I am grateful to my maternal grandmother, Lorna Froberg, for being the musician in the family and for planting in my heart a love of music. Although she died 21 years ago, I remember her fondly every time I pick up her old and beautiful mandolin and play.

Introduction

There is no simple way to explain in words how the arts enrich human lives. Every individual should have stories to tell of being moved by artistic expressions, and every human being has an innate need to produce creative expressions. The arts can bring comfort, or they can stir the tensions of conflict. Unfortunately, they can be and have been co-opted for use in propaganda for forces of oppression and dehumanization; however, they will continue to spring from creative and loving minds who work for social justice and human dignity. The arts can touch our souls and spirits in profound ways that nobody can articulate fully by mere words of prose. They can help us to transcend our preconceived notions of fact and fiction toward finding truths. They come from imagination, and they challenge and inspire humans to use further imagination in new ways with passion and discipline.

I began writing this introduction in late 2015 as an amateur musician with a career in higher education in the field of education. I had been a member of the New York City Labor Chorus (NYCLC) since 2011, the year my wife and I moved from the middle of Long Island to the northwest part of the Bronx. The weekly chorus rehearsals took place in downtown Manhattan, which was near my office at SUNY Empire State College's Metropolitan Center. I left the chorus once in order to try a community chorus closer to home in the Bronx, but after four months I returned to where I knew I belonged.

The NYCLC satisfied my enduring passions for music and activism. At age 13, I went to my first rock concert with a couple of friends. It was Queen in 1975 or 1976, and I was thirteen and thrilled by the feeling that I was somehow experiencing a powerful expression of subversive wisdom and beauty in the face of a suburban experience that was antiseptic and often joyless. It was not much later when I first heard John Lennon's iconic song "Imagine" on the radio with a careful listening to the lyrics.[1] I heard a friend denounce the song as communist, but, somehow, I put the label aside and listened closely. It was nearly ten years later when I first participated as an activist. I was a graduate student at a demonstration on Syracuse University's campus that urged the university to divest from funds benefitting South Africa's apartheid regime. There were speeches and chants, but I was especially moved when the crowd joined a young man with a guitar in singing "Imagine." My activism has taken me to different causes and movements since then, and I have remained fascinated by how social movements and music have fueled each other.

My life as a white heterosexual male with a middle-class and Protestant upbringing has been one of multiple privileges. In my professional and personal life I have been on a journey to overcome my unearned privileges and to be in solidarity with people who experience oppression and who struggle in resistance to demand the dignity that is theirs as humans. I became a high school teacher because I wanted to do something positive for young people after having worked as a paralegal in prison reform, and then I began to understand from reading Paulo Freire how education can be either oppressive or liberating, regardless of one's original intentions.[2] While teaching in an urban high school, I studied for a doctorate in education with a focus on critical pedagogy. While taking courses with a cohort of individuals with diverse backgrounds, I learned to move from political-economy essentialism to an integrated view of the unique spaces among and intersections between anti-racism, feminism, LGBTQ equity, and class struggle. Now, as an educational researcher, I work as someone who is a lifelong learner in becoming wiser and more trustworthy as an ally to people of color, women, the LGBTQ community, and the economically marginalized. I find hope in any movement that fights for freedom with values of participatory democracy, equity, and social justice. I find further hope in social movements when they incorporate the arts.

Music has had a vital role in countless social movements around the world. One cannot understand the power of the labor and civil rights movements in the US, as examples, without the songs that placed imaginative expressions indelibly into people's hearts and minds. The NYCLC exists to keep these songs alive in concert performances and at picket lines of striking workers. In addition to songs from the US labor and civil rights movements, the chorus performs songs of resistance against slavery, from South Africa's anti-apartheid movement, and from the Spanish Civil War, among other historic and current struggles. From more recent and current times the chorus has new songs and some new lyrics added to older songs in support of the Occupy Wall Street, Black Lives Matter, and climate justice movements. Some other songs performed by the chorus have no overt political message but rather a general idea that is uplifting to the human spirit.

This book has at its center an ethnographic study of the NYCLC in its 25th year. My central research question is this: "How does the labor chorus work toward fulfilling its stated purpose 'of bringing the message of workers' history and struggles for social and economic justice through song to people everywhere'?"[3] Volumes exist on music in social movements, and it is important to keep the history in view while navigating the present condition of the arts in social movements. My hope is that this work will provide a worthy contribution to the literature that addresses the powerful force of the arts in activism.

A CHORUS OF AND FOR WORKERS

The NYCLC came into existence in 1991, when unions were continuing to suffer declining enrollments in the aftermath of Reagan's 1981 firing of air-traffic controllers. Three women agreed to start the chorus project, and it has grown to approximately 75 dues-paying members who collectively represent more than 20 unions.[4] Its conductor and artistic director, Jana Ballard, is a music educator at LaGuardia High School, which is New York City's premier public school for the arts. The piano accompanist, Dennis Nelson, is organist and choir director for Trinity Baptist Church in Brooklyn, and he has many accomplishments both as a performer and as a songwriter in support of internationally acclaimed gospel and R&B artists. The leadership of the chorus is a member-elected board of directors, and one of the founding members of the chorus, Barbara Bailey, is president.

The chorus generally has one fundraising performance every other year in a venue with several hundred seats. This concert and other performances, some of which materialize with short notice, keep the chorus busy with weekly Monday-night rehearsals from September to May or June in a large room with a piano on the second floor of a tall building in downtown Manhattan. The entire floor is part of headquarters for the United Federation of Teachers, the union of teachers in the New York City Department of Education. Each two-hour rehearsal is an exercise in working to bring the group's best singing to the spirit and meaning behind the chosen songs.

The chorus membership has some diversity in age, sex, and ethnicity. Most are at or near retirement age, and the ratio of women to men is around three to one. A large majority of members are white, many of whom are of Jewish heritage, and there are about a dozen black members, some with Caribbean heritage. Photos of the chorus in its earliest years show a nearly even representation between black and white members.[5]

An article in the New York Times noted that the chorus would benefit from more voices in the lower ranges (tenors include both women and men) and from an increase in younger members.[6] Some auditions for new members have included announcements that more tenors and basses are in need. In order to appeal to a younger audience, the chorus has brought in some newer songs and new arrangements of older songs. For example, a 2013 recorded performance by the late Roswell Rudd of his jazz interpretation of the classic song *Joe Hill*[7] features several members of the chorus[8] and an original rap titled *The Relentless Walk* by hip-hop artist Reggie Bennett.[9]

I prepared for this ethnographic study of the NYCLC as an insider who had been a member for four years as of the first drafting of this introduction in the Fall of 2015. As an insider, I ran the risk of not seeing the chorus with the fresh and unaltered perspective that an outsider would bring to a study. Using theory to reflect on my findings-in-progress helped me to step back and stay focused on my outside role as researcher even while continuing to participate in the work of the chorus.

THEORETICAL FRAMEWORK

My theoretical conceptualization of this study stemmed from my experiences as an educator involved in theories and practices of education. This framework gave me a critical lens as I gained new perspectives while conducting data collection and analyses. It draws from critical pedagogy in adult education. Critical pedagogy is education for social justice through praxis, which is reflection and action informing each other.

Many educators who identify as researcher-practitioner-activist, as I would identify myself, point to Paulo Freire's *Pedagogy of the Oppressed* as a seminal work in the theory.[10] First published in Portuguese in 1968 and in English in 1970, its current edition during my writing was 2000 with a reprinting in 2007.[11] Freire's influences from socialism and from the liberation theology movement in Catholicism are clear in numerous citations in the book, and there are also citations of sources that come from studies of anti-colonialism and feminism. As a leader in literacy drives in Northeastern Brazil, Freire in this book asserted that education is never politically neutral and called on educators to work in solidarity with oppressed peoples in their struggles for freedom and justice. He urged educators to recognize how education can be either oppressive or emancipatory, offering a process of problem posing and critical dialog as an approach that starts with generative themes from the lived experiences and perspectives of the people living under oppression while moving all—instructor as well as students—toward critical consciousness (taken from the Portuguese word *concientizaçao*). Freire contrasted problem posing with what he called banking—the traditional form of education in which the instructor views students as empty vessels that passively receive deposits of knowledge. In his later career, Freire invited criticism and welcomed scholars in critical education to participate in re-inventing what had become known as Freirian pedagogy. In all his writings until his death in 1997, he continued to challenge and encourage educators to engage in a variety of social movements from within and beyond educational institutions.[12]

Perhaps the most well-known example of arts education based on Freirian principles is in the drama education work of Brazilian Agosto Boal, who developed the concept and methods for what he called "theater of the oppressed."[13] Boal's work invites actors and non-actors to participate in creating scenes that pose a problem and to re-enact the scenes with audience members interjecting to propose changes for the better. Participation in the re-enactment is open to all in the audience, and the result can be a collective view of a problem and of possibilities for solutions. I have used this method in my work with preservice secondary teachers, and it has been an effective way to involve all students in a creative and useful learning process.

A recent example of a Freirian project in music education is from Daniel Shevok, who conducted an auto-ethnographic study on his teaching of a course in jazz improvisation at Pennsylvania State University.[14] Shevok explained how much of music education exists in the banking tradition, and he set out to work with students through Freirian problem posing and critical dialog. He started the course with the hope of creating "a safe environment . . . where students would develop confidence to improvise, experiment, talk, grow musically, and be empowered to make judgments and express musical and verbal positions".[15] He took time to dialog with students individually in a conversational journal in order to learn their musical experiences and interests. Shevok refrained from judging students' mistakes early in the course, and he involved them in some of the curriculum planning. As the semester went on, he released more control of song selection to the students. Class conversations served to foster leadership in each student. As Shevok grew in his understanding of Freirian pedagogy even while implementing it, he made the connection between the student-centered process and the political outcome—the latter being an emerging critical consciousness that moves students and the teacher toward deliberate political action. Shevok explained how his students had been oppressed not only by banking processes of music education but also by a general education of banking that disempowers and dehumanizes students. As the group of students developed trust in a learning community, they learned how to engage in peer assessment without being judgmental. They shared their musical goals with each other, shared improvisational ideas, and eventually created compositions based on themes from their own lived experiences, including feelings of loneliness and alienation in a dominant culture of individualism. Such a humanizing education, as Shevok concluded, is necessary for students to learn that they can express their desires for a better world and can create a space for imagining the possibilities for it.

Critical pedagogy is a concept that emerged from a long history of educational fronts in social movements. The arts, including music, have been involved in countless mobilizations for social justice and equity. Juanita Karpf wrote of an important historic example of a leader in building communities around music and activism in an article about Emma Azalia Hackley, an African American woman who left her career as a musician in the early 20th century to travel across the US and organize community choruses[16]. Amidst a growing community-music movement that limited participation by people of color through *de jure* and *de facto* segregation, Hackley taught what became known as voice culture to many thousands of African Americans of all ages and varying musical abilities across the country. The community choruses that resulted from her efforts performed sometimes with audiences in the thousands, and audience participation was often a part of the performance when there was a familiar spiritual or folk song. In 1919, three years before her death, Hackley helped to form the National Association of Negro Musicians. Along with other African American leaders in music education, Hackley played an important role in cultivating the power of music for social activism.

Lee Higgins noted Hackley's example among many others in his work on the theory and practice of community music.[17] In exploring a history of the concept of cultural democracy, Higgins portrayed a tension between two views. One is that music is art only when it is composed and performed masterfully by professionals; the other is that music, as an art form, is meant to have broad participation from ordinary people. The latter comes from a belief that people need to be participants in the arts and not only consumers of the arts, and that culture is something the people have without receiving it from a group of experts. In addition to citing Freire's influence on community music, Higgins noted how Derrida's concept of deconstruction played a role in democratizing music and the arts. Derrida claimed that deconstruction fit within a continuous process of intervention in which an individual or group constructs, deconstructs, and reconstructs knowledge.[18]

Because the NYCLC is a labor chorus, this study necessarily addresses theories of political economy. Many of the lyrics sung by the chorus have the themes of a Marxist critique of capitalism: alienation, commodity fetishism, hegemony, and class consciousness. Marx's central premise on capitalism is that it extracts surplus value from the labor of the working class, or *proletariat*, in order to enrich the capitalist class, or *bourgeoisie*.[19] Alienation is what workers experience when they do not own the means of production. They sell their labor to a business owner, who determines working conditions and wages under the guise of supply and demand for labor. Many workers are further alienated when their wages do not allow them to purchase the very things that they make. Commodity fetishism is the view that all goods and services are a part of the market. Workers, themselves, become commodities, and, if they organize to demand higher pay or better work conditions, the corporation can move their jobs to another region or country where people are desperate for any kind of job. Hegemony, a concept developed by Italian Neo-Marxist dissident Antonio Gramsci, who wrote from prison in the 1920s and 30s, is the process by which the oppressed give consent to the social relations in which they live.[20] Those with capital and power offer just enough rewards and incentives to keep the masses from revolting, and, if the masses do revolt, there is a military/police apparatus ready to punish them. Finally, class consciousness is what workers gain when they begin to comprehend how capitalism works to enrich the few at the expense of the many. Many of the lyrics sung by the chorus have class consciousness as a central theme, but these other themes from Marxism are present as well.

It is likely that many and perhaps most NYCLC members would not self-identify as Marxist or anarchist. The labor movement all along, though, has been a coalition of liberals, anarchists, and Marxists, and not everyone identifies with only one of these labels. In the contemporary world, there is a broad resistance movement against neoliberalism. The movement of economic liberalism in the late 19th century allowed capitalism to break free from the power of monarchs, aristocrats, and churches; the neoliberalism that dates back to the 1970s is a global movement to fortify private corporations through government policies of deregulation, privatization, and reduced public social services. Occupy Wall Street was an outpouring of activists of many ideological stripes against the neoliberal response to the 2008 recession that neoliberalism caused, but it was a group of anarchist activists that conceptualized the movement in its beginnings.

Anarchism in leftist traditions draws from many theories. Peter Kropotkin's mutual aid upholds solidarity and cooperation as central conditions of dignified humanity while dispelling the assumption that competition and domination are inevitable and desirable parts of human nature.[21] Michael Bakunin critiqued the alliances between religion and state while envisioning an alternative society based on a religion-free ethos of liberty and equality.[22] Emma Goldman's feminist anarchism has helped to empower women by addressing the intersections of gender, sexuality, and political economy.[23] Anarcho-syndicalism, as explained in depth by Rudolf Rocker after the Spanish Civil War, focuses on class struggle toward a decentralized society in which workers engage in direct democracy without hierarchy.[24] These are just some of the branches of anarchism, and anarcho-syndicalism is the one with a direct connection to the labor movement.

Critical theory, born in the 1920s from intellectuals of the Frankfurt School interested in both social psychology and political economy, examines the unique and separate spaces that race, gender, and class (among additional signifiers of difference) occupy. It also examines the intersections between these three. While the songs of the NYCLC generally focus on class, there are also many with themes of anti-racism and feminism. The membership of the chorus is another matter that brings a challenge. As noted above, there are disproportionately high representations of white and female members. Why are there so few people of color in the chorus when New York City is such a racially diverse place? Why are there so few men? These are questions that the chorus will need to explore in its efforts to recruit and retain more people of color and more men, being mindful of intersections and border crossings between race, gender, and class.

The NYCLC is an organization of adult education with a practice that comes from critical theory and from centuries of song expressing the human need for dignity. The power and beauty of the music come from all the elements of history that must include the music of resistance from African Americans before and after emancipation from slavery, from Native Americans singing around the heartbeat of a sacred drum, from women marching for the right to vote, from international freedom fighters joining forces in Spain to battle against fascism, and more.

METHODOLOGY

Because I am a researcher working with the method of ethnography for the first time, I have found the need to study in detail what this work involves. Ethnography is concerned with the culture of a group of people. The NYCLC has developed a culture of its own in its more than two dozen years of rehearsals and performances, and the purpose of my study is to uncover many roots, the trunk, and branches of this culture. Several questions emerged as I prepared for the study. What brought people together to form this group in 1991? What has kept the chorus growing and going over the years? What are the codes of conduct? How does the chorus select leaders, and how do the leaders lead? How can all members participate in decision making? How does the chorus raise and spend its funds? How diverse has the chorus been in terms of race, ethnicity, sex, gender identity, sexual orientation, age, abilities and even/especially class? How diverse has it been in terms of ideology, political affiliation, and activist experience? How diverse has it been in terms of musical talents, preferences, and experiences? What tensions have arisen, and how has the chorus worked through them? Do chorus members all agree on the organization's stated purpose? How do members view the level of effectiveness in the chorus's work toward its purpose? How do non-chorus union members view the chorus's level of effectiveness? These questions and more were in my mind as I anticipated the work of conducting the study.

As a researcher with an interest in critical pedagogy, I crafted this study into a critical ethnography. I worked to find emancipatory themes not only in political economy but also in critical race theory, feminism, and queer theory. Critical race theory provides a narrative for understanding systemic racism and for advancing the struggle for racial justice. Feminism confronts patriarchy while working for the emancipation of women. Queer theory exposes homophobia and heteronormativity while supporting struggles of the LGBTQ community for equity and social justice. Among race, gender, and class, each can stand alone as a social construct with a long history of oppression. The social movements behind each can be blind to the others, or they can build bridges to overcome the divide-and-conquer strategies of powerful conservatives. The NYCLC still exists because classism and class struggle are realities still in the neoliberal 21st century; therefore, my project by necessity was a critical ethnography. Furthermore, while conducting this research, I could not detach myself from my own world view with affinities toward democratic socialism, feminism, queer theory, and anti-racism. This, therefore, also became a work of autoethnography.

What is critical ethnography? Jim Thomas, in his seminal book titled *Doing Critical Ethnography*, offered this definition:

> Critical ethnography is a type of reflection that examines culture, knowledge, and action. It expands our horizons for choice and widens our experiential capacity to see, hear, and feel. It deepens and sharpens ethical commitments by forcing us to develop and act upon value commitments in the context of political agendas. Critical ethnographers describe, analyze, and open to scrutiny otherwise hidden agendas, power centers, and assumptions that inhibit, repress, and constrain. Critical scholarship requires that commonsense assumptions be questioned.[25]

This definition ties the critical researcher to a social responsibility of valuing human rights while confronting power relations that are oppressive. This was not a simple task in 1993 when Thomas wrote this; nor is it now. Researchers with careers in higher education have to find their way to tenure and grants, and the thought of being perceived as too radical can generate fear and self-censorship; therefore, a key word in Thomas's definition is *commitment*.

What is autoethnography? Co-authors Tony E. Adams, Carolyn Ellis, and Stacy Holman Jones wrote, "Autoethnographic stories are the artistic and analytic demonstrations of how we come to know, name, and interpret personal and cultural experience."[26] They recognized four ideals to inform the work of autoethnography: 1) acknowledging limits of scientific knowledge in explaining personal and cultural matters, 2) connecting personal experience to larger contexts, 3) committing to storytelling with a balance between intellect and aesthetics, and 4) addressing ethical issues with regard to oneself, participants, and readers.[27] Using these as guidelines, I have tried to weave self-disclosures into my work in ways that reveal how my experiences, understandings, interpretations, and cautions have factored into my process and product.

Ethics

Conducting critical ethnography, autoethnography or any ethnography involves serious attention to ethical standards. D. Soyini Madison illustrated the ethical stakes in ethnographic study with an example of a seemingly noble documentary film about one young woman in Ghana who escaped genital mutilation by fleeing to the US.[28] Madison, who had lived and had conducted research in the rural region in Ghana featured in the film, questioned the filmmaker about her complete overlooking of the undeniable grassroots efforts there to defend women's and indigenous rights. This film, with all good intentions behind it, in Madison's critical view became one more of many sources that depict an African culture as backward and as lacking an organic movement to save itself. Madison went on to raise five questions that apply to ethics in ethnographic study as follows in direct quote:

1. How do we reflect upon and evaluate our own purpose, intentions, and frames of analysis as researchers?
2. How do we predict consequences or evaluate our own potential to do harm?
3. How do we create and maintain a dialog of collaboration in our research projects between ourselves and Others?
4. How is the specificity of the local story relevant to the broader meanings and operations of the human condition?
5. How—in what location or through what intervention—will our work make the greatest contribution to equity, freedom, and justice?[29]

Each of these questions is critically important, and the fifth sets critical ethnography apart from conventional ethnography. Since I have proclaimed that my project is one of critical ethnography, I have an ethical obligation to deliver work that has intention toward social justice.

Regarding Madison's first question above, I gave plenty of thought to my purpose, intentions, and scope of analysis.[30] My purpose was to present multiple findings on how the NYCLC works toward its mission to bring the music of workers' struggles to the public. I set out to report all relevant findings without letting my own biases interfere. My scope of analysis was a lens that focused on agency for social change, and I strived to be attentive to all perspectives among chorus members regarding the means toward that end.

Madison's second question is one that I discussed with the chorus's board of directors before gaining their permission to conduct the study.[31] I acknowledged how I had the potential to do harm to the chorus. Misrepresenting a testimony could exacerbate misunderstandings and mistrust that already exist. Neglecting to report a significant finding could contribute to an incomplete or distorted view of the chorus. If I promise confidentiality to a participant and then reveal the person's identity in some direct or indirect way, then I have breached trust and have left the person vulnerable to retaliation from other chorus members or possibly even from an employer. If a participant were to request a withdrawal from the study only to be pressured to continue, then I would have violated the need for voluntary participation. The final guideline is that I need to respect and honor every participant regarding privacy and truthful reporting of findings from all relevant data.

Madison's third question goes to the heart of effective qualitative research.[32] A dialog of collaboration could only result when I, as researcher, had gained the trust of prospective participants. In my four-plus years as a member of the NYCLC upon my announcement to the board of my proposed study, I had established a decent level of rapport with many of my fellow members, especially in the tenor section. Still, I needed to be mindful that it would be all too easy to fall into the trap of becoming the academic colonizer who views human subjects simply as data providers. I had become part of the NYCLC culture and, dare I say, "family," so I needed to be myself with the group. I needed to see myself as conducting research *with* the chorus rather than *on* it. This was challenging research that involved risks, and I knew that I would need to apologize for mistakes. I went forth with it because I was confident that the benefits would outweigh the risks.

The potential benefits of this study are in Madison's fourth question.[33] This study of one local community chorus has the potential to contribute to the literature on the arts in social movements. The arts, and sometimes especially music, have had an important role in explaining and inspiring the work of ordinary people in progressive social movements. There is a long history of this, and there is a present that has the NYCLC as an important example.

Hopefully, there will be a future in which the arts will continue to play a vital role in social movements that uphold human rights and dignity. If my study with the NYCLC contributes in any capacity to this hopeful future, then I will be thrilled to have done this challenging work.

This brings me back to Madison's fifth and final question.[34] My study with the chorus was not only about what the chorus is. It was about how the chorus engages in song to contribute to equity, freedom, and justice in the labor movement in the 21st century. My motivation was the same as that of the chorus members and their governing board. We believe that music adds beauty and power to movements for social justice. Our singing to me was a form of play and a form of work. We worked hard every Monday evening to make the songs more beautiful, more powerful, and worthy of representing the overall work of the labor movement from history to today. Our work was a commitment toward making a difference from local struggles for living wages and humane work conditions to the global movement that defies neoliberalism with a vision for a more democratic and just political economy.

These ethical concerns encompassed all phases of data collection and analysis. Staying focused on my purpose, remembering the ways in which my work can do harm, and maintaining a collaborative dialog were my constant guidelines while collecting data. During my analysis of data, I needed to stay mindful of how this local study has significance and limits toward explaining the general human condition. Additionally, I needed to keep my lens for social justice intact in order to honor the integrity of a critical qualitative research project.

Data Collection and Analysis

During the chorus's 25th anniversary year, I collected data from various sources. As a participant in the chorus, I wrote fieldnotes during and after rehearsals and after performances. I conducted interviews and a focus group to capture testimonies of chorus members. I invited non-chorus union members familiar with the chorus's work to an interview, but none replied to my written invitation. I collected information about each song that the chorus performed for the 25th-anniversary concert. Additionally, I searched archives for writing a brief history of music in the labor movement in order to place the chorus in historical perspective.

Participating in the chorus while taking fieldnotes presented unique challenges and opportunities. Emerson, Fretz, and Shaw presented four implications of using fieldnotes in qualitative research.[35] These are connecting methods and findings, pursuing indigenous meanings, writing fieldnotes contemporaneously, and recording interactional detail. Each of these merits a paragraph of reflection on my work.

First, the fieldnotes serve as the connection between method and findings.[36] How I reached my findings was a central factor in what I found. Taking fieldnotes while participating in rehearsals was challenging but necessary, and during performances my notetaking had to wait until immediately after the event ended. I had read that a photographer takes hundreds of photos to find one that has lasting value. It cannot be the same with ethnographic fieldnotes, but too many details would be less troubling than not enough. My fieldnotes needed as much attention to detail as I could provide so that my findings would more accurately reflect what had transpired.

Second, my fieldnotes needed to honor indigenous meanings above my own biases and preconceptions.[37] The chorus had a culture of its own that developed long before I arrived as a member, and I learned more about it than I had imagined before starting the study. At the same time, every individual had a unique perspective on the work and value of the chorus. In the end the findings are from my interpretations through data analysis, but my goal was to be aware that I can capture more authentic representations of the true chorus if I write fieldnotes with the intention of respecting indigenous meanings, even and especially when they run counter to my own biases.

Third, my writing of fieldnotes was a contemporaneous process that occured alongside my interviews and my casual interactions with fellow chorus members.[38] I needed to address my changes in insights and perspectives as they developed. The chorus, itself, had undergone changes that were usually subtle and gradual, and I needed to be attentive to the signs that specific changes were in process. The clues, whether subtle or overt, needed to make their way into my fieldnotes so that I did not miss a beat.

Fourth and finally, my fieldnotes needed to show interactional details as clearly as possible.[39] Placing interactions in context of a situation was important. Capturing not only words exchanged but also emotions was another imperative. The chorus rehearsals were rich in commentary from the conductor and the members. I did not audio-record the rehearsals because I did not want anyone to sacrifice spontaneity for a concern about how one's words would sound in a recording. I wrote direct quotes when I decided that it was necessary, but mostly I had time only to jot down key words and phrases. When a rehearsal ended, I did not always rush out to catch the first subway train home. Sometimes I sat in a quiet space and wrote expanded notes from my jotted fieldnotes in order to commit more details to memory.

With the wisdom of Emerson and colleagues as my guide, I worked intentionally to bring data to life in a way that, hopefully, does justice to the chorus's work.[40] Field observations ran concurrently with interviews and one focus-group session. I had interviews and the focus-group session transcribed. My interviews with individual chorus members were mainly open-ended conversations. I started each interview by collecting information from the individual, such as pseudonym preference (if any), age, union affiliation, gender-pronoun preference, self-identified race or ethnicity or nationality, self-identified social class of upbringing, and number of years in the chorus. I then invited the interviewee to speak openly about her/his experience with the chorus. I facilitated the conversation with questions about the member's life experiences as a musician (amateur in nearly all cases) and as an activist, and about the member's thoughts on the chorus's effectiveness toward its stated purpose.

I conducted one focus group in order to allow a rich group conversation to unfold. All chorus members, including board members, conductor, and accompanist, received the invitation to participate. I asked each chorus member to discuss why she/he joined the chorus and why she/he had stayed. I also asked all participants to discuss openly the chorus's effectiveness toward its stated purpose.

Another source of data came from content analyses of present and past writings about the chorus. These included the chorus's own writings in performance programs. Also included were journalistic and other reports that either featured or mentioned the chorus. I spent time at the Tamiment Library and Robert F. Wagner Labor Archives at New York University to conduct this search, and I found other documents online. In addition, chorus board president Barbara Bailey gave me copies of many documents that she had.

To recap, my data came from the following list of items to study:

- How the chorus rehearsed and performed
- What individual chorus members thought and felt about the chorus's work
- What themes emerged in a focus group and interviews of chorus members
- How performance programs and journalistic reports depicted the chorus

My data analysis followed an intentional process for validity. Carpecken wrote of the importance in critical social research of developing "truth claims" before making "validity claims"—the former requiring consensus from the standards for truth in a culture, and the latter requiring a trust from that culture regarding the credibility in the process of collecting and analyzing data.[41] Carspecken's three ontological categories, aligned in part with Habermas's theory of communicative action[42], are the objective realm, the subjective realm, and the normative/evaluative realm.[43] The first deals with observed communications and actions, the second with multiple perspectives among group members of a concept, and the third with position-taking.

Carspecken charted ways to enhance validity in each realm within a process of five stages.[44] Stage One is building a primary record.[45] This focuses on the objective realm with early observations and fieldnotes. I improved validity in this stage by jotting accurate fieldnotes, being present consistently for all rehearsals that I could attend, and using accessible vocabulary in my fieldnotes and journal. Stage Two is preliminary reconstructive analysis.[46] This involved the early applications of coding as the normative/evaluative realm entered the picture. I enhanced validity by inviting members to check my records and coding, inviting researcher-peers to debrief my work, and analyzing the significance of negative cases or anomalies. Stage Three is the analysis of dialogical data.[47] This was when interviews and focus groups become more frequent, and it involved an interaction of the subjective and normative/evaluative realms. My work here became more valid when I checked for consistency between data from interviews and from observations, provided non-leading questions, invited interviewees to examine samples of fieldnote reconstructions, used the participants' terminology, and prepared to experience the pains that can accompany new learning and personal change for myself. Stage Four is analysis of systems relationships.[48] This was about making connections between the culture in focus and the surrounding world. I built validity in this stage by searching whether other studies' findings complemented mine, inviting researcher-peers to debrief my work, and inviting subjects to check whether my reasoning was congruent with their views. Stage Five is application of macro-level social theory.[49] This involved connecting findings with contemporary world views. The validity of my work in this stage depended on how I presented my findings coherently in context of theory. Validity checks in Stage Four applied here as well. As Carspecken's approach shows, critical ethnography requires careful attention to a variety details in the quest for validity.

The final challenge came in bringing valid findings to an effective publication. The NYCLC is a complex organization that had a history of a quarter century, and this study called for book-length product. Placing the history of the chorus within the context of the broader history of organized singing for organized labor was a must. It was also necessary to connect past and present developments of the chorus with its members' hopes and ideas for its future. This book is only one link of a chain of literature on the arts in activism, and my hope is that many more links will follow from many activists within and beyond academia.

CHAPTERS

This introductory chapter provides an overview of the work of the chorus and gives the scope of the qualitative study's purpose and approach. The six chapters that follow combine to address historical currents before and during the time of the chorus, to present findings of the study, and to advance discussions of the meanings of music in the labor movement of the 21st century.

Chapter One gives a brief history of song in the US labor movement. It addresses when, why, and how music became an important part of the movement from its roots to its branches. The time frame begins with the music of African slaves and the abolitionists, and it ends with the time leading up to the NYCLC's birth in 1991. The emphasis is on efforts to organize the songs and singing as a tool in activism.

Chapter Two is an account of the 25-year history of the chorus—its birth, its growth, its lasting traditions, and its changes. It draws information from personal testimonies, including those from founding members and leaders. It also cites written sources from chorus programs to media reports.

Chapter Three offers a close look at the songs sung by the chorus in its 25th-anniversary concert—from the historic to the contemporary. It gives details of the composers, arrangers, and lyricists, placing each song in its historical context of the US labor movement or, in some cases, of another social movement. The entire library of songs held by chorus members is too large to address, so the focus is on only the songs performed by the chorus in the concert marking 25 years.

Chapter Four is a close look at the chorus and many of its members during the 25th-anniversary year. This gives a summary of developments and phases through the year with details from rehearsals and performances. There is an account of how the chorus looked back at its 25-year history while also looking forward to continuing its work of music and activism into the future.

Chapter Five connects findings with themes based on interviews and the focus-group session. The six themes that emerged were community; diversity; activism/education; quality of music; remembering past members, leaders, and events; and current leadership. These themes reflected the topics that were common also in my reflections from fieldnotes informing the previous chapter.

Chapter Six has my final discussion and conclusions. It provides final thoughts on the future of the chorus from my perspective and from those of participants in the study. It poses questions for ongoing consideration. After its first 25 years, how does the chorus have momentum for continued relevance in New York City and beyond as an example of the arts in a social movement? How will the chorus look and sound in another five years, and in another 25 years?

NOTES

1. John Lennon and Yoko Ono, "Imagine," 1971, Lenono Music.
2. Paulo Freire, *Pedagogy of the Oppressed*, trans. Myra Bergman Ramos (New York: Continuum, 1970/2000).

3. New York City Labor Chorus, *Who We Are*, http://www.nyclc.org/whoweare.shtml.

4. Ibid.

5. Ibid.

6. Clyde Haberman, "The Message of Labor, Proclaimed through Song," *New York Times*, March 24, 2011.

7. Alfred Hayes and Earl Robinson, "Joe Hill," 1938, Bob Miller, Inc.

8. Roswell Rudd (arrangement), "Joe Hill," On CD "Trombone for Lovers," performed by Rudd with NYC Labor Chorus, Sunnyside Communications, Inc.

9. Reggie Bennet, "Joe Hill—The Relentless Walk," on CD "Trombone for Lovers" by Roswell Rudd.

10. Freire, *Pedagogy*.

11. Ibid. A 2018 edition for the book's 50th anniversary became available after I had started my drafting.

12. Judith J. Slater, Stephen M. Fain, and Cesar Augusto Rossatto (eds.), *The Freirian Legacy: Educating for Social Justice* (New York: Peter Lang, 2002).

13. Augosto Boal, *Theater of the Oppressed* (New York: Theater Communications Group, Inc., 1979).

14. Daniel J. Shevok, "Reflections on Freirian Pedagogy in a Jazz Combo Lab." *Action, Criticism, and Theory for Music Education* 14, no. 2 (2015), 85–121.

15. Ibid., 98.

16. Juanita Karpf, "For their Musical Uplift: Emma Azalia Hackley and Voice Culture in African American Communities." *International Journal of Community Music* 4, no. 3 (2011), 237–256.

17. Lee Higgins, *Community Music: In Theory and in Practice* (Oxford: Oxford University Press, Inc., 2012).

18. Jacques Derrida, *Positions* (London: Athone Press, 1981).

19. Karl Marx, *Capital: A Critique of Political Economy* (New York: Charles H. Kerr & Co., 1906).

20. Antonio Gramsci, *Selections from the Prison Notebooks* (New York: International Publishers, 1971), 53.

21. Peter Kropotkin, *Mutual Aid: A Factor of Evolution*, The Anarchist Library, https://theanarchistlibrary.org/library/petr-kropotkin-mutual-aid-a-factor-of-evolution.

22. Michael Bakunin, *God and the State* (Project Gutenburg e-Book), http://www.gutenberg.org/files/36568/36568-h/36568-h.htm.

23. Emma Goldman, *Living My Life: In Two Volumes* (New York: Dover Publications, Inc., 1970).

24. Rudolf Rocker, *Anarcho-Syndicalism* (London: Pluto Press, 2015).

25. Jim Thomas, *Doing Critical Ethnography* (Newburgh Park, CA: Sage Publications, Inc., 1993), 2–3.

26. Tony E. Adams, Carolyn Ellis, and Stacy Holman Jones, *Autoethnography* (Oxford, UK: Oxford University Press, 2015), 1.

27. Ibid., 25.

28. D. Soyini Madison, *Critical Ethnography: Method, Ethics, and Performance* (Los Angeles: Sage Publications, Inc., 2012), 2–4.
29. Ibid., 4-5.
30. Ibid., 4.
31. Ibid.
32. Ibid.,5.
33. Ibid.
34. Ibid.
35. Robert M. Emerson, Rachel I. Fretz, and Linda L. Shaw, *Writing Ethnographic Fieldnotes* (Chicago: University of Chicago Press, 2011), 15–18.
36. Ibid., 15–16.
37. Ibid., 16–17.
38. Ibid., 17.
39. Ibid., 18.
40. Ibid., 15–18.
41. Phil F. Carspecken, *Critical Ethnography in Educational Research: A Theoretical and Practical Guide* (New York: Routledge, 1996), 55–58.
42. Jürgen Habermas, *The Theory of Communicative Action: Volume One: Reason and the Rationalization of Society* (Boston: Beacon).
43. Carspecken, *Critical Ethnography*, 64–84.
44. Ibid., 41–43.
45. Ibid., 44–92.
46. Ibid., 93–153.
47. Ibid., 154–194.
48. Ibid., 195–202.
49. Ibid., 195–197, 202–206.

Chapter One

A Brief History of Singing for Justice in the US Workplace

There is a rich history in the US of singing about work and about justice in the workplace, and the NYCLC performs songs from a long span of time—from some well-aged standards inspired by the spirituals of slaves to contemporary compositions about current social movements. This chapter gives a brief overview of the history with an emphasis on group singing by workers and activists. It starts with the music of slaves and the abolitionist movement, and it continues through significant eras of the labor movement—from early growth to the recent decades of decline in union membership. The focus is not on recording artists but rather on ordinary workers who have sung together about their struggles and hopes.

SONGS OF SLAVES AND ABOLITIONISTS

The savage cruelty of chattel slavery in the Southern US knew no bounds—from permanently separating babies from their mothers, to long hours of daily toil, to inhumane living conditions, to the torture of the bullwhip, to rape of female slaves by masters. Some slaves risked torture with attempts to escape. Some were driven to armed rebellion. Facing such cruelty, slaves found ways to flee, fight, or build resilience for a long struggle. Singing, as Frederick Douglass explained to northerners, became an important form of expressing suffering.[1] As slaves created and sang the spirituals together, they bonded in community and received strength to resist oppression, identifying themselves as God's new chosen people for deliverance from slavery.[2]

Testimonies of former slaves appear in various sources, and they contain many accounts of singing. Norman R. Yetman edited a collection of such testimonies.[3] Nearly half of the 100 former slaves interviewed in this volume mentioned music. The extent to which slave owners allowed slaves to sing varied. Many interviewees spoke of having to hide in order to sing and pray. Some were permitted to sing only while working in the field. Others were permitted to sing at occasions such as church services, baptisms, funerals, and festivals. Singing or dancing at forbidden times resulted in punishments that included severe beating. The songs sung ranged from work songs approved by masters to spirituals with hidden or explicit themes of longing for freedom. An example of efforts made to sing in hiding is in the testimony of Fannie Moore, interviewed at age 88 by Marjorie Jones in Asheville, North Carolina. Moore remembered that slaves would go to the woods to pray and would sing into pots in order to not be heard.[4] She also spoke about an evening in the slave quarters that involved laughing and lively singing until patrollers entered and started grabbing the merrymaking slaves. Her uncle, who had endured many beatings, decided to fight back until the invaders restrained him, whipped him, and then killed him by cracking his skull with a stick.[5]

More than 100 pages containing 136 slaves' songs were transcribed in music and lyrics and then published in 1867 in New York City by A. Simpson & Company with editors William Francis Allen, Charles Pickard Ward, and Lucy McKim Garrison. This volume, titled *Slave Songs of the United States*, now appears as an electronic book, published in 2011 by the University of North Carolina Press. In the introduction the editors explained that putting the songs on paper could never do complete justice to the complexity of the songs in their various renditions, often with improvisations added, as heard in performances by former slaves as individuals or in groups.[6] Many group performances involved a single leader whom the others followed in call-response form while adding irregular rhythms, countermelodies, and sometimes shouting. The editors noted that lyrics of most songs were taken from the Bible or from hymns heard in churches. They explained in detail how the songs and singing varied across regions of the South. They transcribed lyrics phonetically in order to preserve the original sounds. Here is the first of two verses from the song titled "Blow Your Trumpet, Gabriel":

> De talles' tree in Paradise,
> De Christian call de tree of life;
> And I hope dat trump might blow me home
> To the new Jerusalem.
> Blow your trumpet, Gabriel,
> Blow louder, louder;
> And I hope dat trump might blow me home
> To de new Jerusalem.[7]

Like most of the songs in the volume, it has a time signature of 2/4 and a melody that moves quickly with mostly eighth notes and some syncopation. Although this song does not have a chorus in addition to verses, many songs do. The editors did not identify the tempo of this song, but they stated in the volume's brief "Directions for Singing" section that tempo depends on the "spirit of the music".[8]

While slaves created music of their own, the abolitionist movement also brought music into its work. William Wells Brown escaped from slavery in 1834 and became a leading abolitionist in his work as a lecturer and writer. By the middle of the 1840s, Brown often sang in the middle or end of his speeches.[9] He went on to compile a collection of anti-slavery songs that was published in 1848 in Boston by Bela Marsh Printing House with the title *The Anti-Slavery Harp: A Collection of Songs for Anti-Slavery Meetings*. The Project Gutenburg digitized this collection in 2003. Brown's brief preface begins with this statement: "The demand of the public for a cheap Anti-Slavery Song-Book, containing Songs of a more recent composition, has induced me to collect together, and present to the public, the songs contained in this book."[10] The volume includes the lyrics, without the musical scores, of 48 songs. Examples of song titles are "O, Pity the Slave Mother," "Emancipation Hymn of the West Indian Negroes," "I Am an Abolitionist," and "Fugitives' Triumph."

Frederick Douglass mentioned in his writings the importance of songs in the abolitionist struggle: "They are heart songs, and the finest feelings of human nature are expressed in them. 'Lucy Neal,' 'Old Kentucky Home,' and 'Uncle Ned,' can make the heart sad as well as merry, and can call forth a tear as well as a smile. They awaken the sympathies for the slave, in which anti-slavery principles take root, grow, and flourish."[11] Many northerners held misconceptions over the nature of slaves' singing, and Douglass addressed this also in his writings: "I have often been utterly astonished, since I came to the north, to find persons who could speak of the singing, among slaves, as evidence of their contentment and happiness. It is impossible to conceive of a greater mistake. Slaves sing most when they are most unhappy. The songs of the slave represent the sorrows of his heart; and he is relieved by them, only as an aching heart is relieved by its tears."[12] Only those who had experienced being a slave, as Douglass had, could have such a heartfelt understanding of slave songs.

The pain that gave birth to slave songs brought a unique life to what has become known as American roots music.[13] The spirituals created and sung by slaves influenced gospel music, blues, and country music; and without these branches there would be no jazz, folk, rock, or hip-hop. These various forms of music have played parts in the music of protest in different eras, and each carries some DNA of the music that African American slaves made as part of their survival.

SINGING IN THE EARLY LABOR MOVEMENT, 1865–1928

The 13th Amendment of 1865 abolished slavery except for punishment for a crime. Exploitation of African American workers in the South continued in the new era of sharecropping through debt peonage and a discriminatory justice system that unjustly imprisoned, and thus enslaved, many African Americans. W. E. B. Du Bois wrote of the ongoing struggles of African Americans in his classic work *The Souls of Black Folk*, first published in 1903. Each chapter begins with the lyrics and a brief musical score of a song, identifying either the name of a composer/arranger or adding the phrase "Negro song." The final chapter, titled "The Sorrow Songs," is a heartfelt tribute to the central place of music in African Americans' past and ongoing struggles against racism. Du Bois wrote of how the slave songs he had heard stirred his soul. He wrote that the slaves' music, though often misunderstood, "still remains as the single spiritual heritage of the nation and the greatest gift of the Negro people".[14] He praised the Fisk Jubilee Singers for bringing the power and beauty of the songs to the world.

Fisk University was established by the Freedmen's Bureau in 1866 as an African American college. A group of 11 ex-slave students formed in 1871 to raise funds for the struggling school, and they called themselves the Fisk Jubilee Singers.[15] Their performances of slave songs such as "Steal Away" and "Swing Low Sweet Chariot" earned them a growing audience, and they eventually toured much of the US and Europe.[16] By 1878, they had raised $150,000 for the college and had broken a racial barrier by achieving commercial success for their music. The spirituals that they sang became the catalyst for the growing genre of gospel music. As the market for spirituals grew, so did the popularity of racist blackface minstrel shows, which eventually were replaced by Tin Pan Alley. W. C. Handy, in his autobiography titled "Father of the Blues,"[17] stated that in a twist of irony these racist representations played a role in the survival of the spirituals.[18]

The themes of protest and longing for freedom continued to appear in the lyrics of many African American spirituals during the decades following the breakthrough by the Fisk Jubilee Singers. The song "Go Down, Moses" had its beginnings during slavery and became a standard that appeared in many collections of spirituals.[19] It became a tribute to the heroic work of Harriet Tubman, who had become known as "Moses" and the "conductor" of the caravan leading hundreds of slaves to freedom. Another song, though not a spiritual, that continued growing in popularity among ex-slaves and former abolitionists was "John Brown's Body," sung to the tune of the "Battle Hymn of the Republic."[20] This song advanced the message of Brown's martyrdom for decades, and it became one of the standards in the civil rights movement when there was need for a marching rhythm.

The shameful *Plessy vs. Ferguson* of 1896 set the stage for legal segregation in the South. The Great Migration of African Americans from the South to the North began before 1900 but accelerated with the prospect of factory jobs for production to support the Great War, which became known as World War I. Upon reaching northern cities, African Americans could only take the most menial and backbreaking jobs. They faced ubiquitous racism—forced into deteriorated housing and kept out of many of the labor unions. Through the new struggles they kept their roots music from spirituals and work songs, and what followed was the grand expansion of musical forms from gospel to blues to jazz.[21] All of these branches of music have contributed immeasurably to the music of social movements in the US.

As industrialization changed landscapes and lifestyles across the country, the growing working class found the need to struggle for humane working conditions. When workers expressed their struggle in songs, from the beginning they borrowed from the musical traditions of both African American spirituals and European forms of folk and classical music. By the 1870s, when strikes and depressions became more common, labor songs found their way into some newspapers and songbooks. The first labor songbook to gain international usage was *Labor Songs Dedicated to the Knights of Labor*, published in 1886 in Chicago by James and Emily Tallmadge.[22] Among its 29 songs, "Our Battle Song," which later took the title "Hold the Fort," became a labor classic.[23] The Noble and Holy Order of the Knights of Labor became the first major union in the US.[24] The group formed in secret in 1869 and grew to a reported 700,000 members by 1886. The Knights of Labor regularly sang in groups, and they adapted gospel and secular songs with new lyrics to fit their struggle.

The turn of the century was the middle of the third wave of immigration to the US, mostly from southern and eastern Europe and Asia. Singing songs with simple refrains became helpful in learning English, and dancing became an activity that many could share when they were unable to speak to each other.[25] As immigrants toiled together in often horrid conditions, they looked to labor songs as expressions of hardship and hope. One immigrant from Sweden became a leader among the creators of labor songs.

Joel Hägglund took the name Joe Hill after arriving in the US in 1902.[26] As he traveled to find work, he became active in the Industrial Workers of the World (IWW), commonly known as the "Wobblies." With ties to anarchists and socialists, the IWW, founded in Chicago in 1905, was a radical alternative to the American Federation of Labor (AFL), which was the mainstream national union that had grown after splitting from the Knights of Labor in 1886.[27] The AFL, which by the 1890s organized only those they deemed as skilled workers, became an organization of mainly white males who openly discriminated against workers of color and impeded women's efforts to organize as workers. The IWW by contrast, with a syndicalist dream of "one big union," openly welcomed all workers, including the unemployed and underemployed, to its ranks. The Wobblies embraced singing in their activism, and Joe Hill stood out as their most prolific writer with songs such as "The Preacher and the Slave," "There is Power in a Union," and "Casey Jones, the Union Scab." Hill often brought new lyrics to familiar tunes, ranging from hymns to excerpts from European classical music. As the Red Scare spread and struck reactionary fear throughout the US in the early 1910s, a violent repression from the state and vigilantes against the IWW ensued. Following a double murder in Salt Lake City 1914, the prosecution brought charges against Hill with dubious arguments and a lack of substantial evidence. The jury convicted Hill, and the execution went forth in 1915 despite worldwide protests. A tribute to Hill's legacy is in the classic folk song "Joe Hill," written as a poem in 1930 by Alfred Hayes, put to music in 1936 by Earl Robinson, and recorded by many artists beginning in 1938.

The Wobblies printed a pocket-size collection of songs called the "Little Red Songbook," and there were 37 editions in the 20th century.[28] There were an estimated 50,000 copies within four years of its first printing in 1909.[29] Several songs of Joe Hill appeared along with songs by other authors. Ralph Chaplin's "Solidarity Forever," written in 1915 and sung to the tune of the "Battle Hymn of the Republic," became an anthem for the labor movement. Here is one verse:

> When the Union's inspiration through the worker's blood shall run,
> There can be no power greater anywhere beneath the sun.
> Yet what force on earth is weaker than the feeble strength of one?
> But the Union makes us strong.[30]

Songs of the Little Red Songbook addressed work and the workers' struggles. Wherever the Wobblies traveled or worked together, their singing of songs became not only a pastime but a way of communicating messages of class struggle and hope. Hill and Chaplin are the most renowned Wobbly songwriters, but women also contributed many classic songs to IWW culture. Examples include Ethel Comer's "Stand Up, Ye Workers," Laura Payne Emerson's "The Industrial Workers of the World," Rose Elizabeth Smith's "The Ninety and Nine," Vera Moller's "We Made Good Wobs Out There," written while she was in prison.³¹ Women among IWW organizers were leaders in major strikes involving mostly women workers, such as the New York shirtwaist strike of 1909 and the "Bread and Roses" strike in Lawrence, Massachusetts in 1912, where a picketer's sign inspired the writing of the classic song "Bread and Roses."³²

The US entered The Great War, now known as World War One, amid controversy, but the AFL threw its support behind the war effort. Many on the left, including the IWW, proclaimed in protest that it was an imperialist war, and others held pacifist principles. While music had a role in the US propaganda for the "War to End All Wars," there were some protest songs, too. One song that spread among protesters was "I Didn't Raise My Boy to Be a Soldier," written by Alfred Bryan and Al Piantadosi in 1915. The lyrics are from a mother's point of view, and the concluding line is "Remember that my boy belongs to me!".³³ A song like this was persuasive when women were rising as a mass movement to demand voting rights.

The women's suffrage movement's songs are not as familiar as songs of other movements in US history; however, singing was a frequent activity during activist meetings. From the Seneca Falls Convention of 1848 to the 1920 victory of the 19th Amendment, singing helped women to build solidarity in challenging the traditions that oppressed them politically, economically, and socially. Sheryl Hurner studied how themes of suffrage songs connected with women's identities.³⁴ Examples of song titles addressed in this study are "Let Us Speak Our Minds if We Die for It" (Brough, 1863), "Female Suffrage" (Cohen, 1867), "The Suffrage Flag" (Adkinson, 1884), and "Marching on to Victory" (Greene, 1913). Hurner concluded that "Protest song is indeed a powerful expression of faith, hope, and resistance" and added that more research is necessary to explore the possibilities and limits of protest music in strengthening a social movement.³⁵

IWW membership faded in the mid-1920s due to ongoing repression from the second Red Scare and tensions from internal conflicts. The organization still exists, and its website, as of early February of 2016, featured the Joe Hill 100 Road Show Tour, in which groups of musicians performed in 33 US locations during 2015 to mark the 100th anniversary of Hill's execution.³⁶ The report stated, "While some of the crowds were small and others large, all shows on the tour were spirited events with lots of audience participation, enthusiasm, and laughter, all infused with the spirit of labor solidarity." The IWW, headquartered in Chicago, has local branches throughout the US, Canada, Europe, and Australia.³⁷ Several songs of its vintage period and Joe Hill have remained icons to the labor movement, and all songs from every *Little Red Songbook* and some more are collected in *The Big Red Songbook*.³⁸

With the rise of unions came the advent of labor colleges, which, although generally not affiliated directly with unions, prepared students to become union leaders. These schools, like the IWW, valued singing as part of labor culture. Terese Volk identified four prominent schools as the Work People's College, founded in 1907 at Duluth, Minnesota; Brookwood College, founded in 1921 at Katonah, New York; Commonwealth Labor College, founded in 1922 near Mena, Arkansas; and Highlander College, founded in 1932 at Monteagle, Tennessee.[39] Students learned labor songs, "taught them in assemblies, and sang them in sing-alongs, on picket lines, and in road shows in churches and union halls to help educate working people."[40] There were several labor songbooks in print, among them different versions of the Little Red Songbook, and these were the main texts of the music education in these schools. Some labor colleges, like Brookwood and Commonwealth, were residential schools while most of the urban schools provided spaces for meetings outside of work hours.[41] Many of these schools remained active during the Depression years, and some published their own labor songbooks.[42]

SINGING FROM GREAT DEPRESSION TO MCCARTHYISM

The Roaring 20s met the Great Depression with the stock-market crash of 1929, and the US entered the worldwide depression that had already affected many nations. African Americans faced the twin hardships of systemic racism and labor surplus, and music remained an important resource for their struggle and faith.[43] White homesteaders in the plains suffered the ecological disaster of depleted soil and devastating dust storms. Woody Guthrie, who was one of multitudes of "Okies" to make the journey from the dustbowl of Oklahoma and surrounding states to the Golden State of California in search of work, chronicled in songs the hardships and hopes of ordinary working people during this period. Several other prolific songwriters also contributed songs to the struggle, and the labor movement continued to embrace singing through World War II and beyond.

During the early years of the Depression, music became an important tool for workers in many regions as they organized and sometimes went on strike. Roscigno and Danahar wrote in great depth about the role of singing in the southern textile strikes of the early 1930s. They examined how the increased accessibility to radio brought not only President Roosevelt's fireside chats but also many songs—some about work—into the homes of many working families in the villages with textile mills: "In the textile-manufacturing South, the industrial working class was targeted by programmers because this group was much more likely than farmers to have access to radios. Astute programmers provided musical entertainment aimed directly at the concerns and cultural preferences of their specific broadcast audiences."[44] Some mill workers wrote songs about their hardships with working conditions and low pay, and a few performers were able to support themselves with their music. Spontaneous group singing was common during and after work hours. Protest songs such as the Dixon Brothers' "Weave Room Blues" and Dave McCarn's "Cotton Mill Colic" found their way to some radio stations.[45] During the General Textile Strike of 1934, the singing of these songs and others was an important part of demonstrations and picket lines throughout the South.

One of the most prolific songwriters to represent the hardships of the Southern millworker in the late 1920s was Ella May (or Ella Mae Wiggins by many accounts), whose songs filled the air in 1929 during a series of strikes in Gastonia, North Carolina.[46] May was a spinner and a union member in Bessemer City, North Carolina, who had suffered four of her children dying due to poverty. She wrote and performed many songs, some of which survived long after company thugs shot and killed her in September of 1929 during a strike. During the mass funeral in Bessemer City, people joined together to sing some of her songs: "Toiling on Life's Pilgrim Pathway," "Chief Aderholt," "The Big Fat Boss and the Workers," "Two Little Strikers," and "Mill Mother's Lament."[47] Her biography has been written by Kristina Horton, her great-granddaughter.[48]

Two more women who emerged as important labor songwriters were Aunt Molly Jackson and Florence Reece, both active in ongoing coal miners' strikes in Harlan County, Kentucky in the late 1920s and early 30s. Aunt Molly, as Jackson was called, was the most important songwriter to emerge from these strikes. She traveled to New York City and other cities to sing in order to raise funds for the striking miners.[49] Reece wrote "Which Side Are You On?" based on the hymn "Lay the Lily Low" in 1931 during the long miners' strike in Harlan County, Kentucky.[50] Strikers soon sang it on the picket line, and it grew to become a standard in the labor movement. Chapter Three includes the story behind the song and the songwriter.

The radical and revolutionary left took music seriously during the depression years. The Workers' Music League, established in 1931 by affiliates of the American Communist Party, included more than 20 musicians' groups.[51] Judith Tick wrote a biography of Ruth Crawford Seeger, a musical composer and stepmother of the legendary folk musician Pete Seeger. Crawford and her husband, Charles Seeger, were moved to activism upon seeing massive poverty alongside conspicuous wealth: ". . . the homeless men and women in the streets selling apples, rain and snow falling on the heated grates crowded with bodies, the Rolls Royces that still went up and down the streets of New York City."[52] Tick provided a wealth of information about singing of labor songs during the Depression in her chapter titled "Music as a Weapon in the Class Struggle."[53] Pete, as a child, recalled his father and stepmother working feverishly with others to advance the music of proletarian culture. By 1933, they took Pete to meetings of a local music group in New York City called the Pierre Deguyter Club, and Pete recalled joining with the group in singing the communist anthem "The Internationale" among other songs. Many choruses performed songs of class struggle in and around New York City. Among the chosen songs were compositions by Crawford and others by her husband. Crawford had two songs that became popular among labor choruses. One was a tribute to Sacco and Vanzetti, the legendary martyrs of the First Red Scare; the other, titled "Chinaman, Laundryman," portrayed proletarian interests in the Chinese Revolution along with the exploitation of immigrant labor in the US. Most of the workers' choruses sang in their native languages from various parts of Eastern and Southern Europe. Crawford and Seeger contributed songs in English as a minority language.

Music became helpful to unions that welcomed multiculturalism in their ranks. Daniel Katz, in his archival study of the International Ladies' Garment Workers' Union (ILGWU) in New York City during the 1930s, found that the immigrant Jewish unionists who had worked in the garment factories used music as a way to integrate African American women and immigrant women of other languages who were joining the union.[54] Music programs within the union formed choruses and orchestras, and they provided instruments and lessons free to the workers and their families. Singing became a way to help pass the time during work, and musical performances outside of work helped to foster a culturally diverse community. ILGWU concerts featured revolutionary songs of class struggle, folk songs in native languages from various parts of Europe, and African American spirituals. Orchestras and ensembles played challenging works from classical to jazz. The union also had its own radio station, which included diverse music programming.

The economic hardships of the Depression brought artists and intellectuals across the country together in search of a culturally pluralistic national identity. Rachel Clare Donaldson examined this trend of a folk revivalist movement and focused on the role of music. Revivalists ranged in ideology from centrists to New Deal liberals to radical leftists, but they all shared an interest in projecting a national identity of cultural diversity. Folk festivals flourished, and the first day of the first National Folk Festival (NFF) in 1934 in St. Louis "commenced with Kiowa Indians from Oklahoma and moved on to French folk songs and songs from Vermont, and closed with Southern African American spirituals."[55] Diverse musical performances continued for two more days, and the NFF has continued annually in different locations across the US. In subsequent years of the 1930s the NFF became more inclusive of recent immigrant groups and more determined to attract the best African American performers, including the Fisk Jubilee Singers, who sang in the second festival in Chattanooga.[56]

Not every strain of folk music could be captured in a single national festival, but John Lomax and his son Alan traveled the nation together in the 1930s to collect songs that were unique to their respective regions. They received help from other folklorists, including Zora Neale Hurston and Mary Elizabeth Barnicle.[57] John had begun his work before 1910, when he was tracing links between centuries-old Anglo-Saxon music and cowboy music of the western US.[58] Alan worked with super-prolific songwriter Woody Guthrie in the later years of the Depression to compile songs for a collection titled *Hard-Hitting Songs for Hard-Hit People*, which was not published until 1967, when folk-music icon Pete Seeger added musical transcriptions. Bison Books, a subsidiary of the University of Nebraska Press, reprinted this volume in 2012. The book contains 197 songs in 13 sections. Perhaps the most well-known song penned by Guthrie in the collection is "Union Maid," for which the author wrote this introduction:

> Peter [Seeger] and me was fagged out when we got to Oklahoma City from New York, but not too fagged out to plow up a Union Song. Pete flopped out acrost a bed, and I set over at a writing machine, and he could think of one line and me another'n until we woke up an hour or two later with a great big 15-pound, blue-eyed Union Song, I mean Union—named the Union Maid. Whim, wham, and the mule throwed the governor. [Paragraph break] Here's another one comin' out of chute #7, Rider #19. This is an older one made up by the I.W.W.'s to the same tune—an old Indian song. But I don't think the Indians will mind. Fact is they're in the Union same as the rest of us. (What are you guards and deputies gonna sing? Let's hear you sing!).[59]

This note tells a little about Guthrie's and Seeger's travels together before they joined with others to form the Almanac Singers. Guthrie's introductory notes for the songs range from a single sentence to multiple paragraphs with a story to tell. The songs are diverse—from old IWW songs to African American Spirituals to blues.

Recordings of blues grew during the Depression, and lyrics of many songs addressed unemployment or government jobs from the Civil Works Administration and the Works Progress Administration.[60] Although the Depression hit African Americans much harder than white people, the night clubs of major northern cities attracted racially mixed audiences for blues and jazz performances. Religious, middle-class, and educated urban African Americans tended to look down on blues as "nigger music."[61] They associated it with the rural South while projecting their new hopes on the northern cities. Still, the blues flourished during the 1930s as an extension of the African-American oral tradition with southern roots. Blues performer Big Bill Broonzy said the following during an interview in the Mississippi Delta during World War II with Alan Lomax:

> And the thing that has come to a showdown, that we really want to know why, and how come, a man in the South *have* the blues. I worked on levee camps, extra gangs, road camps and rock camps and rock quarries and every place, and I hear guys singin *uh-hmmmm* this and *mmmmm* that, and I want to get the thing plainly that the blues is something that's from the heart—I know that, and whensoever you hear fellows singing the blues—I always believed it was really a heart thing, from his heart, you know, and it was expressing his feeling about *how* he felt to the people.[62]

The blues touched on many of life's situations, and the topic of hard work under dreadful conditions was quite common. The Lomaxes made stops at several prisons in the South to write about work songs sung by prisoners. At the Angola prison in Louisiana they met a prisoner named Hubbie Ledbetter, better known as Lead Belly. Gifted as a songwriter, singer, and guitarist, Lead Belly traveled with Alan after he was released. In 1936, the Lomaxes published "Negro Folk Songs as Sung by Lead Belly."[63] Lead Belly went on to become one of the premier composers and performers of blues and folk music.

A pivotal year for labor was 1935. The passing of the Wagner Act (now known as the National Labor Relations Act) established the National Labor Relations Board and thus confirmed the right of unions to exist. Racism and sexism continued to be rampant in the AFL, the nation's most powerful union.[64] The Congress of Industrial Organizations (CIO), founded in 1935, by contrast welcomed women and workers of color. The CIO unions, like the IWW that had faded, valued singing in a variety of settings. They rewrote lyrics to many of the spirituals and sang in meetings and on picket lines. One pre-Civil War spiritual in particular, "Oh Freedom," became popular in CIO gatherings. Each verse ends with these words: "And before I'd be a slave, I'd be buried in my grave / And go home to my Lord and be free."[65] As CIO unions continued to join forces with African American workers, especially in the South, they worked together to transform many spirituals into labor songs. In their travels Woody Guthrie and Pete Seeger helped to introduce these songs to unions across the country.

An African American poet and songwriter who became a leader among labor organizers in the rural South was John L. Handcox. He wrote of the injustices endured by sharecroppers and tenant farmers, who risked prison if they fled while in debt to a landowner under conditions not unlike slavery in the debt peonage system. Handcox joined with other sharecroppers along with tenant farmers and wage laborers in 1934 to organize all into one collective that became the Southern Tenant Farmers' Union (STFU).[66] The AFL endorsed the STFU but did not recognize it as a member organization.[67] The STFU later became affiliated with the CIO, but internal conflict brought an end to the union in 1939 while most members continued with the CIO's cannery workers' union.[68] During the STFU years, Handcox contributed many poems and songs to the struggle. One of his songs, "Roll the Union On," became a classic in the labor movement.[69] The Almanac Singers' recording of it is on YouTube.[70]

Singing became especially important during the sit-down strike of 1936 and 1937 at the General Motors plants in Flint, Michigan.[71] While occupying the factories, the striking workers of the United Automobile Workers Union composed and sang songs to lift spirits and escape boredom. Many of these new songs found their way into songbooks used by glee clubs and bands newly formed within the union. Supporters of the strikers, including the Women's Emergency Brigade, also sang songs like "We Shall Not Be Moved" and "Hold the Fort" in picket lines outside of the plants. The strike survived violent attempts by police to overpower it and ended after 44 days with important concessions to the workers.[72]

While unions struggled to bring equity to the workplace, African Americans continued to face racism from day-to-day discrimination to the terrorism of lynching. After the Daughters of the American Revolution refused to allow Marian Anderson to sing in Constitution Hall, she performed her famous concert in 1939 at the Lincoln Memorial on Easter Sunday.[73] A song recorded by Billie Holiday, also in 1939, addressed the scourge of racist lynching across the nation, especially in the South.[74] Written by a Jewish communist named Abel Meeropol, "Strange Fruit" was a bold protest song like no other that had gained the public's attention.[75] Another song confronting racism was Lead Belly's "Bourgeois Blues," which he wrote in 1938 after an eventful evening in Washington, DC with his wife Martha along with Alan Lomax and his fellow folklorist Mary Elizabeth Barnicle.[76] Neither a white restaurant nor a "colored" (term used then as in Lead Belly's lyrics) one would serve the racially integrated group, and Lead Belly commemorated the shameful event in song.

Unions continued growing throughout the Depression years, and they played an important role when the nation suddenly entered World War II. Production shifted to support war efforts, and many women took jobs traditionally held by men to replace soldiers. Music continued to have an important place in the stories of work and class struggle. The Almanac Singers became popular with activists in the Popular Front, a coalition against fascism that included liberals, unionists, and the Communist Party. The Almanacs' roster shifted often, and they were a rarity as a biracial group with African American members Brownie McGee, Sonny Terry, and Josh White.[77] The group's early works had a split between peace songs and union songs, but they replaced their peace songs with pro-war and anti-fascist songs after the Pearl Harbor attack and the US entry into the war.[78] The Almanacs found some commercial success until some newspapers attacked their union songs as communist. The group disbanded after Seeger and Guthrie joined the military.[79]

African Americans fought and made sacrifices against fascism and racism in the war, and then they returned to their country still oppressed by Jim Crow laws in the South along with *de facto* racial inequality and discrimination in other regions. Lead Belly wrote and recorded the song "Nobody in the World Is Better than Us" to draw attention to the ongoing post-war racism.[80] Membership in the NAACP grew by 900 percent following the war.[81] The organization continued its tradition of singing spirituals and African American protest songs, and its youth council started using the name "Freedom Songs" by the mid-1940s.[82]

The CIO continued to work on organizing African American workers in the Jim Crow South, and one important example of progress in this struggle was with the tobacco workers of R. J. Reynolds in Winston-Salem, who organized in the Food, Tobacco, Agricultural and Allied Workers of American in North Carolina in the 1940s. Robert R. Korstad, focusing on this case study in his broader examination of what he called "civil rights unionism," highlighted the importance that black workers placed on singing in numerous passages. While they toiled in the most menial and punishing tasks, many sang together to defy the soul-crushing working conditions. When away from the factory, some formed choral groups and clubs.[83] When there were strikes, there was singing of spirituals and protest songs at the picket lines.[84] Although some white workers joined in the struggle at Winston-Salem, most took sides with the company and denounced the CIO, claiming it was run by outsiders and communists.[85] Union dances, true to Jim Crow form, divided whites and blacks with a rope.[86] On the other hand, there was biracial organizing and singing from the Highlander Folk School in Tennessee, where the black spiritual "I will overcome" became the anthem "We Shall Overcome."[87]

The end of World War II marked the beginning of the Cold War against the Soviet Union and its allies. The music of the labor movement continued to flourish in the late 1940s until another Red Scare returned and developed into McCarthyism. A collective called People's Songs formed in 1946, and it attracted members of the Almanac Singers and other musicians committed to making music for progressive change.[88] Meanwhile, the Highlander Folk School had a growing music program under the direction of Zilphia Horton, the wife of the school's co-founder Myles Horton.[89] Highlander brought music, among other resources, to the struggles for racial justice and workers' rights throughout the South.

By 1948, the Red Scare had returned with a vengeance and People's Songs disintegrated.[90] *Sing Out!*, a journal with songs and information for professional and amateur activist-musicians, emerged in 1950 and survived threats from Senator Joseph McCarthy's anti-communist crusade. The Weavers had become a popular folk-music group with a successful cover of Lead Belly's "Goodnight Irene," but they came to an end within a year after an FBI investigation and the media labeled three of their members communists in 1952.[91] Unions, already injured by the restrictions in the Taft-Hartley Act of 1947, bent over backwards to show the public that they were not communist sympathizers.[92]

McCarthyism targeted all artists with any leftist or progressive message in their works or daily lives, and one of the most poignant examples is in Paul Robeson. Born in 1898 to a father who had escaped slavery, Robeson had immense talents as an athlete, lawyer, actor, activist, and writer, but he mainly achieved popular and critical acclaim as a bass singer who brought powerful interpretations to many of the black spirituals. While in Spain in 1938, he was inspired to sing for the Lincoln Brigade of US fighters against Franco's fascist forces.[93] He continued to travel the world throughout the 1940s and performed wherever people welcomed him. His friendly relationship with people in the Soviet Union, though, which never included an endorsement of Stalin and his brutal authoritarianism, brought the wrath of the Red Scare, and the US government annulled his passport in 1950.[94] Robeson wrote his autobiography in 1958, when his passport finally was reinstated. He became one of many influential African American writers to confront racial segregation, and his legacy continues to inspire the NYCLC and other groups that bring the arts and activism together.

The post-war Red Scare was a terrible shock to organized labor, and the attacks against unions have continued in the following years and decades. The explicit paranoia of McCarthyism might be gone; however, a steady decline in union membership and a lasting anti-union sentiment prevail. The history of strong unions that brought important reforms through hard struggle is available, though, for scholars and workers of all kinds to learn. Will the media, schools, and remaining unions learn from this history?

SINGING FOR SOLIDARITY IN CONTEMPORARY ERA OF UNIONS IN DECLINE

Union membership in the US has been in steady decline since 1983, the earliest year in which the Bureau of Labor Statistics could gather comparable data. The union membership rate among workers was 21.1% in 1983, and the rate dropped to 11.1% by 2015.⁹⁵ In 2015, the median weekly income for union workers was $980, and for non-union workers it was $776, or 79% of the income of union workers.⁹⁶ In recent decades capital moved manufacturing jobs from the union-strong North to the anti-union South, and then to so-called developing countries, where wages and standards for working conditions were much lower still. Neoliberalism, the global movement in which international trade organizations and governments enact deregulation of corporations and mass privatization of public services, emerged from the 1973 US-backed coup that toppled the democratically-elected socialist government in Chile and has prevailed globally since the Reagan-Thatcher 1980s.⁹⁷ This global shift has brought disaster to organized labor in the US and in many parts of the world.

New music of the labor movement faded after the post-war Red Scare; however, singing of spirituals and protest songs became ubiquitous in the civil rights movement for racial equality. From the year-long Montgomery bus boycott begun in December of 1955 to the rise of the Black Panther party in the late 60s, music played a large role as a creative expression of indignation and hope. The documentary films *Eyes on the Prize: America's Civil Rights Movement*⁹⁸ and *King: A Filmed Record: Montgomery to Memphis* captured the powerful sights and sounds of civil rights activists singing while marching or holding demonstrations.⁹⁹ It is truly a wonder to see the faces beaming with dignity, to hear the passion and boldness in the voices, to ponder the poetic lyrics of emancipation, and to behold the beauty of the melodies, harmonies, and rhythms.

There were hymns, spirituals, folk classics, and new protest songs sung by thousands in some demonstrations and by groups of all sizes in countless meetings and gatherings. The Montgomery bus boycott successfully desegregated the city's buses but only after a year of great sacrifices from ordinary African-American residents who generated resilience through grassroots organizing supported by soulful singing. Martin Luther King found inspiration while hearing the singing, and his sermons and speeches often used the language of the hymns and spirituals sung by worshippers and by activists.¹⁰⁰ The Highlander Folk School brought black and white activist musicians together in Monteagle, Tennessee to build up the music program behind the movement.¹⁰¹ Other social movements have risen since the civil rights movement of the 1950s and 60s, but none has developed a comparable culture of singing.

The later part of the 1960s saw the rise of the anti-war and Black Power movements. Martin Luther King disaffected many of his closest companions of the civil rights movement as he increasingly spoke out in his last year not only against racism but also against the Vietnam War and against the classism that dehumanized workers.[102] Desperate living conditions for African Americans resulted in so-called race riots in many cities. Joe Street identified a "culture war" within the Civil rights movement as music and plays created by radicalized African Americans took on an explicit edge against white supremacy and sometimes capitalism.[103] Bernice Reagon and the Student Nonviolent Coordinating Committee (SNCC) led the politically-charged singing movement from Albany, Georgia.[104] Inspired by her "African American singing and fighting Mothers," especially Bessie Jones of the Georgia Sea Island Singers, Sojourner Truth, and Harriet Tubman, Dr. Bernice Johnson Reagon has built upon their legacies with her work in the SNCC Freedom Singers followed by her founding of the African American all-female singing group Sweet Honey in the Rock.[105]

After the victories in the Civil Rights and Voting Rights Acts of 1964 and 1965, further struggles for racial justice went forward. The Black Panther Party had recording artists in Elaine Brown and a group called the The Lumpen.[106] The Black Power and Black Pride movements in the late 1960s also produced a network of poets and musicians in Harlem called the Last Poets, who performed poems with music of funk rhythms and helped to set the stage for hip-hop. The group's history and contemporary performances are captured in the documentary film "The Last Poets: Made in Amerikkka."[107]

The labor movement sadly was not a dependable ally to the civil rights and women's movements. Racism and sexism in the craft unions had an impact on who did the work for public and private contractors.[108] Nixon and his strategists knew how racism was the weakness that could divide the working class when Republicans adopted the Southern Strategy to go after the votes of white workers in the South. Much was accomplished by the social movements of the 1960s and 70s; however, systemic racism and sexism lived on, and the seeds of neoliberal global capitalism began to take root. Jobs began moving from the unionized North to the anti-union South. Popular music by the mid-70s reflected a change toward diminished activism as fewer songs held overt political themes. Some exceptions, though, have been notable in punk and hip-hop.[109]

In response to this hostile climate of political economy that continues to repress organized labor, working people have gathered together to express resistance in the arts, including music. As noted in the previous chapter, the New York City Labor Chorus was founded in 1991. Since then, additional labor choruses have formed in six other North American cities—San Francisco, Seattle, Minneapolis-St. Paul, Baltimore, Washington DC, and Vancouver. In addition, there are many more choruses with social-justice orientation that include labor songs in their performances. Some organizations and annual events across the nation celebrate the arts in the labor movement, and

I can highlight two here. The Great Labor Arts Exchange, sponsored by the Labor Heritage Foundation since 1983, has brought labor artists and activists together for three days each June since 1979 for workshops and performances.[110] LaborArts, a non-profit organization founded in New York City in 2001, has this mission statement: "To document and celebrate the artistic and cultural heritage of working people and the labor movement, and encourage understanding of their often overlooked contributions to our society."[111] These contributions, indeed, are often overlooked by mainstream media and academia. The next chapter focuses on the artistic contributions to the labor movement by the New York City Labor Chorus over its history preceding the 25th-anniversary year.

NOTES

1. Frederick Douglass, *Narrative of the Life of Frederick Douglass: An American Slave: Written by Himself.* (1845, Reprint, The Gutenberg Project, 2006), http://www.gutenberg.org/files/23/23-h/23-h.htm.

2. Thomas P. Barker, "Spatial Dialectics: Intimations of Freedom in Antebellum Slave Song." *Journal of Black Studies* 46, no. 4 (May 2015): 369–373.

3. Norman Yetman (ed.), *Voices from Slavery: 100 Authentic Slave Narratives* (1970, Reprint, Mineola, NY: Dover Publications, Inc., 2000).

4. Ibid., Fannie Moore, interviewed by Marjorie Jones, 229.

5. Ibid.

6. William F. Allen, Charles P. Ware, and Lucy M. Garrison (eds.), *Slave Songs of the United States* (1867, Reprint, Chapel Hill: University of North Carolina Press, 2011), 9.

7. Ibid., 43.

8. Ibid., 37.

9. Aaron D. McClendon, "Sounds of Sympathy: William Wells Brown's 'Anti-Slavery Harp', Abolition, and the Culture of Early and Antebellum American Song." *African American Review* 47, no. 1 (Spring 2014): 84.

10. William W. Brown, Preface, *The Anti-Slavery Harp: A Collection of Songs for Anti-Slavery Meetings* (1848, Reprint, The Gutenburg Project, 2003).

11. Frederick Douglass, *My Bondage and My Freedom* (1855, Reprint, New Haven: Yale University Press, 2014), 392.

12. Douglass, *Narrative*. Final paragraph of Chapter 2.

13. Bonnie Raitt, Foreword to *American Roots Music*, edited by Robert Santelli, Holly George-Warren, and Jim Brown (New York: Harry N. Abrams, Inc., 2001), 8.

14. W.E.B. DuBois, *The Souls of Black Folk* (1903, Reprint, New Haven: Yale University Press, 2015), 189.

15. Robert Darden, Nothing but Love in God's Water: Black Sacred Music from the Civil War to the Civil Rights Movement (University Park: Pennsylvania State University Press, 2014), 18.

16. Claudia Perry, "Hallelujah: The Sacred Music of Black America," in *American Roots Music*, eds. Robert Santelli, Holly George-Warren, and Jim Brown (New York: Harry N. Abrams, Inc., 2001), 84–103.

17. W.C. Handy, *Father of the Blues: An Autobiography* (1941, Reprint, New York: Da Capo, 1969), 62.

18. Darden, *Nothing but Love*, 50.

19. Ibid., 24–30.

20. Ibid., 33–36.

21. Ibid., 54–56.

22. Ronald D. Cohen, *Work and Sing: A History of Occupational and Labor Union Songs in the United States* (Crockett, CA: Carquinez Press, 2010), 4.

23. Ibid. Cohen added that the song "Hold the Fort" originated in the US, traveled to England and Australia, and then returned to the US, where it "became a labor staple."

24. Darden, *Nothing but Love*, 60.

25. Ron Eyerman and Andrew Jamison, *Music and Social Movements: Mobilizing Traditions in the Twentieth Century* (Cambridge, UK: Cambridge University Press, 1998), 50–51.

26. Cohen, *Work and Sing*, 20.

27. Phillip Y. Nicholson, *Labor's Story in the United States* (Philadelphia: Temple University Press, 2004), 116.

28. Cohen, *Work and Sing*, 20.

29. Rob Rosenthal and Richard Flacks, *Playing for Change: Music and Musicians in the Service of Social Movements* (New York: Taylor & Francis, 2011), 4.

30. Ralph Chaplain, "Solidarity Forever," lyrics as printed by David A. Carter, "The Industrial Workers of the World and the Rhetoric of Song." *The Quarterly Journal of Speech* 66 (1980): 371.

31. Franklin Rosemont, *Joe Hill: The IWW and the Making of a Revolutionary Workingclass Counterculture* (Oakland: PM Press, 2015), 283.

32. Ibid., 275–277.

33. Dick Weissman, *Talkin' 'bout a Revolution: Music and Social Change in America* (New York: Backbeat Books, 2010), 18.

34. Sheryl Hurner, "Discursive Identity Formation of Suffrage Women: Reframing the 'Cult of True Womanhood' through Song." *Western Journal of Communication* 70, no. 3, 235.

35. Ibid., 254.

36. Ron Kaminkow, "Joe Hill Road Show Tour Conducts Concerts in Three Dozen Cities," January 25, 2016, https://www.iww.org/content/joe-hill-100-road-show-tour-conducts-concerts-three-dozen-cities.

37. Industrial Workers of the World, "International Directory," https://www.iww.org/branches.

38. Archie Green, David Roediger, Franklin Rosemont, and Salvatore Salerno, eds., *The Big Red Songbook* (Oakland: PM Press, 2016).

39. Terese M. Volk, "Little Red Songbooks: Songs for the Labor Force of America." *Journal of Research in Music Education* 49, no. 1 (2001), 35.

40. Ibid., 42.
41. Cohen, *Work and Sing*, 89.
42. Ibid., 91–93.
43. Darden, *Nothing but Love*, 88-90.
44. Vincent J. Roscigno and William F. Danaher, *The Voice of Southern Labor: Radio, Music, and Textile Strikes, 1929-1934* (Minneapolis: University of Minnesota Press, 2004), 29.
45. Ibid., 49–51.
46. Ibid., 58–59.
47. Ibid., 89.
48. Kristina Horton, *Martyr of Loray Mill: Ella May and the 1929 Textile Workers' Strike in Gastonia, North Carolina* (Jefferson, NC: McFarland, 2015).
49. Timothy P. Lynch, *Strike Songs of the Depression* (Jackson: University Press of Mississippi, 2001), 64–66.
50. Cohen, *Work and Sing*, 67.
51. Judith Tick, *Ruth Crawford Seeger: A Composer's Search for American Music* (Oxford, UK: Oxford University Press, 1997), 188.
52. Ibid.
53. Ibid., 188–200.
54. Daniel Katz, *All Together Different: Yiddish Socialists, Garment Workers, and the Labor Roots of Multiculturalism* (New York: New York University Press, 2011). 137, 153, 155, 185.
55. Rachel C. Donaldson, *"I Hear America Singing": Folk Music and National Identity* (Philadelphia: Temple University Press, 2010), 27.
56. Ibid., 28.
57. Ibid., 32.
58. Cohen, *Work and Sing*, 6-7.
59. Woody Guthrie with Alan Lomax and Pete Seeger (eds.), *Hard-Hitting Songs for Hard-Hit People* (1967, Reprint, Lincoln: University of Nebraska Press, 2012), 324.
60. Cohen, *Work and Sing*, 51.
61. Eyerman and Jamison, *Music and Social Movements*, 81.
62. Big Bill Broonzy, interviewed by Alan Lomax, in Lomax, *The Land Where the Blues Began* (New York: Pantheon Books, 1993), 460. Emphasis in italics by Lomax.
63. John A. Lomax and Alan Lomax, *Folk Songs as Sung by Lead Belly* (New York: McMillan, 1936).
64. Darden, *Nothing but Love*, 66.
65. *Oh Freedom*, traditional African-American spiritual, lyrics as quoted by Darden, *Nothing but Love*, 70.
66. Michael K. Honey, *Sharecropper's Troubadour: John L. Handcox, the Southern Tenant Farmers' Union, and the African American Song Tradition* (New York: Palgrave McMillan, 2013), 50.
67. Ibid., 64.
68. Ibid., 137.
69. Ibid., 95–96.

70. Adelfred (YouTube username), "Almanac Singers—Roll the Union On," song by John L. Handcox, video recording, 2009, https://www.youtube.com/watch?v=v4YeDI4R9MA.

71. Lynch, *Strike Songs*, 104–108.

72. Ibid., 119.

73. Janell Hobson, "Everybody's Protest Song: Music as Social Protest in the Performances of Marian Anderson and Billy Holliday." *Signs: Journal of Women and Culture in Society* 33, no. 2 (2008), 443.

74. Angela Y. Davis, *Blues Legacies and Black Feminism: Gertrude "Ma" Rainey, Bessie Smith, and Billie Holiday* (New York: Vintage Books, 1998), 181–197.

75. Dorian Lynskey, *33 Revolutions per Minute: A History of Protest Songs, from Billy Holiday to Green Day* (New York: HarperCollins Publishers, 2011), 4–13.

76. Weissman, *Talkin' 'bout a Revolution*, 195.

77. Darden, *Nothing but Love*, 99.

78. Lynskey, *33 Revolutions*, 27–28.

79. Weissman, Talkin' 'bout a Revolution, 197.

80. Ibid., 196.

81. Darden, *Nothing but Love*, 102.

82. Rebecca de Schweinitz, *If We Could Change the World: Young People and America's Long Struggle for Racial Equality* (Chapel Hill: University of North Carolina Press, 2009), 303.

83. Robert R. Korstad, Civil Rights Unionism: Tobacco Workers and the Struggle for Democracy in the Mid-Twentieth-Century South (Chapel Hill: University of North Carolina Press, 2003), 89.

84. Ibid., 312, 317–318.

85. Ibid., 345–348.

86. Ibid., 349.

87. Ibid., 238–240.

88. Cohen, *Work and Sing*, 119–130.

89. Darden, *Nothing but Love*, 120–121.

90. Ibid., 106.

91. Lynskey, *33 Revolutions*, 36–38.

92. Nicholson, *Labor's Story*, 252–253.

93. Paul Robeson, *Here I Stand* (1958, Reprint, Boston: Beacon Press, 1988), 53–54.

94. Ibid., 63–73.

95. Megan Dunn and James Walker, "Union Membership in the United States," Bureau of Labor Statistics, September 2016, 2, https://www.bls.gov/spotlight/2016/union-membership-in-the-united-states/pdf/union-membership-in-the-united-states.pdf.

96. Ibid, 7.

97. Naomi Klein, *The Shock Doctrine: The Rise and Fall of Disaster Capitalism* (New York: Picador, 2007), 72–76.

98. Henry Hampton, executive producer, *Eyes on the Prize: America's Civil Rights Movement 1954–1985* (1994; Arlington, VA: Public Broadcasting Service), documentary film.

99. Ely Landau, producer, *King: A Filmed Record: Montgomery to Memphis* (1970; New York: The Martin Luther King Film Project and Kino Classics), documentary film.

100. Darden, *Nothing but Love*, 36, 95.

101. Ibid., 120–121.

102. Tavis Smiley, *Death of a King: The Real Story of Martin Luther King, Jr.'s Final Year* (New York: Little, Brown, and Co., 2014), 11–21.

103. Joe Street, *The Culture War in the Civil Rights Movement* (Gainesville: University Press of Florida, 2007), 24, 26, 127–129, 164.

104. Ibid., 42–48.

105. Bernice Johnson Reagon, *If You Don't Go, Don't Hinder Me* (Lincoln: University of Nebraska Press, 2001), 100–141.

106. Street, *Culture War*, 157–159.

107. Claude Santiago, producer, *The Last Poets: Made in Amerikkka* (2012; Lussas, France: AndanaFilms), documentary film.

108. Nicholson, *Labor's Story*, 271.

109. Priya Parmar, Anthony J. Nocella II, Scott Robertson, and Martha Diaz (eds.), *Rebel Music: Resistance through Hip-Hop and Punk* (Charlotte: Information Age Publishing, Inc., 2015), xix–xxviii.

110. Labor Heritage Foundation, *GLAE Poster 2010*, http://www.laborheritage.org/wp-content/uploads/2010/03/glaeposter2010.pdf.

111. Labor Arts, Our Mission, http://www.laborarts.org/.

Chapter Two

A History of the NYC Labor Chorus

The NYCLC came into existence 10 years after President Reagan fired striking air traffic controllers in 1981. The firing of thousands of striking members of the Professional Air Traffic Controllers Organization (PATCO), who were protesting an increased work pace, high stress levels, and worsening workplace facilities, became a turning point from which organized labor has not recovered.[1] The firings came after PATCO had endorsed Reagan during his campaign in 1980.[2] The lack of a unified response of protest by organized labor to the firings enabled attacks against unions to continue. The chorus became an organization of resistance to the ongoing attacks against workers' rights. The idea of bringing workers of multiple unions together to unite in singing was new to this era of decline in union membership and strength.

THE BIRTH AND GROWTH OF THE CHORUS

Three founding mothers—Barbara Bailey, Laura Friedman, and Bobbie Rabinowitz—shared the idea to create the chorus and the will to do the hard work of organizing it. Of these three, only Bailey became a singing member. My attempts to contact Rabinowitz went unanswered. I was able to contact Friedman during the summer of 2018, and I interviewed her by phone in October.[3] Bailey, the long-time president of the chorus, shared with me in an in-person interview her memories of the beginnings in 1991.[4]

Barbara Bailey, age 77 at the time of our interview before a rehearsal in March of 2017, self-identified as a black woman. She is retired from the NYC Police Department as a supervisor who represented the union Communication Workers of America (CWA) Local 1180 in resolving grievances and later helped to create a division for retirees' benefits. She was the sixth of six children, and her mother was a church organist in St. John's Baptist Church, which was founded by her grandfather in a Long Island community. Bailey described her neighborhood as "mixed" with Italian and Swedish families, stating "we lived next door to each other and everyone respected each other and got along . . . played on the street and we had a community center, we all congregated there." She credited this environment of her upbringing as the source in why she is "comfortable being around people."

Bailey stated that Bobbie Rabinowitz, a social worker, had the original idea to start a labor chorus. Rabinowitz shared her plan with Laura Friedman, a CWA member who then asked Bailey to make it a team of three founders. The three were concerned that new union members knew little about the history of unions' struggles, and they saw a multi-union chorus as a vehicle for uniting workers to learn part of that history through songs. Bailey also mentioned that rock music had become much more popular than the music that Pete Seeger and other folk artists had made, the latter often with lyrics upholding the labor and civil rights movements. The three founding mothers hoped that the labor chorus would help to revive these songs that were neglected by commercial media. They sent recruitment notices to many unions in New York City, and Bailey recalled that there were 15 to 20 members that first year.

Laura Friedman was 65 years old and self-identified as white when I interviewed her by phone in fall of 2018.[5] She was retired as a union organizer for the Legal Services Staff Association, which became affiliated with District 65 of the United Auto Workers. She also had worked as executive director of the Fund for Labor Education, which helped unions develop their leaders. In her upbringing her family went from middle class to poor after her father died. Although she was never a singing member of the NYCLC, she was active in helping the other two founding mothers launch the organization. The three of them first decided to work together on creating a labor chorus when they were in Laura's kitchen together for a different meeting among unions. Laura's motivation for forming a labor chorus was what she saw as a lack of opportunity for rank-and-file members across unions to gather together while leaders among unions often were able to do so. All three founding mothers loved music and saw a chorus as the way to bring union members together in a supportive organization. Laura claimed that she had few people she saw as heroes, but she exclaimed that Pete Seeger was at the top of her short list as someone who was "a humble man who did great things, and from his singing to his organizing he never stopped; it's who he was."

Seeger recommended that the founders hire Geoffrey Fairweather, a black Jamaican-native musician, as conductor. Bailey, along with several other long-time members that I interviewed, remembered Fairweather as an excellent conductor who helped the chorus grow to more than 100 members. Sadly, shortly after leaving the chorus in 2003 for a sabbatical, an illness led to his death in 2005.[6] Patricia Logan, a soprano who is blind and self-identifies as white, was age 67 and employed at New York University's Tamiment Library when interviewed. She recalled, "[Fairweather] used to make me feel very good by talking about the fact that, when he was teaching on his home island when he had a chorus, that none of the people could sight-read and they were all learning by listening, and so he thought it was a very normal and usual experience."[7] Ann Gael, another soprano and a retired grants manager, was age 71 and self-identified as "white, Scottish-Welsh." She stated, "Geoffrey Fairweather had charisma that dripped off his fingernails. He was just amazing. When he said, 'Just sing it for me this way,' you wanted to say, 'Oh, I will do it, or I will die in the attempt.'"[8] Denise Jones, an alto and frequent soloist who self-identified as African American, was age 53 and working as a social worker when interviewed. She spoke with a beaming smile: "Geoffrey Fairweather, he saw the solo in me, I didn't see it [laughing]. And he had believed in me and gave me a try, so when I tried, I was like huh, I said, 'Geoffrey, this is not going so well,' and he is like, 'Get working on it.' So I got working on it and now it's better."[9] Having heard many times the dynamic solos by Jones in performances and rehearsals, I was surprised to learn that she was not already a seasoned soloist upon joining the chorus. Her ongoing work in the chorus is a testament to Fairweather's legacy.

As much as the founding mothers and Fairweather did to launch the chorus, there was a perception that a larger body of leaders could help further in managing the workload. A board of directors formed during the first year. Betty Reid, a postal worker and one of the original board members, shared some of her earliest memories of the leadership group.[10] Reid, who self-identifies as a black woman, was 67 years old when I interviewed her. When she went to her first rehearsal, she was the only person to attend in addition to the three founding mothers and Fairweather, who assigned her to be a soprano after her audition. Eventually, after membership grew, Reid ran for the board successfully as an at-large member. The late Ginger Pinkard, the original treasurer on the board, was unfamiliar with a newly adopted program called Quick Books. Reid had worked with the program as treasurer in her union, so she stepped in as treasurer for the chorus after Pinkard voluntary stepped aside. Reid recalled that the board paid a part-time bookkeeper "for quite a while." Jeffrey Vogel, a retired respiratory therapist and member of 1199 SEIU United Healthcare Workers East, was another original member of the board.[11] Vogel, who identified himself as a "spiritual socialist Jewish atheist," was 69 years old and a retired respiratory therapist when interviewed. The board welcomed him because of his relationship to his union, which had been one of the chorus' best sources of financial support. Vogel stated, "Sometimes there have been little conflicts occasionally arising between board members, but for the most part it's been very constructive." He added that keeping the chorus going for 25 years was a great accomplishment. Although Vogel never had an official title within the board, he claimed to have been leading efforts in publicity and searches for performance opportunities over the years.

Another essential role from the start has been accompanist. Eustace Johnson played piano for the chorus until leaving in 2002 to meet an increasingly demanding schedule as accompanist at his church.[12] Upon leaving, Johnson included Dennis Nelson on a list of possible replacements. Nelson took over and continues as accompanist as of this writing. I have more information on both accompanists later in this chapter. Denise Jones commented that both are excellent musicians who supported her development as a soloist.[13]

The debut performance of the chorus was at the 1199 Bread & Roses Conference on November 9, 1991.[14] Conference participants included filmmaker-novelist John Sayles, historian Studs Terkel, and Pete Seeger. Moe Foner, while working as an executive officer for Local 1199 in 1979, had established Bread & Roses as a union cultural program.[15] The program brought singers and actors to hospitals and nursing homes, printed posters, and produced a musical about health-care work titled "Take Care." The 1991 conference, according to UE News, "brought together workers and artists in an effort to regain labor's voice and militancy." It was an appropriate event for connecting the chorus with the existing labor-arts community.

The chorus continued into 1992 with public performances. An event listed as "Sing Along with Pete Seeger" appears on the NYCLC website's list of performances.[16] The place was Hunter College, but no exact date appears. An Internet search of "Sing Along with Pete Seeger" led me to a Library of Congress video of Seeger in 2007 leading a room full of people in singing songs.[17] Seeger wrote in 1993, "It all boils down to what I would most like to do as a musician. Put songs on people's lips instead of just in their ears."[18] Also listed on the NYCLC website as a 1992 performance is the Democratic Party National Convention, which was held July 13 to 16 in New York City. Co-founding-mother Laura Friedman recalled that a Baptist choir also performed at the convention. When this choir and the NYCLC members were together while passing each other backstage, the Baptists chanted, "Go labor, go labor!" NYCLC members in return chanted, "Go Baptists, go Baptists!"[19]

The premiere Benefit Concert for the NYCLC took place on the evening of Saturday, June 19, 1993, and such concerts have continued every other year since then. The journal for the concert, which was the main source of revenue for the chorus through advertisements, includes a list of members' names and union affiliations.[20] There were 33 sopranos, 25 altos, 11 tenors, and six basses. The tenors included five women, assuming names that are traditionally female were, indeed, women. Overall, the chorus appeared to have only 12 men among 75 members. Also found in the journal are brief biographies of Geoffrey Fairweather and Eustace Johnson as conductor and accompanist, respectively.[21] Separate paragraphs name Fairweather's accomplishments as a musician in Jamaica and the US. He was currently an assistant professor of music at John Jay College. Johnson, who was also working as music director for the Praise Ensemble and choir director at Trinity Baptist Church, was once a pianist for Chuck Berry. Another bio appears for Henry Foner, narrator for the concert. Foner, who died in 2017 at age 97, had a long history in the labor movement as organizer, teacher, and songwriter. The concert-journal bio noted that he currently was a member of the Editorial Board of *Jewish Currents* magazine. Brief biographies also appear in the journal for three guest performers: Pete Seeger, John D. Anthony, and Pat Humphries.[22] Seeger's paragraph noted his work of more than 50 years in singing for schools, unions, rallies, and marches. Anthony, a vocal bass soloist and actor who had performed at the Metropolitan Opera and with orchestras in Europe, sang the lead for "Ballad for Americans"[23] with the chorus. Humphries, a singer-songwriter in the folk tradition, was noted for her songs that had become standards at rallies worldwide.

There are a few other performances listed for the next two years of the chorus in either/both the chorus website[24] or/and the 25th Anniversary journal.[25] One was at an event titled "Everybody Says Freedom" that was part of Central Park Summerstage series on June 26, 1993. The next event listed was the Rainbow Coalition Conference on May 12, 1994, at the Waldorf Astoria Hotel. Also listed was a rally for national health care on June 8, 1994, in Washington, DC. On April 27, 1995, the chorus sang at UN headquarters for the First Anniversary Celebration of the New South Africa. My online searches for detailed information on these events were unfruitful.

The chorus performed its second benefit concert on June 11, 1995, at Great Hall on the campus of The Cooper Union for the Advancement of Science and Art, commonly known as Cooper Union.[26] Eighty-three members were listed by name and union affiliation, including 37 sopranos, 28 altos, 12 tenors, and six basses.[27] There were two guest artists.[28] Listed first are Ossie Davis and Ruby Dee, an African American husband-wife team who often performed together from their works as poets, playwrights, actors, and activists. Also listed is Thokoza with Thuli Dumakude, a South African group of four women who sang songs from traditional and contemporary sounds of South Africa's black townships.[29]

A major event for the chorus in 1996 was the 60th Annual Anniversary Dinner to honor Veterans of the Abraham Lincoln Brigade (VALB), who had left their homes in the US to fight for the Republican forces in the Spanish

Civil War. This was held on April 21 at the Sheraton in Midtown Manhattan, and the admission was $50 to benefit the Abraham Lincoln Brigade Archives (ALBA).[30] Listed at the top of the program were the names of eight readers who voiced "a dramatic reading of *Madrid 1937: Letters of the Abraham Lincoln Brigade from the Spanish Civil War*, edited by Cary Nelson and Jefferson Hendricks with songs by the New York City Labor Chorus." Among the readers were Harry Belafonte and Susan Sarandon. Speakers were William Sussman, Vice Chair of ALBA; Milton Wolff, Bay Area Commander of VALB; and Henry Foner, listed as retired president of the Fur and Leather Workers Union, United Food & Commercial Workers. The program flyer did not list the songs sung by the chorus, but at least one song in Spanish from the Spanish Civil War, "Si Me Quieres Escribir" (If You Want to Write to Me), was still in the chorus repertoire during the decade of the 2010s.[31]

The chorus had another eventful year in 1997. The third benefit concert, on June 1, included guest performances by Pete Seeger again and Guy Davis, a blues musician and actor who is the eldest child of Ruby Dee and Ossie Davis.[32] Then came a tour of Sweden from June 25 to July 10—the first of four trips by the chorus over the years to perform in other countries.[33] Several chorus members spoke of memories of the trip in my interviews with them. Velma Hill, a retired city worker in social services who was 77 years old at the time of the interview and identified herself as a "southern black woman," joined the chorus just before the trip and then went. She recalled with delight, "We have learned . . . people's culture, even the songs, then the history behind the songs . . . When we went to Sweden we went to Joe Hill's house—the house that he was born in. That was a little house, oh lord [laughter]. But, you know, to learn in different cultures and the history of people fighting for the jobs and the unions."[34] I was glad to learn from Velma that the country of Joe Hill's birth has made the effort to preserve his memory. Rona Armillas, a retired teacher and school administrator who was 73 when interviewed and who self-identified as a "Jewish American with Eastern European grandparents," included the following in her testimony of the trip: "We got to sing with, and listen to, choirs from all over, not all over the world. They were mostly Scandinavian and some from the Baltic states, like Estonia . . . And some songs, so many people knew, like *Siyahamba* [a South African song]. We'd all get together and people would be singing *Siyahamba* together. It was funny."[35] These two interviewees and others clearly were still moved by their travel experience after nearly 20 years had passed.

Among the most important events in the NYCLC's history was the 100th anniversary of Paul Robeson's birth. The chorus sang with Pete Seeger at a tribute to Robeson on May 30, 1998, at the New York Historical Society.[36] A much larger event, though, was on November 30, 1998, at Carnegie Hall with the title *Gala Centennial Salute: Paul Robeson: Ol' Man River*. A poster announcing the event lists the chorus among the performers, including Muhammad Ali, Harry Belafonte, Ossie Davis, Ruby Dee, Danny Glover, Whoopi Goldberg, Pete Seeger, and the South Wales Onllwyn Male Voice Choir, among others.[37] The Paul Robeson Foundation sponsored the gala, and ticket prices ranged from 20 to 500 dollars. Another event with the NYCLC's singing was "Songs of Struggle and Protest: A Paul Robeson Centennial Anniversary Concert" on February 6, 1999, in the Hudson Valley city of Poughkeepsie, New York.[38] The list of songs performed by the chorus included the epic "Ballad for Americans,"[39] featuring bass member and retired postal worker Percy McRae as soloist. Robeson had recorded the song in 1940, and it was the best-selling of all his recordings.[40] Its uplifting words brought a message of unity to the nation during the 1940 campaigns for the presidency.[41]

Some chorus members in interviews spoke of Robeson and how the chorus marked his legacy. Bobby Greenberg, a retired secondary history teacher and the vice president of the chorus board who was 78 years old when interviewed, and who identified himself as Jewish but not religious, recalled, "We spent a year on his music and we went everywhere, we went to Rutgers, we sang at Carnegie Hall in concert with Pete Seeger on–just on [Robeson's] music and his life."[42] Jeff Vogel spoke of how his parents, who were persecuted during the McCarthy years for their membership in the Communist Party, raised him on the music of Robeson. He went on to say with glowing admiration, "that voice of Robeson particularly always thrilled me. It was this amazing deep, deep, beautiful voice. So, that's really inspiration for my singing."[43] Robeson died 15 years before the NYCLC started, but his legacy remains as a cornerstone to the foundation of the chorus.

The chorus performed its Fourth Gala Benefit Concert on the afternoon of Sunday, June 4, 1999, at Haft Auditorium of the Fashion Institute of Technology. The concert program lists the names and union affiliations of 102 members from a total of 24 local unions.[44] One part of the concert offered "a segment of songs celebrating the centennial of the birth of Paul Robeson, including a performance of 'Ballad for Americans.'"[45] Percy McRae sang the solos. He died suddenly on July 31, 2000, after singing the national anthem at Wrigley Field in Chicago for a baseball game, and the NYCLC dedicated the CD of studio recordings of the concert program to his memory.[46] Ann Gael spoke of her memories of McRae:

> He was like 6'6" and big and he had a very deep bass voice. So he sang Paul Robeson parts to the things that we sang and he was just such a lovely, lovely, lovely man in addition to his wonderful voice and he was a postal worker. He went to a postal worker convention in Chicago and they asked him to sing the national anthem at the Cubs game. So he got up, he sang the national anthem

and sat down and died of a heart attack, but imagine how wonderful that you die doing what you love."[47]

The CD liner notes end by stating of McRae, "We will miss his great presence, his tremendous voice and his wonderful and gentle spirit."[48] Having listened to the CD, I can attest that he, indeed, had a tremendous voice.

The NYCLC has not performed only as a concert chorus. Its website includes this statement prior to its contact information: "Please contact us to have the Chorus sing at your picket line, rally, meeting or other event."[49] Included in the list of performances are "Transport Workers Union Local 100 Rally at MTA [Metropolitan Transportation Authority]" in 1999 and "Picket Line in Support of Citarella [dock] Workers" in 2000.[50] Some of these non-concert events have involved only a fraction of the chorus membership with neither conductor nor accompanist, but they represent intentional actions to bring singing back to the front lines of workers' struggles. Some chorus members expressed a desire to focus more on these events and less on concerts. Marilyn Taylor (pseudonym) stated, "I don't find [preparing for concerts] very exciting. My disappointment is that we almost never go to a union hall anymore. We almost never go to a picket line anymore. We're always too busy preparing for a concert. I don't want to be in a concert choir. I want to be a labor chorus."[51] Other members, though, are concerned more about music quality than political actions. Debbie Zanca, an accomplished soprano who is blind and self-identifies as Caucasian and Jewish of Russian and Polish descent, was age 65 when interviewed and had worked for the Lighthouse, an organization providing services for the blind and visually impaired. She stated, "People used to ask me, 'Don't you think [the NYCLC] is a step down from what, the way you used to sing?' I said, 'No, it is a different genre of music, it is a different style of music and some classical is incorporated. And so, I am not into marching on picket lines and things like that. I have to be honest; I am in it strictly for the music."[52] However difficult the conflict might be, the tension between emphases on singing quality and activism perhaps can lead to a healthy balance in which the results are picket lines and rallies with better singing and concerts with livelier narration that connects songs to current actions.

The NYCLC celebrated its tenth year in 2001. The chorus joined with the Queens College Chorus and Orchestra at Judson Memorial Church on April 18 to perform a program titled "Celebrating American Labor Songs of the 1930s."[53] Constructed in the 1890s and located next to Washington Square Park, the building has housed a Protestant congregation with an early history of service to immigrants in poverty that has expanded to a general commitment to social justice.[54] On June 27, the NYCLC performed its 10th Anniversary Concert at The Town Hall in Midtown Manhattan.[55] An organization of suffragists called The League for Political Education had the idea of building a place to support political education, and architects McKim, Mead & White oversaw the 1921 construction of The Town Hall.[56] The venue has continued in its support of the arts in education and in its commitment to social justice.[57] These are only two examples of many in how the chorus has sought to perform in buildings that offer a history of service to justice in addition to attractive décor and high-quality acoustics.

The schedule of the chorus after the turn of the century only became busier. The chorus website reports a total of 10 performances during 2002 and 13 in 2003.[58] According to the website, the chorus returned to The Town Hall to perform in 2002 and 2003 programs titled "Yiddish in America." The event was produced by the Workmen's Circle, an organization committed to Jewish identity-building and social justice since its 1900 inception.[59] My online search for information on the NYCLC's participation led to the 2003 performance for the second annual "gala celebration" of the event, with a November 6 date.[60] Emcee was film and Broadway star Lainie Kazan. There were nine performances that evening, and the finale was announced as follows: "The New Yiddish Chorale, the New York City Labor Chorus and the Jewish People's Philharmonic Chorus will join in a rousing finale to celebrate Yiddish."

Many of the NYCLC members I interviewed included their Jewish heritage when asked how they identify themselves in terms of race, ethnicity, and/or nationality. Kelly Wilmeth, a retired school social worker of age 67 when interviewed, replied, "White Eastern European Jewish but I don't know if that's . . . that's not really ethnicity but a cultural. . . . I'm a Buddhist but a cultural Jew but I practice Buddhism."[61] Like several others interviewed, she separated cultural Judaism from religious Judaism and identified with the former. Bobby Greenberg, in response to the same question at the start of a focus-group session, replied, "Identify certain terms of race, well, I think race is a—it's a construct that doesn't make any sense. Ethnicity Jewish, nationality Jewish, I mean that I think of myself as ethnically Jewish, not religious, not practicing and never had practice."[62] Greenberg also mentioned that he sang as a teenager in a chorus affiliated with the Jewish People's Fraternal Organization, which he described as "a left-wing Jewish organization." Eugene Hamond, a bass who was age 72 and a retired health and safety officer when interviewed, replied "I always put down human," in response to my race-ethnicity-nationality question.[63] He was raised in a mostly middle-class and Jewish suburb of New York City. He remembered a sense of community that seemed to be lost: "Yeah, [there were] Union Halls and then there were Irish community groups and Italian and Jewish and neighborhood community centers where people would go for meals. They would go for music and dances. They probably go for places where kids who get tutoring help with their homework. That just doesn't exist anymore. It's a very—people are very isolated now." Our discussion turned to the growing crisis of heroin addiction that seemed to be a result of the lack of community in so many places—urban, suburban, and rural.

The NYCLC also has participated in events for the African American community. On February 21, 1996, the chorus sang in the Black History Month Celebration at the Apollo Theater,[64] the venue in Harlem famous for helping to launch the careers of many African American performers since opening in 1914 and starting its amateur nights twenty years later.[65] Three other NYCLC performances for black history appear from 2003 to 2009 on the website list.[66] No date appears for the 2003 event, which took place at Lincoln Hospital. An event listed as "Black History Month Concert at the Ethical Culture Society" appears under 2005-2006 without a date. The dateless listing under 2009 is "Black History Month Celebration for CWA 1180 [Communication Workers of America]." My Internet search for details on these events was unsuccessful. The next chapter addresses the African American and African roots of some of the songs sung in the 25th Anniversary concert.

Six of the 28 chorus members that I interviewed identified themselves as either black or African American. As noted above, Barbara Bailey[67] and Betty Reid[68] identified themselves as black women, and Velma Hill[69] as a southern black woman. Denise Jones, as mentioned above, identifies herself as African American.[70] Inez West, a retired teacher who was age 65 when interviewed, identified herself as a black woman.[71] Dennis Nelson, mentioned above as the accompanist for the chorus since 2002, self-identified as both African American and Caribbean American, noting the Jamaican heritage of his family.[72] Nelson clarified, "So it is kind of fluid but basically I see myself born in this country and my cultural heritage is more of Caribbean—Jamaican." Also, as noted above, the original conductor of the chorus, Geoffrey Fairweather, was a black immigrant from Jamaica.

Fairweather left for a sabbatical from the chorus in 2003 to work with the New Jersey Philharmonic on building a new community chorus in Newark.[73] Due to health issues leading to his death in 2005, he never was able to return to the NYCLC. The chorus membership had grown to more than 100 under Fairweather's work as director and conductor. Fairweather's successor would have the challenges of leading a large group in either familiar or new directions.

A NEW ERA FOR A MATURING CHORUS

The interim conductor of the NYCLC during Fairweather's sabbatical was Peter Schlosser. He joined the chorus not knowing that he would end up replacing Fairweather to become its second long-term conductor. Only a few members mentioned Schlosser in interviews. His legacy in the chorus continues in several of his song arrangements that remain in the repertoire.

Schlosser arrived early enough in 2003 to conduct the 12th Anniversary concert on May 30 at the Fashion Institute of Technology.[74] The concert program listed 78 members, which was down considerably from prior counts. A brief biography in the program listed some of Schlosser's accomplishments, including many years as conductor of the Jewish People's Philharmonic Chorus, performances in Broadway and off-Broadway plays, and his then-current position in teaching speech and music at the Center for Worker Education of the Community College of New York. The concert was also the first major NYCLC performance for accompanist Dennis Nelson, who replaced Eustace Johnson shortly before Fairweather's departure.[75] Nelson's bio mentioned several accomplishments, including performances and tours with renowned gospel artists, many years as organist for Trinity Baptist Church in Brooklyn, and his then-current work as a music teacher in a New York City public school. Also appearing in the program was a bio for guest musician Charlie King, an award-winning artist who had "been at the heart of American folk music for over 35 years."[76]

This is the earliest concert program that I was able to access as a complete document.[77] Bound in heavy yellow paper, it has 36 unnumbered black and white pages. The cover includes a drawn image of a dove carrying a musical note. Named as presenter was Laura Friedman, one of the three founding mothers of the chorus. Brian McLaughlin, president of the New York City Central Labor Council, served for greetings. The 18 songs for the evening appeared on a list with credits to each song. A few pages showed photos of chorus members in their sections and in other settings. Members in the photos wore a white T-shirt with the chorus name under an image of a fist holding a musical note, superimposed on an apple (New York City being the "big apple"). Some photos also show members wearing union hats. The last 24 pages are where unions, individuals, and a few small businesses paid for advertisements, greetings, or announcements from a single line to 1/8 page and up to a full page. The full back cover had this message in bold: "The 237,000 united members of 1199 SEIU proudly salute the New York City Labor Chorus. Here's to many more years of bringing to life the passion and power of our labor movement with song!"

The chorus continued to stay busy with performances. Thirteen events appear on the website list for 2004 to 2005.[78] A highlight of 2004 was participation by many chorus members in the Great Choral Convergence at the Great Labor Arts Exchange on June 19 in Washington, DC. Following the idea of one of the NYCLC's founding mothers, Bobbie Rabinowitz, six labor choruses performed in a concert at the Washington Ethical Society that was recorded for a CD.[79] Joining the NYCLC were the Brooklyn Women's Chorus, the DC Labor Chorus, the Fruit of Labor Singing Ensemble (from Raleigh, North Carolina), the San Francisco Bay Area Labor Heritage Rockin' Solidarity Chorus, and the Seattle Labor Chorus. The NYCLC contributed four of 20 songs by single choruses on the CD, and the final song featured all choruses together. The liner notes include an essay by Rabinowitz, who ended it stating, "Choral singing—songs of workers performed by working people—is very powerful modality, representing the collective working together for an outstanding sound, and is an example of how we can all work together for the cause of a just and peaceful world." The CD became available after Fairweather's death, and the liner notes include in bold, "Dedicated to the memory of Karl Geoffrey Fairweather (October 13, 1942—May, 11, 2005), founding Choral Director, New York City Labor Chorus."

The NYCLC performed its 7th Gala Benefit Concert on June 11, 2005, at The Graduate Center of the City University of New York. The concert program includes a full-page tribute to the memory of Fairweather.[80] After noting many highlights of Fairweather's career and his leadership for the chorus, the final paragraph states, "We are proud and grateful for all that Geoffrey Fairweather gave to us. He has been our friend, mentor, teacher, and conductor. Our highest tribute is the dedication of this concert to his memory." The chorus performed again on November 10, when John Jay College held its Concert Celebrating the Life of Geoffrey Fairweather.[81]

The program of the 25th Anniversary concert lists two events for 2006 performances and another two for 2007.[82] First in 2006 was February 10 for the Martin Luther King, Jr. Celebration in the Long Island City area of Queens, and second was March 26 for the Garment Industry Exhibit at the Center for Jewish History. First under 2007 was February 12 for the Commemoration of the Abolition of Slavery in Great Britain, held at the British Consulate. Then on March 23 there was the Labor History Education Program at Middle School 180 in the Rockaway Park section of Queens. This last event is the only one I could find in records regarding performances in elementary or secondary schools. Several members, when interviewed, mentioned the importance and/or challenges of performing in schools. Barbara Bailey stated, "When we sang in the schools, the kids were fascinated and we were well received. It's just like you know you used to be able to go to the school and use the school facilities for meetings, and all that's cut out now and it's a shame because it makes it difficult to get to the children who are really the foundation for the next generation."[83] Patricia Logan commented, "We got a grant one year to sing at some senior centers. That was excellent, but . . . we need to get invited to perform in more schools because since children don't hear as much about or know as much about unions as they should . . . it's really important that we, if we can do that, and I guess we have to reach out to teachers and administrators to get invites."[84] I will return to this idea of the chorus performing in schools in the final chapter.

The chorus performed its 8th Gala Benefit Concert on June 16, 2007, at the Ethical Culture Society Auditorium, across from Central Park near its southwest corner. The program's first page, which gives a summary of the chorus' work in its 16 years, includes these words: "The New York City Labor Chorus holds the distinction of being the forerunner of labor choruses in the country."[85] Songs for the evening appeared under five thematic sections: Coal Miners' Story, The Desire for Freedom, The Reality of War, Our Precious Planet, and Our Union Heritage.[86] The names and union affiliations of 82 members appear next to photos of each section.[87] There were 30 sopranos, 27 altos, 17 tenors, and 8 basses. A photo of the three founding mothers, all smiling and arm in arm, fills one page with their note of congratulations to the chorus.[88] A guest performance was by the Impact Repertory Theatre, described as "one of the oldest Black, not-for-profit theatre companies founded in 1997" and with the purpose to promote "the healthy development of young people ages 12 to 19 by providing a learning environment that encourages, nurtures, and challenges its students."[89] This was an example of the chorus connecting with youths, and it shows that performing in schools is not the only way to make such connections.

The chorus continued to stay busy in 2008 with seven performances listed on its website.[90] It was 2009, though, that held a series of particularly large events. One of these was the Lincoln Bicentennial Gala Concert on February 12 at Riverside Church, the grand Gothic cathedral built in the late 1920s in Harlem, where Martin Luther King and Nelson Mandela gave historic speeches.[91] The conductor was Maurice Peress,[92] who had worked closely with Duke Ellington and was conductor of the student orchestra at the Queens College Aaron Copland School of Music for 33 years until his death in 2017.[93] The NYCLC performed Lampell and Robinson's "Lonesome Train"[94] with actors Ruby Dee and Sam Waterson.[95] National Geographic created a webpage to announce Lincoln bicentennial events across the country, noting the following for this event: "The Riverside Church will host the Lincoln Bicentennial Gala Concert to benefit the Riverside Food Pantry. The Riverside Inspirational Choir, the New York City Labor Chorus, and the Orchestra of the Aaron Copeland School of Music at Queens College will perform."[96]

The chorus also performed twice in 2009 for Cooper Union's "Great Evenings in the Great Hall" series.[97] The first was the April 21st inaugural event titled "Abolitionism and Civil Rights." Broadway World's website announced the performances as follows: "The New York City Labor Chorus will perform songs of protest, freedom and justice. Rev. Dr. Calvin Butts of the Abyssinian Baptist Church, actors Barbara Feldon, Marina Squercieati and David Strathairn, and novelist Thulani Davis, who as a child, witnessed her grandfather 'auctioned' on the stage of The Great Hall as part of an abolitionist rally, will offer readings and reenactments from the era."[98] The chorus returned to Cooper Union on September 17th to perform in the event titled "Workers' Rights." Theater Mania announced the evening with these words: "Tony Award winner MaryAnn Plunkett will join the previously announced Maria Tucci for *Workers' Rights*, part of Cooper Union's *Great Evenings in the Great Hall* series, to be presented on September 17. The evening—which will revisit America's labor movement as seen through the eyes of both its advocates and opponents—will also feature journalist Pete Hamill and The Triangle Fire Remembrance Coalition, and the New York City Labor Chorus."[99]

Another grand event for the chorus in the later part of Spring in 2009 was the celebration of Pete Seeger's 90th birthday. This festive gathering, on May 3 at Madison Square Garden, had the chorus appearing "with singers such as Bruce Springsteen, Joan Baez, and Dave Matthews."[100] Billed as the "Clearwater Concert," it supported "Hudson River Sloop Clearwater, a non-profit environmental advocacy and education organization founded by Pete Seeger and others [in the 1960s] that is dedicated to protecting the Hudson River and creating new environmental leaders."[101] Jeff Vogel recalled how Seeger helped the chorus by appearing in some of its early events, including a couple of the fundraising concerts: "He was very, very, very helpful to the chorus. And as a result, we got invited to sing in his 90th birthday party at Madison Square Garden."[102]

The NYCLC held its 18th Anniversary Gala Benefit Concert on June 13, 2009, at the Ethical Culture Society Auditorium.[103] The concert program brought attention to events earlier in the same year, ending with this note of anticipation: ". . . and culminating in a long hoped for singing tour of Wales in connection with our long relationship with several Welsh choirs." Many chorus members went on a tour of Wales from June 25 to July 10. Nine members mentioned this trip to me in interviews as a highlight among memories of the chorus, and I will give two examples. Jesse Kasowitz, a retired attorney at age 77 when interviewed, identified himself as "white, Jewish of Lithuanian origin." He recalled, "We did a commemoration for Spanish Civil War Heroes and veterans. There were American heroes, so the Abraham Lincoln Brigade, there were Welsh heroes and we sang with the Red Chorus there and also with other choruses in Wales. It is a big choral tradition in Wales. We were invited by the Pontarddulais Chorus, which is a region of Wales, and we sang with them and they came here and sang with us."[104] Bobby Greenberg was keeping count of the Welsh choruses that they met: "We made a trip to South Wales to sing with mining choruses. We actually spent 13 days and we sang with 11 different choruses."[105]

As chorus members have sung and traveled together, they have formed friendships with each other. The NYCLC's website list of performances marks the loss of one of its members and a friend to many in the chorus and beyond.[106] The celebration of Julius Margolin's life of 93 years was on October 16, 2009, at the Local 1199's Martin Luther King Auditorium in Midtown Manhattan.[107] Margolin sang with the NYCLC and also recorded and performed music for many years with fellow chorus member George Mann. A World War II veteran and retired film electrician, Margolis continued to be active in the labor movement beyond age ninety.[108] I was fortunate to see and hear him sing live with Mann in 2007, when I attended the How Class Works Conference at Stony Brook University. He was still singing with plenty of spunk and clarity at age 91, and I never would have guessed then that he was even older than eighty.

A final note on 2009 is that Peter Schlosser resigned as conductor sometime after the Gala Benefit concert in June. He helped to keep the chorus together after the departure and untimely death of Fairweather, but his time to leave came after six years. Some chorus members in interviews mentioned that Schlosser did not have the bond with chorus members that Fairweather had. Bobby Greenberg stated of Schlosser, "He was a very intense guy and difficult to work with sometimes but . . . I don't know what it was finally, but I think it was like the lack of discipline of the group sometimes. He didn't have the ability to bring a group together like Jana [Schlosser's replacement]."[109] Denise Jones commented that she had a good relationship with Schlosser (and also with his predecessor and successor) and that he "had excellent arrangements and we still use some of, I think, Peter's arrangements as well."[110] As I mentioned above, I will address the NYCLC's ongoing use of some of his arrangements in the next chapter.

NEW DIRECTIONS WITH A THIRD CONDUCTOR

After a search for Schlosser's replacement, Jana Ballard became the NYCLC's conductor in Spring of 2010.[111] Her bios on the chorus website, posted Fall of 2010, and in the 25th Anniversary concert program of 2016 give brief overviews of her musical achievements.[112] She credits her early growth in musicianship to "good music teachers from elementary school on" in Bowling Green, Kentucky, where she grew up. After completing undergraduate and master's degrees in music education from Western Kentucky University, Ballard taught elementary and then high school vocal music in Bowling Green. She moved to New York City in 2005 and has been a teacher since 2007 at LaGuardia High School for the Performing Arts. Ballard's leadership experiences in music education include her 2010 conducting of the Baltimore County High School Honors Chorus, her 2011 conducting of the Kentucky Music Educators Association All-State Junior High Treble Chorus, and her more recent (current as of 2016) service as the Repertoire & Standards Senior High School Chair for the Eastern Division of the American Choral Directors Association. The earlier bio states, "She intends to help us improve our rehearsal and performance skills and our sound."

Unlike Schlosser but like Fairweather, Ballard did not come to the chorus with a background of activism in the labor movement. Bobby Greenberg stated, "[Fairweather] came from a classical musical tradition, not a labor tradition at all and, but he was open–which is interesting, in our chorus two out of our three directors did not come to the labor movement—Jana and Geoffrey."[113] Experience in activism was not the priority in the search to replace Schlosser, though, and Ballard's commitment to improving the sound of the chorus has been a breath of fresh air for many. Eugene Hamond stated, "I find the chorus really just like a real family. I mean it really is. And I also love it since Jana has come. She makes us work!"[114] Terry Weissman, an early-childhood educator who was 75 years old when interviewed and self-identified as "Caucasian" and American-born to an immigrant father from Poland, expressed her appreciation of Jana's work as well: "I think I've seen just an enormous change in the chorus under Jana's direction, and I love what's happening in terms of the music quality of the group. I think I've become a better singer because of her and that's very satisfying to know that you can be 75 and getting better at something [*laughter*]."[115]

I interviewed Ballard in the Spring of 2017, on a late Monday afternoon when she was in a bit of a hurry to join a meeting with the chorus board of directors.[116] She had much to say, though, for the brief time that she was available. Regarding her limited experience with political activism, she noted that there had never been much activism happening in Bowling Green during her years there from childhood to young adulthood. She added, "I was brought up in a Democrat household. My mom and dad were Democrats. I, as a youngster, was a little bit more conservative, actually. And then as I came into my adult years, I embraced my parents' political choice . . . I am very strong-willed and I was taught to stick up for myself, but I never really was part of anything." Like Hamond, she used the word "family" to describe the sense of community she felt with the chorus: "I think just in general now the choir has really become—it's like a family. I feel like I know so many of the members well just from seeing them every week for years." She contrasted her lasting relationships with the chorus to those with her high school students, who graduate and then are gone. Ballard spoke of the challenge she has in working with many chorus members who never learned to read music, but she added, "I'm surprised at how well some people remember the music just based on what they hear every week." When I asked her what she found most rewarding in directing the chorus, she replied, "The year after year developing, growing, and just going back and listening to recordings and from years ago, oh my goodness, we sound so much better now and just to see the faces of the choristers being pleased and happy with themselves, too. It's very rewarding for me to see that you guys also know that you've improved and are doing a good job."

The chorus had its first two performances with Ballard as conductor later in the Spring of 2010. The first was the "Concert for Nuclear Disarmament" at Riverside Church on May 3, featuring 100 singers from Japan.[117] I was unable to find details on the Internet for this. The second event was on June 4, titled "New York City Labor Chorus in Concert with Six Choirs from Wales."[118] Eustace Johnson returned to be accompanist for the NYCLC in this event held at the First Reformed Episcopal Church in East Midtown. The choruses from Wales were Ystradgynlais Male Choir, Gyrlais Choir, Llandovery Male Choir, Morriston RFC Choir, Onllwyn Miners' Welfare Choir, and Pontarddulais Male Choir. This event occurred just a year after the NYCLC made its trip to Wales to perform with various choirs.

After a year of transition in 2010, the chorus had a highly eventful year in 2011 with 12 events listed.[119] The first major event was March 25 for the 100th anniversary of the Triangle Shirtwaist Fire, the historic disaster in New York City in which 146 workers, mostly young immigrant women of Italian or Jewish heritage, lost their lives. The chorus had performed at this annual commemoration in prior years, but the centennial brought a much larger calendar of events not only in New York City but across the country.[120] Betty Reid recalled the Triangle Fire commemoration as a regular annual event of the chorus at which sometimes school children would join in singing with the chorus, with or without handouts with the lyrics printed.[121] In Chapter Four I give my report after participating with the chorus at this event in 2017.

With memories of the Wales trip still fresh, the chorus made a trip to Cuba for a week in April of 2011. The chorus website lists the trip as "Performances & exchanges with many groups in Cuba."[122] Twenty-three of the 28 members that I interviewed as individuals mentioned the trip; some noted that they missed the trip because they joined the chorus after the trip. One of the members on the trip was Mariana Gastón. When I asked her how she identifies herself in terms of race, ethnicity, and/or nationality, she replied, "I'm Latina, I'm white Latina. Cuban. Born in Cuba and half Cuban and half Mexican, my mother is Mexican. By national I'm an immigrant. I'm a naturalized citizen of the United States."[123] She was age 67 at the time of the interview and was working as a school administrator in bilingual education. Her family moved to the US in 1961 because her parents did not agree with the Cuban Revolution that triumphed in 1959. She joined the chorus shortly before the Cuba trip but had been on the Wales trip as Bobby Greenberg's partner. Gastón had not done much singing since her youth, when she would often join with Cuban-immigrant friends and family in singing Cuban songs informally, but she regularly included singing in her lessons as an elementary and middle school teacher. She was involved as a teenager in protesting against racial discrimination and the US War in Vietnam and joined organizations in solidarity with the Cuban Revolution. When her testimony turned to the NYCLC's Cuba trip, she stated, "And then we, they started going to Cuba, you know, I said, 'Okay, I should give them a hand.' Because together we went to Cuba to hook up the chorus with the organization that would host. . . . Because, you know, I would help them have a good trip."

Several chorus members did express that it was a good trip and a highlight among memories in the chorus. Barbara Schwimmer, a retired social worker who was age 87 when interviewed and who self-identified as Caucasian with a Russian-Jewish background, said of the trip, "I just can't forget it. It was particularly meaningful to me because we spoke to people, we performed, and they performed for us."[124] Denise Jones stated, "We got to sit in with the chorus members in the Cuban trade union chorus and they were pretty, like, militant. But they liked us and we swapped songs, they sang the song, so that was wonderful. And we went from town to town and we sung for children and saw the children's faces light up. It was really beautiful."[125] More testimonies about the Cuba trip and some footage of singing by Cubans and the NYCLC appear on the DVD that the chorus and filmmaker Carlos Rafael Betancourt Martin produced.[126]

I missed the Cuba trip because I did not join the chorus until September of 2011, after moving from the middle of Long Island to the Bronx. I was one of two who went to audition on a Monday afternoon at the site where the chorus held rehearsals. Two chorus members sat in back rows to listen, and Jana had me sing a few scales while she accompanied on piano. I knew from the website announcement that I would also need to sing an unaccompanied solo of any song of my choice, and I sang four verses of "The Ballad of Joe Hill."[127] Jana then said, "You're a tenor." The other newcomer and I received news later that we were accepted into the chorus, and we were there for rehearsal the following week.

On November 5, 2011, the chorus performed its 20th Anniversary concert at Town Hall with all seats filled. After two months of hard work in weekly two-hour rehearsals, we sang 23 songs split among five sections by themes listed as "Hold the Fort," "Songs of Freedom," "Cuba!," "The World We Hope For," and "Finale."[128] Guest performers were GQ, an R&B group from the Bronx. The concert journal included two pages for newly written reflections by each of the three founding mothers.[129] Another page read, "This page is dedicated to the memory of our chorus members who have passed away since 1991. It is hard to understand why people are taken from us, but we find comfort in knowing they were a special part of the chorus family."[130] I remember well the rehearsal following the concert, when we started with spoken thoughts about the performance. Ballard and many members were pleased with the progress of our sound, and we all knew that it came with plenty of focus and diligence in rehearsals.

A highlight of 2012 was in the recording sessions with jazz trombonist Roswell Rudd, which I addressed in the introduction.[131] It is important to note four concerts that have been repeat performances over the years for the chorus in addition to the Triangle Shirtwaist Fire commemoration. I address all four in Chapter Four for their performances during the 2016-2017 calendar year. One is the annual conference for nurses who are members of United Federation of Teachers, a second is the holiday concert each December at the MetLife building in Midtown, a third is participation in the People's Voice Café series at the Community Church of New York, and a fourth is the annual Clara Lemlich Awards for women who have been outstanding leaders in struggles for social justice. In Chapter Four I also note that two members of the chorus have been recipients of the Lemlich Award.

Two more gala benefit concerts occurred between the 20th and 25th anniversaries. One was the Spring Gala Concert on May 18, 2013, at the Tribeca Performing Arts Center on the campus of the Borough of Manhattan Community College; the other was the 23rd Anniversary on November 15, 2014, at Ethical Culture Society. I have the concert program only for the latter, which had as part of the intermission a tribute "Remembering Pete Seeger."[132] Seeger had died on January 27, 2014, at age ninety-four. Seven of the 22 songs on the program involved Seeger as composer, adaptor, writer of additional lyrics, or source of inspiration. The concert journal listed a total of 79 members. My wife was in the audience, and she had not heard the chorus perform since its 20th Anniversary concert—a lapse of three years. She told me that she could not believe it was the same chorus, that the improvement in sound was incredible. That says something about Ballard's work as conductor and director.

During the NYCLC's calendar year of 2015-16, there was plenty of anticipation for the upcoming 25th anniversary. A performance that was especially important was on the day before Martin Luther King Jr. Day—January 17, 2016—at Trinity Baptist Church in Brooklyn, where Dennis Nelson has been organist and choir director for many years. I regretted missing this event while away on vacation. Many chorus members spoke highly of the experience while time was given for debriefing in the next rehearsal. Parts of the concert, like parts of many other performances by the chorus, appear in YouTube videos.

In June, I joined about a dozen chorus members in attending the Great Labor Arts Exchange (GLAE) in Silver Spring, Maryland. Many of these members had been to GLAE many times already, and it was my first time. I conducted a songwriting workshop to pay tribute to Ella May (sometimes with second last name Wiggins), a labor organizer, singer-songwriter, and martyr whom I addressed in Chapter One. I was delighted that many of the NYCLC members and others participated with positive energy. I enjoyed the entire four-day event, and it was refreshing to see and hear performers of diverse cultures and a wide range of ages. It was an uplifting end for my fifth year with the chorus, and I looked forward to the approaching 25th-anniversary year.

NOTES

1. Philip Yale Nicholson, *Labor's Story in the United States* (Philadelphia: Temple University Press, 2004), 300.
2. Joseph A. McCartin, "The Strike That Busted Unions," New York Times, August 2, 2011, https://www.nytimes.com/2011/08/03/opinion/reagan-vs-patco-the-strike-that-busted-unions.html.
3. Laura Friedman, interview by the author, October 10, 2018.
4. Barbara Bailey, interview by the author, March 6, 2017.
5. Laura Friedman, interview.
6. Tina Susman, New York City Labor Chorus Gets Better with Age. Los Angeles Times, December 19, 2012. http://articles.latimes.com/2012/dec/19/nation/la-na-labor-chorus-20121220
7. Patricia Logan, interview by the author, October 6, 2016.
8. Ann Gael, interview by the author, October 6, 2016.
9. Denise Jones, interview by the author, October 11, 2016.
10. Betty Reid, interview by the author, June 5, 2017.
11. Jeffrey Vogel, interview by the author, January 25, 2017.
12. Dennis Nelson, interview by the author, March 27, 2017.
13. Denise Jones, interview by the author, September 29, 2016.
14. New York City Labor Chorus, *25th Anniversary*, 2016, 4.
15. United Electrical, Radio & Machine Workers of America, "Moe Foner Dies; Promoted Working Class Culture," UE News, February 2002, http://www.ranknfile-ue.org/uen_0202_foner.html.
16. New York City Labor Chorus, "Past Performances," http://www.nyclc.org/performances.shtml.
17. Library of Congress, "Sing Along with Pete Seeger," 2007, https://www.loc.gov/item/ihas.200197114/.

18. Pete Seeger, *Pete Seeger in His Own Words*, eds. Rob Rosenthal & Sam Rosenthal (Boulder, CO: Paradigm Publishers, 2012), 252.

19. Laura Friedman, interview by the author.

20. New York City Labor Chorus, *Benefit Concert*, eds. Bobbie Rabinowitz, Betty Reid, & Denis Berger, 1993, 3.

21. Ibid., 6.

22. Ibid., 7.

23. Earl Robinson (music) and John LaTouche (words), with revised lyrics by New York City Labor Chorus, "Ballad for Americans."

24. New York City Labor Chorus, "Past Performances."

25. New York City Labor Chorus, *25th Anniversary*.

26. New York City Labor Chorus, *Benefit Concert*, ed. Bobbie Rabinowitz, 1995.

27. Ibid., 2.

28. Ibid., page from photocopy illegible.

29. Donna Bryson, "South African Music Hints at Gospel, Jazz," Los Angeles Times, May 13, 1989, http://articles.latimes.com/1989-05-13/entertainment/ca-2883_1_thokoza-townships-gospel.

30. Abraham Lincoln Brigade Archives, "60th Annual Anniversary Dinner," program/flyer, 1996.

31. "Si Me Quieres Escribir," music and lyrics transcribed for New York City Labor Chorus, 2007.

32. New York City Labor Chorus, *25th Anniversary*.

33. Ibid.

34. Velma Hill, interview by the author, May 22, 2017.

35. Rona Armillas, interview by the author, February 7, 2017.

36. New York City Labor Chorus, *25th Anniversary*.

37. Gilbert Fletcher, designer of poster titled *Gala Centennial Salute: Paul Robeson: Ol' Man River*, 1998.

38. New York City Labor Chorus, program flyer for event "Song of Struggle and Protest: A Paul Robeson Centennial Anniversary Concert."

39. John LaTouche (words) and Earl Robinson (music), "Ballad for Americans."

40. Faith Petric, "The Folk Process," *Sing Out!* 49, no. 2 (2005), 82.

41. Ben Shapiro, "'Ballad for Americans' Sent 'Message of Unity' in 1940 Presidential Race," transcript to radio broadcast of "All Things Considered," National Public Radio, November 5, 2015.

42. Bobby Greenberg, interview by the author, February 7, 2017.

43. Jeff Vogel, interview by the author.

44. New York City Labor Chorus, *Fourth Gala Benefit Concert*, 1999, no page number.

45. Earl Robinson (music) and John LaTouche (words), with revised lyrics by New York City Labor Chorus, "Ballad for Americans," on CD titled *Worker's Rise: Labor in the Spotlight*, 2000, recorded by New York City Labor Chorus at Mirror Image Studios, New York City.

46. New York City Labor Chorus, liner notes to CD titled *Worker's Rise: Labor in the Spotlight*, 2000.

47. Ann Gael, interview by the author.
48. New York City Labor Chorus, liner notes to CD.
49. New York City Labor Chorus, http://www.nyclc.org.
50. New York City Labor Chorus, "Past Performances."
51. Marilyn Taylor (pseudonym), interview by author.
52. Debbie Zanca, interview by author, November 17, 2016.
53. New York City Labor Chorus, *25th Anniversary.*
54. Judson Memorial Church, "History: Overview," http://classic.judson.org/Historical-Overview.
55. New York City Labor Chorus, *25th Anniversary.*
56. The Town Hall, "History," http://thetownhall.org/history/#town-hall-history.
57. The Town Hall, "Arts in Education," http://thetownhall.org/arts-in-education/.
58. New York City Labor Chorus, "Past Performances."
59. The Workmen's Circle, "Who We Are: Our History." https://circle.org/who-we-are/our-history/.
60. Ari Davidow, "Yiddish in America, NYC, Nov 6," The Klezmershack Calendar, 2003, http://www.klezmershack.com/calendar/2003_11.php
61. Kelly Wilmeth, interview by author, February 7, 2017.
62. Bobby Greenberg, focus group conducted by author, May 10, 2017.
63. Eugene Hamond, interview by author, March 13, 2017.
64. New York City Labor Chorus, *25th Anniversary.*
65. Apollo Theater, "Apollo Theater History," 2016, https://www.apollotheater.org/about/history/.
66. New York City Labor Chorus, "Past Performances."
67. Barbara Bailey, interview by the author.
68. Betty Reid, interview by the author.
69. Velma Hill, interview by the author.
70. Denise Jones, interview by the author, September 29, 2016.
71. Inez West, interview by the author, April 30, 2017.
72. Dennis Nelson, interview by the author, March 27, 2017.
73. New York City Labor Chorus, *12th Anniversary Concert*, 2003.
74. New York City Labor Chorus, *12th Anniversary Concert.*
75. Dennis Nelson, interview by the author
76. New York City Labor Chorus, *12th Anniversary Concert.*
77. Ibid.
78. New York City Labor Chorus, "Past Performances."
79. Bobbie Rabinowitz (Producer) and Labor Heritage Foundation, *The Great Choral Convergence: Live!* (Compact Disc, multiple artists, recorded June 19, 2004, Washington Ethical Society, Washington, DC).
80. New York City Labor Chorus, *7th Gala Benefit Concert*, 2005.
81. New York City Labor Chorus, *25th Anniversary*, 5.
82. Ibid.
83. Barbara Bailey, interview by the author.
84. Patricia Logan, interview by the author.
85. New York City Labor Chorus, *8th Gala Benefit Concert*, 2007, 1.

86. Ibid., 2-3.
87. Ibid., 4-5.
88. Ibid., 9.
89. Ibid., 13.
90. New York City Labor Chorus, "Past Performances."
91. Riverside Church, "History and Architecture," https://www.trcnyc.org/history/.
92. Virginia Chang Chien, "La Valsa de Virginie: A Blog That Covers Music, Life, Art, Travel," 2016, http://whispering-of-eternity.blogspot.com/p/work-info-present-un-unsrc-symphony.html.
93. Neil Genzlinger, "Maurice Peress, Conductor Who Worked with Ellington, Dies at 87," New York Times, January 4, 2018,
94. Millard Lampell (text) and Earl Robinson (music), "Lonesome Train," Abraham Lincoln Online, http://www.abrahamlincolnonline.org/lincoln/education/lonesome.htm.
95. New York City Labor Chorus, *18th Anniversary Gala Benefit Concert*, 2009, 1.
96. Meg Weaver, "Celebrate Abe's 200th Birthday," National Geographic Society, 2009, https://www.nationalgeographic.com/travel/intelligent-travel/2009/02/11/celebrate_abes_200th_birthday/.
97. New York City Labor Chorus, *25th Anniversary.*
98. Broadway World, "'Great Evenings in the Great Hall' Series Begins at Cooper Union 4/21," April 17, 2009, https://www.broadwayworld.com/article/GREAT-EVENINGS-IN-THE-GREAT-HALL-Series-Begins-At-Cooper-Union-421-20090417.
99. Andy Propst, "MaryAnn Plunkett to Join Maria Tucci in Cooper Union Event," Theater Mania, September 16, 2009, https://www.theatermania.com/new-york-city-theater/news/maryann-plunkett-to-join-maria-tucci-in-cooper-uni_20497.html.
100. New York City Labor Chorus, *18th Anniversary Gala Benefit Concert.*
101. Hudson River Sloop Clearwater, "Pete Seeger 90th Birthday Concert DVD Now on Sale," December 16, 2009, https://www.clearwater.org/latest-news/pete-seeger-90th-birthday-concert-dvd-now-on-sale/.
102. Jeffrey Vogel, interview by the author.
103. New York City Labor Chorus, *18th Anniversary Gala Benefit Concert.*
104. Jesse Kasowitz, interview by the author, May 26, 2017.
105. Bobby Greenberg, interview by the author.
106. New York City Labor Chorus, "Past Performances."
107. kwilder (username), "Friday, October 16: Memorial Events for Labor Activist/Musician Julius Margolin," OnTheWilderSide (weblog), October 3, 2009, http://www.onthewilderside.com/tag/george-and-julius/.
108. George Mann and Julius Margolin, "Bio," http://georgeandjulius.com/?page_id=38.
109. Bobby Greenberg, interview by the author.
110. Denise Jones, interview by the author, September 29, 2016.
111. New York City Labor Chorus, "In the Spotlight," http://www.nyclc.org/archive.php?spotlight=inthespotlight_09-11.html.

112. New York City Labor Chorus, *25th Anniversary*, 6.
113. Bobby Greenberg, interview by the author.
114. Eugene Hamond, interview by the author.
115. Terry Weissman, interview by the author, January 23, 2017.
116. Jana Ballard, interview by the author, March 13, 2017.
117. New York City Labor Chorus, *25th Anniversary*, 5.
118. New York City Labor Chorus, flyer for "Concert with Six Choirs from Wales."
119. New York City Labor Chorus, "Past Performances."
120. Remember the Triangle Fire, "The Triangle Factory Fire, 1911-2011: Calendar of Events, http://www.rememberthetrianglefire.org/images/TriCoNewspaper.pdf.
121. Betty Reid, interview with the author.
122. New York City Labor Chorus, "Past Performances."
123. Mariana Gastón, interview with the author, February 7, 2017.
124. Barbara Schwimmer, interview with the author, December 19, 2016.
125. Denise Jones, interview with the author, October 11, 2016.
126. Carlos Rafael Betancourt Martin (filmmaker) and New York City Labor Chorus, *Solidarity: New York City Labor Chorus in Cuba, 2011* (DVD, recorded April 17-24, 2011, in multiple locations in Cuba).
127. Alfred Hayes (lyrics) and Earl Robinson (music), "The Ballad of Joe Hill," 1938, by Bob Miller, Inc., http://unionsong.com/u017.html.
128. New York City Labor Chorus, *20th Anniversary*, 2-3.
129. Ibid., 12-13.
130. Ibid., 5.
131. Roswell Rudd with guests Reggie Bennett and the New York City Labor Chorus, "Joe Hill," on CD "Trombone for Lovers" (Ivan Rubenstein-Gillis, producer; 2013, Sunnyside Communications, Inc.).
132. New York City Labor Chorus, *23rd Anniversary*, 5.

Chapter Three

Songs of the 25th-Anniversary Gala Concert

The main event of the NYCLC's 25th year was a concert held on November 12, 2016, at Skirball Center for the Performing Arts on the campus of New York University. Selecting the 20 songs that would end up on the program of the 25th-Anniversary Gala Concert was no simple task. The Arts & Culture Committee (ACC) made the suggestions, and the board of directors issued final approval. I go into details about the ACC and the gala concert in Chapter Four. This current chapter focuses on the chosen songs and the four themes into which each was placed. Some of the songs could have a chapter unto themselves, but this chapter can only give a brief introduction to each.

As the chorus leadership had done with previous gala concerts, it divided this one into themes. The four chosen themes this time were struggle, peace, joy, and 25 years. Each theme consisted of five songs. The concert program included under each song title the credits for words and music, adding also, where appropriate, a name for arrangement.[1] My introduction to each song includes background into its creation and its places in the respective theme and in the labor movement in general.

STRUGGLE

Class struggle is a central theme in the labor movement. The quote in the program for this section was by Dr. Martin Luther King, Jr.: "The arc of the Universe bends toward justice."[2] The five songs selected for this theme portray the hard work and high hopes that go into a long fight for social justice. They remind everyone that victories in social movements have come only after bitter struggle. They are from different traditions, including lyrics from three languages. Songs such as these help current movements see connections from history to the present and from global to local.

Oh, Freedom

"Oh, Freedom," an African American spiritual, set the stage for an evening of beautiful and powerful songs. The arrangement credit is to Carl Haywood, and the copies for the chorus added different verses.[3] This is an example of a "zipper" song, which involves a verse repeated in its entirety except for a change of a single word or short phrase. The words include a message that death is preferable to a return to slavery. The words "Oh, freedom" opened the first verse, which the chorus sang quietly. The second and third verses, also sung quietly, substituted "No more moanin'" and "No more weepin'," respectively. The fourth and fifth verses, which the chorus sang loudly and more rapidly, substituted the phrases "There'll be singin'" and "There'll be shoutin,'" respectively. The final verse returned to "Oh, freedom" while maintaining the louder volume and faster tempo but in a higher key. It was the right song to open the event with the audience clapping and singing along.

This classic spiritual became one of the most important songs of the Civil Rights movement.[4] It was among the songs that Coretta Scott King remembered singing with fellow activists before meetings for carrying out the Montgomery bus boycott.[5] Prior to the Civil Rights movement, the interracial group Union Caravan included "Oh, Freedom" in its pro-union performances throughout Iowa in the fall of 1949.[6] An even earlier account of the song's use is from the New Era School in December of 1936 in Little Rock, Arkansas, where African-American union organizer and songwriter John L. Handcox led a biracial group of union organizers among tenant farmers in singing.[7] It is one among many spirituals that helped form song lists for both the labor and Civil Rights movements.

El Pueblo Unido (The People United)

The *nueva canción* (new song) movement of the 1960s and early 70s brought songs with politically conscious lyrics, intricate melodies, and lively rhythms from all corners of Latin America to the world. "El Pueblo Unido," with words and music by Sergio Ortega, is an example from Chile, where music was an important part of the protests in resistance to Agosto Pinochet's right-wing military dictatorship that violently overthrew Salvador Allende's democratically-elected socialist government in 1973 with a US-supported military coup.[8] The NYCLC sang an arrangement by Peter Schlosser, who, as noted in the previous chapter, was director of the chorus from 2003 to 2009. The rhythm is a driving march, and the arrangement has interweaving melodies. The first verse is in Spanish, and the second is its English translation. Each verse ends with a loud piano-supported chant, which exclaims that a united movement will never lose. The song continued the intensity level where the opening song had left off.

The original recording of "El Pueblo Unido" was by the Chilean group Quilapayún, the group behind many recordings by the legendary singer-songwriter Victor Jara, whom military commanders murdered shortly after the coup.[9] Quilapayún was touring Europe at the time of the coup, and they remained in exile in France.[10] A search of the song in YouTube results in many performances from professional and amateur musicians around the world and in different languages. The chant contained in the song continues to be a favorite in marches and rallies for various progressive causes.

Tina Sizwe (The Brown Nation)

The third song of the concert, "Tina Sizwe," was the third song from South Africa that the chorus had performed in recent times, and it was new in the NYCLC repertoire. It is listed in the program as a "South African (Zulu) freedom song."[11] The sheet music, which did not identify a publisher, had a note under the title that included these words: "This song, one of the favorites of Chief Albert Luthuli, President of the African National Congress, is destined to be known around the world, we feel. This tune is taken from a hymn, and should be sung with rich harmony." The score is in ¾ time and has three-part harmony and interwoven melodies with sopranos and tenors taking the main part. The words are in the indigenous language, and the score gives the English translation of the message calling for racial justice to replace white people's control of the land.

An internet search shows that the common spelling is "Thina" instead of "Tina." Smithsonian Folkways Recordings has the English translation of the title as "We the Africans" and lists the language as Xhosa.[12] The 30-second sample of the song sung by South African refugees on the Smithsonian website gives a tempo much slower than how the NYCLC sang it. Another difference is that the Smithsonian recording is without instrumental accompaniment while the labor chorus sang with Dennis Nelson's piano support. "Thina Sizwe" also is one of 29 songs on the soundtrack to the documentary film "Amandla! A Revolution in Four-Part Harmony."[13] The film, which I saw on a big screen in the open air of a summer evening in 2016 in Brooklyn's Prospect Park, portrays the powerful ways in which singing helped to fuel the indigenous movement against the apartheid regime.

Give Me Your Tired, Your Poor

Appearing in the concert program at the end of the listed songs is an inset with the heading "Introduction to 'Give Me Your Tired, Your Poor'." The three chorus members credited with writing the introduction were Ricky Eisenberg, Tom Karlson, and Jeff Vogel. The text had the following: "As a workers' chorus, as a nation of immigrants, we want to affirm Emma's welcome to the 'huddled masses yearning to be free'. People of every color and nationality must be given full citizenship in the house of Labor. United we stand, divided we fall. We sing to a future where people are not forced to flee their homes because of wars of empire, political oppression, or hunger."[14] These words effectively set the stage for singing a powerful song honoring those who have no choice but to flee from danger or injustice.

"Give Me Your Tired, Your Poor" was the final song of Irving Berlin's 1949 musical comedy "Miss Liberty," and the words, which appear on the Statue of Liberty, came from the 1883 sonnet "The New Colossus" by Emma Lazarus.[15] The four-part choral arrangement with piano accompaniment, also copyrighted 1949, was by Roy Ringwald. The score has a single verse that repeats twice. The first time is in unison, the second in harmony softly, and the third in a different harmony with a bold finale. The score begins with the words "Broadly, with majesty," and that is the sound that the chorus strived to attain in the rehearsals and the concert.

The song, like the poem, has the message that immigrants and refugees—no matter how destitute—are welcome. Throughout US history, there has been a broad xenophobic reaction to each wave of immigrants. Before the 2016 election, many immigrant-rights activists called President Obama the "deporter in chief" for having presided over more deportations than any previous president. Then President Trump won election after using racist rhetoric, promising a wall across the entire southern border and a travel ban against several Muslim-majority countries. Solidarity among workers has no border, and "Give Me Your Tired, Your Poor" makes that clear. The poem, as well as the song it inspired, will continue to have a poignant space in the movement for immigrants' rights.

Ain't You Got a Right

The finale for the first theme of the night was one of the finest moments of the concert. "Ain't You Got a Right," composed by African American songwriter and community organizer Jane Wilburn Sapp, is a moving work from the gospel tradition.[16] After the third of four verses, there is a sensational bridge that starts with the basses and brings in one more section at a time until the tenors add the final part. In several NYCLC performances of this song, especially the 25th-anniversary concert, the audience was moved to applaud loudly at the end of the bridge, many perhaps thinking it was the song's grand finale. After letting the applause fade, the chorus continued quietly with the fourth and final verse.

There are different songs with the title "Ain't You Got a Right to the Tree of Life." Guy Carawan, a white folk musician who was music director at Highlander Folk School (later renamed Highlander Research and Education Center) from 1959 until his death in 2015, has credit on several internet sites as co-composer with his wife Candie to a song by that title that is not much different from Sapp's song. The Carawans co-authored a book with the same title and the subtitle "The People of Johns Island, South Carolina—Their Faces, Their Words, and their Songs." The publisher stated that the book, "First published in 1966 . . . recorded the thoughts, captured the faces of blacks just beginning to feel the tremors of the civil rights movement."[17] The Carawans' book includes a transcript of the words and music to the song "Ain't You Got a Right to the Tree of Life" with a credit to "The Moving Star Hall congregation."[18] The words are essentially the same as Sapp's version sung by the chorus, but the melody and rhythm are different. Sapp's version is in 6/4 time with alternating parts for sections whereas the version in the Carawan's book is in 4/4 with parts for leader, group, and all. In all its versions it is a stirring spiritual, and it worked tremendously well for the NYCLC to sing it at the end of the first set of songs in the concert.

PEACE

The second theme for the 25th-anniversary concert was peace. The quote in the program for this theme was by John Lennon: "A dream you dream alone is only a dream. A dream you dream together is reality."[19] Many songs in history have called for an end to war and a commitment to peace. The NYCLC chose five diverse songs that represent struggles and hopes for peace with justice. There is a long history of intersections between the labor and peace movements within issues such as imperialism, war profiteering, conscription, and military recruitment in under-resourced public schools, so it was appropriate to include this theme in the concert.

Peace by Piece

The first song of the concert's second theme was "Peace by Piece," composed by Robbie Solomon. The publisher of the score is Transcontinental Music Publications, which identifies itself on the cover of the song as "The world's largest publisher of Jewish music since 1938."[20] The score identifies the genre as "Gospel." It is a slow and moving song in 6/8 time with solos and rich SATB (soprano, alto, tenor, bass) harmonies. A soprano sang the beautifully melodic solo part for the gala concert. The lyrics speak to a long collective struggle for peace.

When the NYCLC board of directors approved this song for performances, they decided to change some of the words at the end, when the tempo slows down for a magnificent finale. The final words in the score use religious language, and the substituted words do not. I do not know whether this was a controversial decision made after much debate, nor do I know whether the board asked the publisher for permission to make the change. It is interesting that the chorus has kept religious lyrics intact for some songs while making changes to secular words for others.

Johnny, I Hardly Knew 'Ya

There are peace songs and anti-war songs; "Johnny, I Hardly Knew 'Ya" is among the latter. Peter Schlosser provided his arrangement of this traditional song in 2006 for the NYCLC. It goes by the familiar tune of "When Johnny Comes Marching Home," which during the US Civil War became a pro-war variation of the traditional Irish anti-war song.[21] Schlosser's arrangement is a march that moves quickly in 12/8 time with SATB parts. Basses and tenors begin by singing "Huroo" in series, giving an effect of bagpipes that continues as sopranos and altos sing the first part of each verse. The four sections sing the lyrics together in harmony then for the latter part. The song ends dramatically with a quiet and harmonized "Och, Johnny," followed by a loud "I'm swearin' to ya" in unison.

An internet search shows many variations of lyrics to this song. Schlosser's arrangement has four verses that tell the story of a badly wounded soldier from the perspective of his wife. The concluding words swear that those who start wars "never will take our sons again" to battle. The song addresses the plight of war veterans who return to their families with physical wounds or the psychic wounds of what today we call Post-Traumatic Stress Syndrome. It is fitting for the NYCLC to include songs that express hope for peace but also others that address the horrors and tragedies of war.

Simple Song of Freedom

The next song under the theme of peace was Bobby Darin's "Simple Song of Freedom," a spirited protest song sung in unison. Many songs sung by the NYCLC have arrangements for harmony, but not this one. Singing well in unison is a different challenge, and the chorus rehearsed it often to build a unified and energetic sound. This is one of three songs from the concert captured on a YouTube recording, and all three show up when doing a search from YouTube with key words "NYC Labor Chorus 2016."[22]

With a copyright of 1969, the song became one of many that questioned or protested the US war in Vietnam. Although Darin wrote "Simple Song of Freedom" in 1969, it only became a minor hit when Tim Harden recorded it in 1974, after the withdrawal of US troops from Vietnam had begun.[23] The song's title does not suggest an anti-war theme, but the refrain ends with words that express a desire of the people to resist war. The lyrics, including additional words by NYCLC-member Jeff Vogel, appeared in the concert program and on the big screen above the stage, and conductor Jana Ballard invited the audience to sing along.[24] The printed version kept Darin's refrain and nearly all of one of his verses (an adjustment showed the number of the world's current population). The other two verses were Vogel's words, one of which directly addressed the peace/anti-war theme. The added words bring realities of 21st-century war to this 20th-century song. The technology of warfare has advanced, but have critical thinking and moral reasoning advanced as well in this era of the terrifying so-called "war on terror," often dubbed the "endless war"?

Imagine

John Lennon and Paul McCartney had a tremendous run of hit songs with critical acclaim during the Beatles years, but "Imagine," arguably, has remained Lennon's signature song. Lennon's partner for conceptualizing the iconic song was none other than his wife Yoko Ono, and the National Music Publishers Association announced in 2017 that going forward she would receive credit as co-writer.[25] Anyone who has ever taken time to read or listen to the lyrics carefully knows that behind the beautiful melody is a message that challenges everyone to consider alternatives to authoritarian traditions behind religions, nation-states, and capitalist greed. The message is subversive, yet the song became a hit even on commercial radio. A poll by Rolling Stone magazine for the 500 greatest songs of all time had "Imagine" at number three, and the editors quoted Ono, who was looking back thirty years after the recording: "It's not like he thought, 'Oh, this can be an anthem.'" "Imagine" was "just what John believed: that we are all one country, one world, one people. He wanted to get that idea out."[26]

The NYCLC performed an arrangement by Mac Huff.[27] The soprano section sang the first part of the first verse, which was marked for a solo in the arrangement, and all joined for the last line. While altos joined sopranos to harmonize the second verse, tenors and basses also harmonized with "ooh" in the background, and then all sang the final line with a crescendo to lead into the chorus. An added crescendo came at the end of the chorus, leading to a key change and bold unison singing for the final verse, repeated chorus, and finale. It is a moving arrangement, and we spent a great deal of time in rehearsals to work on the most challenging parts.

Song of Peace

The final song from the section on peace was "Song of Peace," a hymn with a majestic melody and hopeful lyrics. The words are by Lloyd Stone (first two verses) and Georgia Harkness (third verse), and the music is taken from the song "Finlandia" by Jean Sibelius. The arrangement credit is to Johnnie Carl.[28] Stone (1912-1993) had studied to become a music teacher but then joined a circus in Hawaii and remained there for life, composing songs and poems. Harkness (1891-1974) was a Methodist theologian who became the first woman to teach in a seminary. She had a passion for the arts and a vision of a world-wide, universal Christianity.[29] Her final verse has the following words:

> May truth and freedom come to every nation,
> May peace abound where strife has raged so long,
> That all may seek to love and build together
> A world united righting every wrong,
> A world united in its love of freedom,
> Proclaiming peace together in one song!
> This is my song, O God, Amen![30]

Sibelius (1865-1957) was a composer from Finland, and his 1899 composition of "Finlandia" helped his fame spread from Finland to around the world. The work of Sibelius became a source of national pride among Finns at a time when Russia was becoming more aggressive in its colonizing hold.[31]

This song is an example of fine poetry matched with stirring music to create a powerful message. It often can be difficult to hold onto hope for peace; however, singing a song such as this with a large group of people reminded me that I was not alone in the struggle to imagine an end to war and to act on a faith that peace is possible. Songs alone will not end wars, but they can help to inspire continued work toward building a more just and peaceful world. This is another song that has a YouTube recording for its performance in the 25th anniversary concert.[32]

Songs of the 25th-Anniversary Gala Concert   73

JOY

The third theme of the concert was joy. The quote in the program for this section was from a poem by John Keats: "A thing of beauty is a joy forever: its loveliness increases; it will never pass into nothingness."[33] Working for social justice is a struggle, but there is joy in sharing the work with others and knowing that the work makes a difference. The NYCLC works diligently to bring its best abilities to the music of the labor movement and other struggles, but there are many moments of laughter and smiles during rehearsals and after performances. The joy of singing and of participating in the labor movement has sustained a community for the chorus, and there is no duration of a quarter century without joy from memories and from the ongoing work.

Ode To Workers

After the intermission, the chorus started the theme of joy with "Ode To Workers," which brought words by Henry Van Dyke, Paul Robeson, and Jeff Vogel to the final movement of Beethoven's Ninth Symphony, also known as "Hymn to Joy" or "Ode to Joy."[34] The melody is one of the most recognized and admired in the history of European classical music. The most widely known lyrics set to the famous melody were by Henry Van Dyke, a Presbyterian minister who in 1907 was inspired by the beauty of Massachusetts' Berkshire Mountains when writing with the title "Joyful, Joyful, We Adore Thee."[35] The sheet music credits Edward Hodges (1796-1867) for adaptation of the song. Hodges was a British composer who emigrated to Canada and then the US, where in 1839 he became music director at Trinity Parish.[36]

NYCLC member Jeff Vogel composed the first verse, which the chorus sang in unison with the following lyrics:

> Workers sing your union anthem 'cross the land and o'er the Earth
> Tell the story of the battles that led to your glorious birth
> Robber barons, Wall Street tyrants, gath'ring wealth is all they know
> Come together, join our forces, and defeat our greedy foe.[37]

The other two verses, sung in four-part harmony, had words that the concert-program writers attributed to performances by Paul Robeson. After the second verse, pianist Dennis Nelson played a beautiful solo that inspired the chorus to sing the final verse with its best energy. The song truly set the stage for the set of songs with the theme of joy.

Common Thread

In keeping with the theme of joy, "Common Thread" is an upbeat song with hopeful lyrics. The composer is Pat Humphries, who was a guest performer for the NYCLC's first benefit concert in 1993 and who became one of two singer-songwriter partners of Emma's Revolution. The NYCLC sang a 2009 arrangement by Peter Schlosser. The lyrics speak to the hope of uniting across social movements to rise together. Sopranos sang the first verse, tenors and basses the second, altos the third, all the fourth, and all joined together in the chorus between verses and at the end.

I had no luck finding Humphries singing her own song on YouTube, but there are several versions by other singers and groups. The Common Thread Community Chorus of Toronto took their name from the song.[38] Their 2010 version does not sound much different from Schlosser's arrangement for the NYCLC, but the latter has more syncopation. All memorable songs bring out a special response, and this song brings out the hope, pride, and joy of working with others for social justice.

How Can I Keep from Singing?

The title "How Can I Keep from Singing?" expresses what is in the hearts and minds of NYCLC members when they take a subway trip to a rehearsal or performance. The singing comes from both necessity and joy. The credits to the song in the concert program read, "Traditional Folk Hymn, arranged by Andy Beck; Additional words: Pete Seeger and Jeff Vogel."[39] Beck's arrangement of this beautiful hymn with four-part harmony starts with quiet singing (*piano*), builds to a high volume (*forte*), and ends very quietly (*pianissimo*).[40]

The verses in Beck's arrangement have no overtly political message. They simply work with the melody and harmonies to evoke the joy of singing. Jeff Vogel contributed two lines of revised lyrics. It is a joy to sing this song with a large chorus led by a conductor and accompanist who are highly talented and passionate professionals. As the song ends quietly, it leaves the peaceful feeling that sometimes only singing can bring. It is a work of art that upholds the power of singing to elevate the soul, and its place in the NYCLC's repertoire is important.

If You Can Walk You Can Dance

The title "If You Can Walk You Can Dance" contains one of the only two lines in the entire song. The other substitutes "talk" and "sing" for "walk" and "dance," respectively. These words come from a Zimbabwean proverb. Elizabeth Alexander composed the music for a choir with four-part harmony.[41] A note at the top of the score reads, "With gentle marcato and precise rhythmic energy." The opening piano passage sets the marked rhythm, and the entire piece flows with an upbeat energy. It is difficult to stand still while singing to the danceable rhythm. There are various passages in which the four sections trade singing the lead, including one in which sopranos and altos snap fingers while tenors and basses sing quietly. Near the end the music stops suddenly after the word "talk," and all talk out loud with their own chosen words until the conductor signals to stop. Then the song ends with an extra-lively finale.

Like the preceding song, this one carries no words with an overtly political message. Its theme is celebration of singing and dancing, and all working people need time to set aside their troubles and celebrate life. It is a joy to sing the song, and the rhythmic music begs for choreography. It is a challenging piece to sing well, though, so adding choreography would bring an additional challenge for rehearsals. Any added feature would be a bonus to this song that inspires joyful singing.

Life on Earth, So Amazing

The set of songs for the theme of joy started with a familiar and celebrated masterwork from the classical era, and so it ended with another. The title and revised lyrics of "Life on Earth, So Amazing" are from 2007 by Jeff Vogel, who was inspired to write the words upon seeing a photograph of the Earth from outer space. The music is John Purifoy's 2001 abridged arrangement of Handel's "Hallelujah Chorus" of the "Messiah Suite."[42] After three bars of a piano introduction, the lively singing in four-part harmony began with the title words taking the place of "hallelujah": "Life on Earth, so amazing, so amazing, a-ma-a-a-zing." Another change is "And peace shall reign forever and ever," replacing "And He shall reign." These are fitting words of joy and celebration to match the festive music. As mentioned in Chapter One, bringing new words to familiar music is an age-old tradition in the labor movement of the US dating back at least to the IWW in the early years of the 20th Century. Lyricists like Vogel are carrying on with the practice. Additional writing by Vogel on the theme of protecting life on Earth appears in the 2015 Earth Day edition of Tikkun Daily, an interfaith blog that promotes progressive politics.[43]

"Life on Earth, So Amazing" also has a video recording of its performance in the 25th-Anniversary Concert on YouTube.[44] Appearing on the large screen above the stage for all the audience to see was the excerpt from John Keats' poem as quoted in the program.[45] At the end of the song there was a hearty applause, and conductor Jana Ballard faced the audience with a smile, a bow, and a wave of the hand to salute the chorus. It was a joyful ending to the concert's section on the theme of joy.

TWENTY-FIVE YEARS

The final theme of the concert was, appropriately, twenty-five years. The entire evening was a celebration of the chorus still going strong after a quarter century. The final five songs of the evening were classics. They were songs that the chorus had performed many times in concerts, on picket lines, and/or in marches. The quote in the program for the theme was by Pete Seeger: "The right song at the right moment can change history."[46] These are songs that not only stood the test of time but also contributed to changing history.

To My Old Brown Earth

The perfect song to give tribute to our mortality along with enduring bonds of community is Pete Seeger's "To My Old Brown Earth." The chorus sang Paul Halley's arrangement, which begins with instructional words "Very slowly and expressively."[47] Seeger composed the words and music in 1964, while there was still a revival in folk music. The poetic lyrics are of an elder encouraging those who follow to keep strong connections to each other and to their home on Earth. It is a short but incredibly beautiful song. The NYCLC sang it under the alternative title "And You Are Still Mine" for the celebration of Pete Seeger's 90th birthday at Madison Square Garden, in which 51 artists performed.[48] An audio recording of this performance by the labor chorus is on YouTube.[49]

This song was the right choice to start the theme of 25 years because it is from the perspective of someone near life's end who is hopeful that others will carry on the important work of moving humanity toward a better world. Although Seeger would live another 50 years after writing this song, he showed in these brief verses a spiritual maturity regarding mortality and the power of a community to grow in commitment despite losing members to death. The chorus lost many members over the course of its first 25 years; keeping them close in memory has been a source of strength for the group. There were very few deaths of members during my six years in the chorus. Although I did not know any of these individuals well, I joined with fellow chorus members in expressing grief and in celebrating each person's life and unique contributions to the life of the community.

Which Side Are You On?

The classic labor song "Which Side Are You On?" has a story behind it. Woody Guthrie, while speaking to Alan Lomax, quoted an anonymous person who knew the two sisters that authored the song: "This song was composed in 19 and 31 by the two children of Sam Reece, two little girls. They're grown up now, but one was nine and the other eleven then. It was made up from the condition of their father, who was organizer in Harlan County [Kentucky] for the U.M.W. of A. . . One night, during the big Harlan strike their home was raided by company thugs, and after that they composed this song."[50] Guthrie then commented on how some of the greatest songwriting comes from ordinary people who never had formal training in the art. He ended his commentary with this line: "Lord pity the scabs, the ginks, the hooded Lizards, and Great Gizzards, that jump on the working folks and beat these songs out of 'em."[51]

The version of the song as transcribed by Pete Seeger has eight verses.[52] The NYCLC sang a version with five on a score that does not name the arranger, but the handwriting matches that which is found in other songs arranged by Peter Schlosser ("El Pueblo Unido" and "Johnny, I Hardly Knew 'Ya"). The score gives these credits: "Words: Florence Reece (1931); Music: Old hymn tune."[53] The refrain involves singing the words of the title eight times with an interweaving pair of melodies—one by sopranos and altos, the other by tenors and basses. The clear message is that there is no neutral ground in class struggle. The verses tell a story of union organizing and resistance against lying bosses, company thugs, and unprincipled scabs. Although the song was penned by a woman (possibly with her sister), the third verse indicates that the perspective is from a miner's son. By contrast, the similar verse and all other verses in Seeger's transcript have no reference to indicate a male perspective.[54] The fourth verse in the score for the NYCLC ends with a correction to bring gender neutrality because the original equates being a "man" with having courage.[55] Some chorus members have added verses on a separate sheet to address additional contemporary issues such as health care, ecology, and racism. My copy has notes in my own handwriting indicating which verses were sung for some performance. I cannot recall which verses we sang for the 25th-anniversary concert (the program did not give credit for words to anyone other than Florence Reece), but this was without doubt one of the liveliest among many spirited songs of the evening.

This Old Hammer

The third song of the final theme was "This Old Hammer," a classic from African-American folklore. The legend of John Henry, still a matter of debate whether it is fiction, is the story of a steel-driving worker in railroad construction who tried to prove that he could outperform the new machine that was placing workers out of a job.[56] The story ends with him winning the contest only to lose his life from heart failure in response to the stress of the work. Numerous versions of different songs pay tribute to the legend. A quick search in YouTube shows that many renowned artists have recorded some version of such a song.

The version performed by the NYCLC is an adaptation by Walter Ehret.[57] The word "Slowly" appears at the top of the score. The tempo is slow, but there is bluesy intensity in alternating passages of soft and bold singing. The opening words, sung only by sopranos and altos in the adjusted score for the chorus, are "This old hammer killed John Henry (repeated twice), but this old hammer won't kill me." The second verse has two interweaving parts with sopranos and altos harmonizing while bases and tenors sing melody. After the second verse, a sensational piano transition leads into a change of key with the printed instruction "With drive" for the third verse: "Take my hammer to the walking boss (repeated twice), tell him I'm gone (repeat)." The final verse and ending then return to soft singing. It was not easy to sing this intense work so late in the program, but it showed how the chorus was prepared well for such a challenge.

Union Maid

"Union Maid" arguably is Woody Guthrie's second most famous song after "This Land Is Your Land." Made popular by the Weavers' version in the early 1940s with Seeger singing lead, it is on everyone's short list of labor classics.[58] The chorus has the indelible sing-along line that expresses no fear with the union's support. When renowned musicians joined together with fans to celebrate the centennial of Guthrie's birth in 2012 in Tulsa, Oklahoma, the group Old Crow Medicine Show performed "Union Maid" and had the crowd singing along with the chorus.[59] Once, around that time, when I was telling a long-time friend in a long-distance phone call that I had joined the NYCLC, he replied with a question that revealed his limited knowledge of labor songs: "What do you do—sit around singing Union Maid?" I think I replied that that was only one of many in the group's repertoire of old and new songs but that it was one of the old favorites.

The concert program credited Guthrie for words and music.[60] The sheet music used by the chorus, though, has the following: "Words by Woodie Guthrie; Tune: Redwing; Arranged by Murray Chase."[61] Composed in 1907 by Kerry Mills (music) and Thurland Chattaway (lyrics), "Red Wing" was a folk song about a Native American woman's love and longing for a warrior who was far away, and Guthrie did take the music directly from it for "Union Maid."[62] The NYCLC did not sing the third of four verses in its score of "Union Maid," which has the narrated note "For history's sake."[63] It contained words that portrayed women as less-than "others" in the union movement. The entire chorus sang the first verse in unison, tenors and basses sang the second verse, and sopranos and altos sang the fourth and final verse, which portrayed activist women in a positive light. An added note for the final verse stated, "A new verse for the 1980s," and a post-script note further added, "I wish I could remember who wrote this one—P.S." No matter how many times the NYCLC performed this song in concerts and marches, it remained a favorite. At least, I never heard anyone complain that we were singing it again.

Bread and Roses

If there is one song that epitomizes the work and message of the NYCLC, it would be "Bread and Roses." It was appropriate to have it as the final song in the program. The program named the composers as Joel Oppenheimer for words and Mimi Farina for music.[64] The correct author of the words was James Oppenheim, as noted on the photocopied sheet music (dated 2004 in handwriting) used by the chorus, which also named the music composer as Mimi Fariña (note the "ñ" instead of "n").[65] The phrase "bread and roses" became a common rally cry after the successful Bread and Roses Strike by thousands of textile workers, mostly immigrant women, in 1912 in Lawrence, Massachusetts.[66] Oppenheim's poem "Bread and Roses," though, preceded that strike with a December 1911 publication in *American Magazine*.[67] The clear message in the poem is that workers need more than just the basics for survival—food, shelter, clothing; we also need the aesthetic qualities that come from the arts and the wondrous beauty of nature. The poem explicitly upholds class struggle against the elites of capitalism: "No more the drudge and idler, ten that toil where one reposes." The verses give special focus to the leading role that women often have played in the fight for necessities and access to the arts and nature's beauty. The beautiful melody and harmonies of Fariña's music complement the message of the poem. Fariña, who died of cancer at age 56 in 2001, was the younger sister of Joan Baez but, as noted in her obituary by *The Guardian*, "was no less a stirring personality and performer."[68]

Hearing this song sung well is an inspiration. There are long stretches with only sopranos and altos singing. During these passages in rehearsals, I would often close my eyes, relax, and marvel at the beauty of the harmony and words. This song is a wonderful gift to the movements for women and labor,

80   *Chapter Three*

but I had never heard it before joining the NYCLC at age forty-nine. Wherever there is a labor chorus, women's chorus, or any chorus with a social-justice orientation, this song will continue to inspire all who sing and hear it.

ENCORE: ROCKIN' SOLIDARITY

Although it was not listed in the program, the prepared encore was "Rockin' Solidarity," an upbeat blues-gospel-rock-infused adaptation of Ralph Chaplin's labor classic "Solidarity Forever." The printout of lyrics used by the chorus shows an arrangement credit of "Rockin' Solidarity" to Dave Welch, whom the Left Coast Labour Chorus of Vancouver, British Columbia, Canada identifies as an activist from San Francisco.[69] The original "Solidarity Forever" places Chaplin's words in the music of the "Battle Hymn of the Republic." Chaplain (1887-1961) was a poet, artist, and editor who was active in the IWW, and he wrote the song, first published in 1915, with hopes that it would inspire revolutionary passion.[70] It has appeared in every edition of the IWW's Little Red Song Book since then. In its rousing and easily-sung chorus are the words "Solidarity forever" three times, followed by "For the union makes us strong."

Whereas the final song listed in the concert program—"Bread and Roses"—was a quieter anthem, the encore gave the audience a revved-up version of another anthem that had many in the audience out of their seats, clapping to the rhythm and singing the chorus out loud. Bringing "Rockin' Solidarity" to its fullest life was soloist Denise Jones, who sang each verse with all the intensity and precision of a seasoned gospel or blues artist. Backing her up was Dennis Nelson with a stirring piano accompaniment along with the chorus that swayed to the rhythm and joined in singing the chorus after each of the three verses. The finale was a slow and ecstatic repeat of the final line of the chorus, upon which all chorus members removed their union hats and waved them in the air. This had been the encore for NYCLC concerts for years, and Denise and the chorus had never failed to end a show on a high note of great passion and skill. The ending of the 25th-anniversary concert was no exception.

CONCLUSIONS ON THE SONG SET

The concert brought 21 songs to the audience on that one evening. The complete repertoire of the NYCLC holds more than 60 songs, and that is only my collection as a member of six years. My folder has 64 songs, still in alphabetical order. To the best of my memory, we sang nearly all of them at least once in rehearsals over that six-year period, and there are only a few that I cannot recall singing in at least one performance. The 25th-anniversary concert was a landmark event, and I can only begin to imagine how hard the Arts & Culture Committee worked along with the board of directors to narrow the concert program down to 21 songs. The result was a group of diverse songs that fit well into the four themes.

Going to weekly rehearsals and often-frequent performances year after year, I often heard fellow members commenting on songs they liked and sometimes on disliking a song. The labor movement is a long enough and large enough part of US history to have brought many different points of view and many works of musical expression to the public. The songs come in the musical genres of spirituals/gospel, European classical, hymns, blues, jazz, country, rock, and hip hop. If one searches hard enough, there probably is a polka with a great message of class struggle. The messages in the songs of the NYCLC repertoire range from having no overtly political stance to making a revolutionary statement, and most are somewhere in the middle of these ends. It is entirely appropriate for the NYCLC to include a song of pure joy but without a firm political message, like "If You Can Walk You Can Dance." To paraphrase the prominent feminist anarchist Emma Goldman, any revolution that bans dancing is one to reject.[71] It is also important to include songs that push the envelope with revolutionary lyrics, and several of the songs introduced above do just that. The notion of ending child labor once was a radical one, but now there is universal agreement that education for youths is a human right. Socialism was a dirty word during the Cold War, but now the concept of democratic socialism holds wide acceptance as seen by the surprisingly strong candidacy of Bernie Sanders in 2016. The NYCLC will have ongoing debates over which songs should get more attention, and that is a healthy process as the organization works to honor the past while affirming changes for the present and future.

NOTES

1. New York City Labor Chorus, *25th Anniversary*, 2016, 12–13.
2. Ibid, 12.
3. Carl Haywood, *The Haywood Collection of Negro Spirituals*, 1992, 225.
4. Richard Newman, *Go Down Moses: A Celebration of the African-American Spiritual* (New York: Roundtable Press, 1998), 103.
5. Robert Darden, *Nothing but Love in God's Water: Black Sacred Music from the Civil War to the Civil Rights Movement* (University Park, PA: The Pennsylvania State University Press, 2014), 125.

6. Ibid., 106.

7. Michael K. Honey, *Sharecropper's Troubadour: John L. Handcox, the Southern Tenant Farmers' Union, and the African American Song Tradition* (New York: Palgrave McMillan, 2013), 111.

8. New York City Labor Chorus, *25th Anniversary*, 12.

9. Sergio Ortega, "El Pueblo Unido," song on studio album "El Pueblo Unido Jamás Será Vencido" by Quilapayún, 1975.

10. Quilapayún, *Historia*, 2018, http://www.quilapayun.com/hexilio.php.

11. New York City Labor Chorus, *25th Anniversary*.

12. N/A, "Thina Sizwe," song on album "This Land Is Mine: South African Freedom Songs," 1965.

13. N/A, "Thina Sizwe," song on the soundtrack to the motion picture "Amandla! A Revolution in Four-Part Harmony," performed by the SABC Choir, 2003.

14. New York City Labor Chorus, *25th Anniversary*, 13.

15. Neil W. Levin, "Give Me Your Tired, Your Poor," liner notes to *Milken Archive of Jewish Music*, 2019, https://www.milkenarchive.org/music/volumes/view/legend-of-toil-and-celebration/work/give-me-your-tired-your-poor/.

16. Jane Wilburn Sapp, "Ain't You Got a Right." http://www.nyclc.org/Lyrics/Ain't%20you%20got%20a%20right.pdf.

17. Guy and Candie Carawan, *Ain't You Got a Right?: The People of St. Johns Island, South Carolina—Their Faces, Their Words, and Their Songs* (1967, Reprint, Athens: University of Georgia Press, 1989), back cover.

18. Ibid., 170.

19. New York City Labor Chorus, *25th Anniversary*, 12.

20. Robbie Solomon, composer of lyrics and music, *Peace by Piece*, 2003.

21. Jonathan Lighter, *The Best Anti-War Song Ever Written* (E. Windsor, NJ: Loomis House Press, 2012), 4.

22. Moonala 123 (YouTube username), "NYC Labor Chorus," video recording of "Simple Song of Freedom," https://www.youtube.com/watch?v=UNmaGCt8mQE

23. Bobby Darin, *Simple Song of Freedom*, recorded as 7" single by Tim Hardin, 1974, https://www.discogs.com/Tim-Hardin-Simple-Song-Of-Freedom/release/4971121.

24. New York City Labor Chorus, *25th Anniversary*, 3.

25. Christopher D. Shea, "Yoko Ono Will Share Credit for John Lennon's 'Imagine,'" *New York Times*, June 15, 2017, https://www.nytimes.com/search?query=ono+imagine.

26. "The 500 Greatest Songs of All Time." *Rolling Stone*, April 7, 2011, https://www.rollingstone.com/music/music-lists/500-greatest-songs-of-all-time-151127/?list_page=10#list-item-50.

27. John Lennon and Yoko Ono, "Imagine" (Lenono Music, 1971). Arrangement by Mac Huff (Lenono Music, 1991).

28. Johnnie Carl, arranger, "A Song of Peace," lyrics by Lloyd Stone and Georgia Hawkins, music by Jean Sibelius (Choristers Guild, 2011).

29. "This Is My Song," Your Daily Poem, 2019, http://yourdailypoem.com/listpoem.jsp?poem_id=497.

30. Georgia Harkness, "This Is My Song", which became Verse 3 of "A Song of Peace." Lyrics printed by permission from Music Services Inc.

31. San Francisco Symphony, "Program Notes: Sibelius: *Finlandia*," 2016, https://www.sfsymphony.org/Watch-Listen-Learn/Read-Program-Notes/Program-Notes/Sibelius-Finlandia.aspx.

32. Carl Vogel, "NYC Labor Chorus 2016 Winter," video recording of "A Song of Peace," https://www.youtube.com/watch?v=bZf9_-W1FRk.

33. New York City Labor Chorus, *25th Anniversary*, 13.

34. Ludwig van Beethoven, final movement of Ninth Symphony, 1824. "Hymn to Joy" adapted by Edward Hodges (1796-1867). Henry Van Dyke, 1907, alt. "Ode to Workers" adapted lyrics by Henry Van Dyke, Paul Robeson, and Jeff Vogel. Sources for this endnote are sheet music used by NYCLC and p. 13 of *25th Anniversary* concert journal.

35. C. Michael Hawn, "History of Hymns: 'Joyful, Joyful, We Adore Thee.'" Discipleship Ministries of the United Methodist Church, 2019, https://www.umcdiscipleship.org/resources/history-of-hymns-joyful-joyful-we-adore-thee.

36. "Edward Hodges," Hymn Time, http://www.hymntime.com/tch/bio/h/o/d/hodges_e.htm.

37. Jeff Vogel, adapted words for "Ode to Workers." Printed by permission.

38. CommonThreadChorus (YouTube username), "Common Thread May 2010 Common Thread Community Chorus of Toronto," video recording of "Common Thread," https://www.youtube.com/watch?v=lOU0w17PRco.

39. New York City Labor Chorus, *25th Anniversary*.

40. Andy Beck, arranger, "How Can I Keep from Singing" (Van Nuys, CA: Alfred Publishing Co., Inc., 2008).

41. Elizabeth Alexander, music composer, "If You Can Walk You Can Dance" (Seafarer Press, 2009).

42. John Purifoy, arranger, "Hallelujah Chorus," George Frideric Handel (New York: G. Schirmer, Inc., 2001).

43. Jeffrey Vogel, "Earth Day 2015," *Tikkun Daily*, April 21, 2015, https://www.tikkun.org/tikkundaily/2015/04/21/earth-day-2015/.

44. Moonala123, "NYC Labor Chorus 2016," video recording of "Life on Earth, So Amazing," https://www.youtube.com/watch?v=21aheK48cdY.

45. John Keats, "Endymion," in *The World's Best Poetry, Volume VI*, eds. Bliss Carmen, et al., (Fancy, 1904), reprinted by Bartleby.com: Great Books Online, https://www.bartleby.com/360/6/154.html.

46. New York City Labor Chorus, *25th Anniversary*.

47. Pete Seeger (words and music), Paul Halley (arranger), "To My Old Brown Earth," (New York: Stormking Music, Inc., 1964).

48. Vintage Vinyl News, "Set List: Pete Seeger's 90th Birthday Show at Madison Square Garden (May 5, 2009), https://www.vintagevinylnews.com/2009/05/set-list-pete-seegers-90th-birthday.html.

49. Adelfred (YouTube username), "06 New York City Labor Chorus—You Are Still Mine," audio recording (May 10, 2009), https://www.youtube.com/watch?v=b1yfnr1AL50&list=PLxLwkHVTgXCbIm_4wfP_fOsTrIny8J_rE&index=4.

50. Woody Guthrie (with Alan Lomax and Pete Seeger), *Hard Hitting Songs for Hard Hit People* (Lincoln: University of Nebraska Press), 176.

51. Ibid.

52. Ibid., Pete Seeger, 176–177.

53. Anonymous arranger/transcriber, "Which Side Are You On," composed by Florence Reece, 1931.

54. Pete Seeger (with Woody Guthrie and Alan Lomax), *Hard Hitting Songs for Hard Hit People*, 177.

55. Anonymous arranger/transcriber, "Which Side Are You On."

56. "John Henry," Library of Congress, https://www.loc.gov/item/ihas.200196572/

57. Walter Ehret, adaptation of "This Old Hammer" (Shawnee Press).

58. Wayne Bledsoe, "Labor Day Celebrated in 25 Unforgettable Songs." *Knoxville News-Sentinel* (September 1, 2017), database: Newspaper Source Plus.

59. Jennifer Chancellor, "Musicians, Fans Celebrate Woody Guthrie's Legacy at Centennial in Tulsa." *Tulsa World* (March 11, 2012), database: Newspaper Source Plus.

60. New York City Labor Chorus, *25th Anniversary*.

61. Woody Guthrie, "Union Maid," arranged by Murray Chase (People's Songs, Inc., 1947), http://www.nyclc.org/Union_Maid.pdf.

62. Dan D. Dirges, "Red Wing," video-recorded performance, https://www.youtube.com/watch?v=IA0v-GgTp2E.

63. Woody Guthrie, "Union Maid."

64. New York City Labor Chorus, *25th Anniversary*.

65. James Oppenheim and Mimi Farina, "Bread and Roses," 2004.

66. Robert Ross, "Bread and Roses: Why the Legend Lives On," in *The Great Lawrence Textile Strike of 1912: New Scholarship on the Bread and Roses Strike*, eds. Robert Forrant, Jurg K. Siegenthaler, Charles Levenstein, and John Wooding (Amityville, NY: Baywood Publishing Company, Inc., 2014), 219–230.

67. Zinn Education Project, "Songs and Poems: Bread and Roses," 2019, https://www.zinnedproject.org/materials/bread-and-roses-song/.

68. Colin Irwin, "Mimi Farina: Talented Folk Singer Overshadowed by her Older Sister, Joan Baez," The Guardian (July 20, 2001), https://www.theguardian.com/news/2001/jul/21/guardianobituaries.

69. Left Coast Labour Chorus, http://www.leftcoastlabourchorus.com/.

70. Jon Bekken, "Solidarity Forever: A Wobbly Labor Anthem," *Anarcho-Syndicalist Review* 55 (2011): 31.

71. Emma Goldman, *Living My Life, Volume One* (New York: Dover Publications, Inc.), 56.

Poster for Paul Robeson Gala Centennial Salute, 1998.
Photographer unknown. Used by permission from NYCLC archives.

Poster for concert in 2000.
Photographer unknown. Used by permission from NYCLC archives.

NYC Labor Chorus members (in red) in cultural exchange, Mantanzas, Cuba, May 2011.
Photo by Mariana Gastón, used by her permission.

Concert at the Tribeca Performing Arts Center, May 2013.
Photographer unknown. Used by permission from NYCLC archives.

Concert at the Tribeca Performing Arts Center, May 2013.
Photographer unknown. Used by permission from NYCLC archives.

Jana Ballard, director and conductor of the NYC Labor Chorus, 2010 to present.
Photographer unknown. Photo provided by Ms. Ballard.

Dennis Nelson, piano accompanist to the NYC Labor Chorus, 2002 to present.
Photographer unknown. Photo provided by Mr. Nelson.

Denise Jones in front singing solo at memorial service for activist Bill Gilson, April 2016.
Photographer unknown. Used by permission from NYCLC archives.

Velma Hill, featured member of "In the Spotlight" on the NYCLC's website.
Photo provided by Ms. Hill to NYCLC archives. Photographer unknown. Used by permission from NYCLC archives.

Cover of 25th-anniversary concert journal.
Photographer unknown. Used by permission from NYCLC archives.

Chorus on stage at 25th-anniversary concert.
Photo by Ellen and Jay Bitkower. Used by permission from NYCLC archives.

Chorus on stage at 25th-anniversary concert.
Photo by Ellen and Jay Bitkower. Used by permission from NYCLC archives.

Participants of focus group, May 10, 2017. Clockwise from left: Tom Karlson, Bobby Greenberg (vice president), Jeff Vogel, Jesse Kasowitz, Inez West, Georgia Wever, Barbara Bailey (president, co-founder), Neil Blonstein.
Photo by the author.

Chapter Four

The 25th-Anniversary Year

When the NYCLC started another calendar year in September of 2016, it was not just another year; it was the year marking a quarter century of the organization's life. So much can happen in a person's life in 25 years. One changes from child to young adult, from young adult to middle-age, or from middle-age to retirement age. Likewise, an organization undergoes changes with the passage of so much time. The chorus had gone from its infancy to a rich maturity. Several original members were still among the most active. In recent years there had been a few new members joining and a few elderly members leaving due to either disability or death, and each death left surviving members in a bittersweet time of mourning while also celebrating the person's life. Like any organization, the NYCLC was continuously making plans for its future while reviewing its history and collective memories to assess its strengths and challenges. The 25th-anniversary year, though, would become a special time for thoughtful reflection and purposeful planning.

STARTING A NEW YEAR
AND PREPARING FOR A BIG CONCERT

On the morning of Saturday, September 10, on the weekend after Labor Day, about 15 or 20 members of the chorus braved the hot, humid weather to march in the Labor Day parade. We gathered around 9:00 at 5th Avenue and 44th Street, wearing white chorus tee shirts, black pants (no shorts), black socks, and black shoes as directed in the email announcement two weeks in advance. Having not seen each other since late spring, our conversations focused mainly on each person's new stories to tell from the summer. One union nearby had a group of bagpipe players and drummers in kilts, and several of us stopped talking to listen to them practice. A couple chorus members were passing out flyers to fellow members and bystanders for Bernie Sanders' presidential campaign. At one point, a woman of around age 50 from the Actors' Equity Association (AEA) came over and asked us what we would be singing. Someone mentioned "Union Maid," and she started singing it loudly and clearly; we instantly joined in.[1] After the second verse, we came to a stop. As our visitor left to rejoin her group, a couple chorus members enthusiastically invited her to become a chorus member.

With two members carrying our banner in front, we marched north to the parade's end point, several blocks north of the southeast corner of Central Park. I took a turn in holding the banner. The crowds on either side were sometimes large but mostly sparse. A few faculty members and staff of CUNY's Murphy Institute for Worker Education and Labor Studies were in front of us. Behind us was a large group from the AEA, whose loud chants occasionally drowned out our singing of "Union Maid." One of their chants was "Fair wage, on stage." As we approached the march's end, there was a band on a stage with a soloist singing "Solidarity Forever."[2] Naturally, we joined in the singing. When we finished, we said "See you Monday" to each other in anticipation of the year's first weekly rehearsal.

The first weekly Monday rehearsal of the chorus's new calendar year occurred at a location other than the usual second floor of 50 Broadway, where the United Federation of Teachers (UFT), the union for teachers in New York City's public schools, provided without charge a large room with a piano for the chorus. The UFT offices were closed, so the NYCLC board of directors chose to rent a large rehearsal studio on the 16th floor of 520 8th Avenue, between 36th and 37th Streets. Rehearsal time, as usual, was 6:00 to 8:00 PM. Early arrivers who had not been at the Labor Day parade were excited to see each other again after the long summer break. The rehearsal started with Barbara Bailey, as president, welcoming everyone back and thanking all who had marched for Labor Day. Bobby Greenberg, as vice president, then thanked those who had already contributed money for the upcoming 25th-anniversary concert's journal, and he asked everyone to think about giving for an ad from each of the four sections—soprano, alto, tenor, and bass. Bobby also identified Bob Harris as coordinator of phone calls to unions and other potential donors. Jana Ballard, as director, then exclaimed, "We should have had a potluck! Everyone's so excited!" She started leading everyone in stretching exercises but then stopped to say, "Look who's here, guys! Dennis!" Our piano accompanist, Dennis Nelson, had been in a horrible car accident late in the prior spring that left him unable to play piano with a wrist fracture. He was able to play again, and everyone welcomed him back with hearty applause. Dennis smiled and thanked everyone for thoughts and prayers, and then Jana led the vocal warm-up. We went on to practice nine songs that were selected to be in either of two sections—"25 Years" and "Joy"—of the 25th Anniversary concert. Jana was mostly pleased with our sound but took time to work on errors, especially from the bass and tenor sections. As usual, she was a demanding but warm teacher who used humor spontaneously. As we worked on "Common Thread," she smiled and said in her southern accent, "If you accidently sing harmony, make it the right harmony," which drew laughter. During the break for announcements, Barbara stated that we could pay annual dues of 35 dollars beginning the following week. Jana then was excited to say, "Twenty-five-year concert! Not many choruses stay together that long, and I'm glad to be with the chorus for six years now." She also was pleased with the venue choice of Skirball Auditorium at New York University. Rehearsal ended early at 7:35, and Jana asked members of the Arts and Culture Committee (ACC) to stay and meet with her.

On the following Monday, rehearsal returned to the usual location. While we worked on "Give Me Your Tired," Jana stopped to encourage everyone to record rehearsals on smart phones.[3] Laughter followed when she said, "Something for when you have nothing to do—practice with coffee and candlelight." Moments later, while working with sopranos on a challenging part, Jana reminded everyone that she was serious about not wasting time: "It's hard to do anything when there's talking going on during rehearsal." Some side talk continued until a member in the alto section spoke out, telling everyone to stop talking while Jana works with a section. As in every rehearsal, there was a break near the middle for announcements. Barbara and Bobby gave reminders: wear the red shirt for photos next week; help to find sponsors for ads in the concert journal. I announced that I had started taking notes for my study; I had first announced my study a couple months before the summer break. Rehearsal resumed with work on "Tina Sizwe."[4] Jana complimented sopranos on their high energy level and expressive faces, and she made clear that everyone needed these qualities. After a second run through the song, Jana cheerfully asked, "How much better was that?" She added that we should be tired after singing, and Barbara replied, "That's why we go to the afterglow," which drew plenty of laughter. The "afterglow" was a tradition that chorus members had learned in their tour in Wales in the summer of 2009. The Welsh singers would celebrate the end of their performances with an afterglow in a nearby restaurant/bar. The rehearsal ended with work on two songs that Jana warned would be challenging: "Johnny, I Hardly Knew Ya"[5] and "Peace by Piece."[6] While we worked on the latter, Jana reminded everyone while smiling, "Watch your s-endings! Don't you know me after six years?" The chorus responded with laughter, knowing how patient Jana had been with the ongoing trouble from uneven singing of words ending in "s." We did better with another try and heard Jana's parting words of the evening: "When we rehearse, I need you to go hard. We have to find what is weak. Most songs end with gusto; make it happen!"

The following Monday was September 26, and we were back at the studio on 8th Avenue for rehearsal again. Velma Hill was sorting our concert tickets from her chair, and later she moved to the end of the studio and received help from Barbara Bailey and Betty Reid. Rehearsal was delayed several minutes due to late delivery of chairs. Barbara took a moment to announce proudly that she, along with a fellow chorus member, had visited the Smithsonian African-American Museum for its opening. We worked quickly through 16 of the 20 songs chosen for the concert, taking a break for photos—one for each section, and one of the entire chorus. Barbara announced that each member would be responsible for selling five concert tickets. When rehearsal ended, Jana was pleased: "Once we finish the hard stuff, the last section will be like [gesture and expression of celebration]! We've done a lot tonight. Good job!"

The next rehearsal was on Wednesday, October 5, again at the 8th Avenue studio. A series of Monday holidays and other situations prevented the chorus from using the UFT location a few times. The New York City Department of Education honors Jewish holidays with school closings, and Monday the 3rd was part of Rosh Hashana. The evening began with Bobby Greenberg reminding everyone to seek organizations and individuals to purchase an ad in the concert journal. He also asked for money from ticket sales and announced that a bass member was first to turn in money for all five of his tickets. After leading us in stretches and vocal warmups, Jana reminded us that we had worked on the 16 easiest songs of the concert during the previous rehearsal, and then she led us in hard work on the other four. She urged anyone not familiar with a song to listen without singing. When we finished for the evening, Jana complimented us on our energy and said that some professional choruses could learn this from us. "It's called heart!" she exclaimed. As rehearsal came to an end, she asked the ACC to stay and work with her.

After skipping another Monday, the chorus was back on regular schedule with rehearsals at 50 Broadway on October 17 and the three following Mondays. Jana worked hard to keep everyone focused on being ready for the November 12 concert. Amidst the serious work there frequent moments of laughter. Jana reminded everyone that she saw one of her high school students in each chorus member, and bass Jeff Vogel said out loud with a smile that he wanted to meet his youthful counterpart. Barbara and Bobby continued to collect money from ticket sales at each rehearsal. Other members collected money from ads to go in the concert journal, encouraging their fellow members to ask borough presidents and the mayor for notes of congratulations to the chorus. Everyone cheered after Bobby announced during the October 31 rehearsal that more than $23,000 had been collected for the journal, which was more than breaking even. Concert ticket sales, though, were lagging. Velma asked members to consider paying for their unsold tickets, and Bobby invited anyone needing extra tickets to check with him. On October 31, Jana arrived at rehearsal only a few minutes late after attending her son's preschool Halloween party, which was after a full day of teaching. She apologized, and many members expressed happiness upon hearing about her son again. While working on the more difficult songs, Jana reminded everyone that it was important for individuals not to sing any part not mastered. "Take one for the team" was her often-repeated phrase for persuading anyone who was struggling to be silent when necessary.

The final rehearsal before the concert was held at the 8th Avenue studio on Wednesday, November 9, the day following the election of Donald Trump as president. Conversations before the 6:00 start ranged in tone from angry disbelief to deep sadness to a glum lack of surprise. Bobby announced to everyone that the chorus was more important than ever and that "we're coming here with joy." The rehearsal did not go so well. At one point, Jana said, "Bad rehearsal, good concert," hoping that we got the problems out of our system that evening. During the final announcements, Jana commended the ACC for their hard work and asked them to stand; a hearty applause followed. She then thanked alto Mimi Bluestone for putting together a slide presentation of photos for the big stage screen during the concert, again bringing an enthusiastic applause. Finally, Jana encouraged everyone to review and practice difficult parts. She stated, "It's your concert, and I want that so much for you, not for me." She left us with three words regarding the quality of music needed for the performance: "beautiful, inspiring, and clean."

TWENTY-FIFTH ANNIVERSARY CONCERT

The concert in honor of the chorus's 25th anniversary was a celebration as much as a performance. Tom Karlson, a member of the bass section, captured the spirit of celebration in his poem titled Twenty Five Years, which was published in the concert program:[7]

>twenty-five years of singing
>songs of labor, civil rights, women's rights
>songs to fight the horrors of war
>nuclear war, drone war, all war
>singing to save mother earth
>songs from gospel

> songs for marching, the picket line
> sweet songs of labor and love
> a quarter century of battling injustice with song
> the new york city labor chorus

On November 12, I arrived around 4:45 at New York University's Skirball Auditorium. It was a cool fall day, and I, like many others, had a red long-sleeve shirt under my short-sleeved red chorus shirt. Along with other members just arriving, I found the waiting room. Following Jana's advice, we brought our own food and water in order to avoid unpredictable delays in restaurants. Jana led vocal warm-ups around 5:00, and then we went to the stage to work on lining up. We went through two songs and then returned to the waiting room for a final rehearsal of all or parts of several songs. Jana spoke words of encouragement as we lined up to walk to the stage for the performance. She said that she was proud of us, that we had worked hard for this, and that it was *our* concert.

Before we entered the stage, Dennis was performing with members of his group, Everton Bailey & the Instrumental Sounds of Praise, which blended sounds of R&B, gospel, and jazz. The audience applauded enthusiastically as they finished their set and while the chorus arrived. I could see that nearly all seats in the large lower part and side balconies of the venue were filled, but the small upper balcony was empty. Bobby welcomed everyone and introduced the master of ceremonies, Steve Kramer, executive vice president of 1199 Service Employees International Union. Steve spoke of his long admiration of the chorus and then introduced the first section of the concert with the theme of struggle. All seemed to be going well with audience response and with Jana's expressions. The final song of this section was "Ain't You Got a Right."[8] Jana had mentioned in our final rehearsal in the waiting room that she might extend the bridge if it was sounding good, and she did this. The audience responded with elation during the brief pause at the bridge's end, and then we continued with the song to its end, enjoying a repeat in applause. Steve then introduced the second section with its theme of peace. "Peace by Piece," the first song, seemed to go quite well, and a soprano took a bow for her solo upon Jana's insistence via body language.[9] All continued to go well according to the audience responses and Jana's smiles. The audience sang heartily with us for "Simple Song of Freedom."[10] When the section ended, the applause was strong, and Jana mouthed the words "Good job!" repeatedly to us from the front and side of the stage. Steve announced the intermission, but the microphone was not working. I overheard talk that maybe some in the audience would leave, thinking that the performance had ended. We returned to the waiting room to rest and drink water, and some of us ate a bit.

When we returned to the stage, Dennis's full group was finishing their set. The brass section left the stage and continued their festive playing as they marched past us in the space behind the back-stage curtain. We then took our places on stage as Dennis finished playing with the rhythm section. Fortunately, the crowd was just as big as it was before we had exited the stage for the intermission, so the malfunctioning microphone was not an issue in the end. Steve introduced our third section, which had the theme of joy. The audience response was especially grand for the energy of the final two pieces: "If You Can Walk, You Can Dance;"[11] and "Life on Earth, So Amazing."[12] Jana continued to look happy about our performance. Steve introduced the final section, titled "25 years." After a few measures of our first song, many in the audience applauded upon recognizing it as one of Pete Seeger's classics—"To My Old Brown Earth."[13] The remaining four of the set were also highly recognizable songs, and the audience continued to respond with enthusiasm through the finale, "Bread and Roses."[14] Barbara then presented a gift to Steve—a framed poster of the concert. Steve announced his special appreciation of the three "founding mothers" of the chorus, including Barbara. Then a woman from the audience read to everyone a declaration of November 12 as NYCLC Appreciation Day, and then she presented the framed script to Barbara. Barbara then presented gifts of French bread and red roses to Jana and Dennis. Jana gave a speech, telling her story of applying for the position of chorus director and proclaiming that the chorus had made her a better musician and a better teacher. Finally, Jana announced that the chorus would end with "Rockin' Solidarity."[15] The rhythm section joined in, and Denise Jones, as she had done so many times, brought much of the crowd to their feet with her powerful, bluesy solos. Taking in the final applause, we all returned to the waiting room to get our belongings before finding our family members and friends who had been in the audience. Many chorus members and those with them then made their way to the afterglow at a nearby restaurant/bar. Exhausted, I decided, instead, to start my 75-minute subway trip home, but later I regretted missing the afterglow.

STAYING BUSY AFTER THE GRAND CONCERT

There was a little time to bask in the success of the success of the 25th-Anniversary Concert, and then the chorus stayed busy with other performances. Even before the first post-concert rehearsal, there were two gigs that did not involve the entire chorus. There were enough volunteers for both, though.

Singing for Workers on the Street

Only four days after the big concert, about a dozen chorus members came together on a Wednesday around noon to sing in support of workers at Ellen's Stardust Diner in Midtown Manhattan at Broadway and 51st Street. While we were there, several people lined up outside to wait for a table. This diner was a place where the staff kept visitors entertained with their singing and dancing talents. We joined in singing with two Stardust employees, who appeared to be in their twenties. With one of the employees on acoustic guitar, we sang "Union Maid,"[16] "Going to Roll the Union On,"[17] and "We Shall Not Be Moved."[18] After Denise Jones arrived, chorus members requested "Rockin' Solidarity."[19] The guitarist did not know the guitar part, and Denise said that she could not sing the solos without instrumental accompaniment. I accepted when offered the guitar, and I was thrilled to be strumming the chords while Denise sang her heart out for each verse and others joined for the chorus. While we sang, a couple chorus members helped to pass out fliers with information about the workers' grievances. When done singing, a few of us stayed a while to talk with the employees. A couple chorus members invited them to join the chorus for the next rehearsal, and they seemed interested. I gave both my written invitation for an interview before leaving for my office, but I never heard from them.

The chorus has a history of singing for striking workers on picket lines, but this was the only similar event of the year for which a group of chorus members gathered to sing. Although the chorus mainly performs concerts and other highly structured performances, there is a commitment to be available for singing on the streets where workers are striking. The chorus's web page includes a space with contact information after the following: "Please contact us to have the Chorus sing at your picket line, rally, meeting or other event."[20] A few chorus members do the extra work to contact all members when an opportunity suddenly arises to sing for striking or demonstrating workers, and this time it was Jeff Vogel who notified everyone via email just two days before the event, attaching a press-release document that summarized workers' grievances at Stardust and providing links to media reports on the situation.

Performance for Nurses

For years, the chorus had performed at an annual meeting of nurses affiliated with the Federation of Nurses, which had done its collective bargaining through New York City's United Federation of Teachers since 1979.[21] On November 18, I participated in this event for the first time. It was held at the Westin Grand Central Hotel on East 42nd Street near Grand Central Station. About 30 chorus members arrived early and enjoyed bagels with coffee and juice in a room adjacent to the meeting room. There was a moment of uncertainty when Denise still had not arrived and it was nearly time to sing. Barbara announced that we would have to sing "Rockin' Solidarity"[22] as the traditional adapted hymn of "Solidarity Forever."[23] Bob Harris then said that he was ready to sing the solos, so we rehearsed "Rockin'" with him on the solos. He did know the words, and he hit the notes well; however, he could not replicate the bluesy rhythm and unique vocal inflections that Denise had always brought to the tune. While Bob sang part of the solo, I saw one member trying to hold back nervous laughter and many others looking a bit perplexed. Fortunately, Denise arrived just as we were lining up to go into the meeting room for the performance. She was quite winded after rushing to arrive on time, but she was as ready as ever to sing the solos. While we were lined up to move into the large meeting room, Bob spoke to me of the need for the chorus to have reserve soloists ready in case an assigned soloist is unable to attend a performance. That would be an interesting proposal for the board to consider. Perhaps songs with solos could have reserve soloists on a case-by-case basis depending on each song's challenges and members' abilities to fill the role.

We lined up to sing at the front of the meeting room. Jana could not be there because she was teaching. In her absence an alto member took over as conductor. Dennis had his electric piano and amplifier set up. We sang four songs and then joined hands and swayed to "Rockin' Solidarity." The audience of nurses had joined us in singing parts of a couple of the earlier songs, but they responded with sheer jubilation to "Rockin'," holding hands, swaying, cheering Denise on with her solos, and singing the chorus with us all. We then left to a delightfully lively applause. I would estimate that there were about 150 nurses in the audience, but they had as much collective energy as any of our audiences of fund-raiser concerts with several hundred to more than a thousand attending. This was an annual gig that I knew would continue well into the future.

Post-Concert Rehearsals

The first rehearsal following the 25th-anniversary concert was on November 21, and we were back at 50 Broadway, where we would be for all remaining rehearsals of the calendar year. Jana started by exclaiming, "Let's give ourselves a round of applause [regarding the concert]! So many things went very well!" In response many members shouted, "Thank you, Jana!" Jana then mentioned that her school students eventually graduate and new ones arrive but "you all stay." Someone from the bass section replied, "You're stuck with us," and a collective roar of laughter followed. Jana invited everyone to share thoughts on the concert. One commented that it was a team effort. Soprano Ann Gael said that her son brought a friend who loved the history and said that we need to recruit young people. Soprano Georgia Wever praised the band. Soprano Terri Weissman said that people in the back could hear every word. An alto said she loved the venue. Someone else said that a friend who had seen us often regarded this as our best concert. Jana then added that her husband had not attended a big concert for three years and that he heard "dynamic contrasts" with the men, especially, sounding better. She also said, "My artsy-fartsy friends loved it." Barbara then read an email from a member of the tenor section that gave a poetic summary of the concert. Jana then turned our attention to our next performance—December 5th for the annual holiday event at the Met Life building. Then she asked, "Oh, how did it go Friday [performance for nurses]?" Barbara replied, "They loved us!" Georgia added that the attendees all stood up for "Rockin' Solidarity." Someone else commented that momentum from the concert was with us for both the nurses' event and the Stardust action. Jana replied that she had seen a video of us at Stardust and liked it. Then she called out "We Shall Overcome" as our first song to rehearse and said, "I have a feeling we'll need to sing this soon."[24] Many laughed at the gallows humor regarding the Trump Administration. After rehearsal of a few songs, there was the break for announcements. Georgia shared that her friend's eight-year-old daughter had asked if there will be separate water fountains again, and many groaned at the sad thought that this could be on a child's mind in 2016. Barbara announced that she would take a break from the chorus until February, and she thanked the alto member who conducted at the nurses' event. Jeff Vogel spoke in some detail about the event at Stardust, and another member added, "We need to do more of these events." After some more singing, Jana brought the rehearsal to closure with thanks to all, especially Barbara, and the chorus applauded Barbara out of thanks for all her hard work.

On the following Monday our rehearsal focused on the songs we would sing for the annual holiday performance at the Met Life Building in Midtown. Jana announced, "I want this concert to be another step forward." During the break, a bass member announced that we had sold about 700 out of 800 tickets for the anniversary concert. He added that we collected $36,000 with the concert and the journal. Bobby then announced that the next morning there would be a nationwide demonstration for the Fight for 15 movement. He asked for a show of hands from anyone who could be at Zuccotti Park (site of Occupy Wall Street) at 5:30 AM. Someone asked why it was so early, and Bobby replied that it was necessary to have it in the news early. Bobby asked whether anyone would hold the chorus banner with him, and there was no reply. There was another announcement for the chorus's annual holiday potluck, and someone stated, "If you like desserts and wine, okay." Jana added, "In other words, eat dinner before." Many laughed, knowing how prior potlucks had been unbalanced in favor of alcohol and sweets. Georgia then asked whether the anniversary concert had been recorded. A bass member affirmed that it would be online but maybe not with all songs. The rehearsal continued and ended with the holiday songs for which the lyrics were changed for a labor theme.

One of the tenors had announced during the November 21 rehearsal that a friend of his had died, and he asked interested members to participate in singing for a memorial ceremony. That event occurred on Saturday, December 3 in Brooklyn at the union hall for the city's Transportation Workers Union. I was one of about a dozen chorus members there. We rehearsed "Joe Hill,"[25] "Union Maid,"[26] and "Ode to Workers"[27] with two string musicians before the ceremony, and then we performed all three about an hour into the ceremony. The chorus member who organized our performance thanked us after we sang, and we all left as the ceremony continued.

Holiday Concert and Party

On Monday, December 5, we performed our annual holiday concert in the lobby of the Met Life Building adjacent to Grand Central Station. Our arrival time was 4:30, and we sat at tables in a waiting room, talking and eating the scrumptious chocolate chip cookies that were provided each year for this event. Security workers escorted groups to restrooms. When we went on stage, it was a challenge to fit everyone. An elderly woman who had been host of this event for years gave the small audience a brief introduction. Meanwhile, crowds of people were streaming steadily through the lobby on both sides of the stage, hurrying on their way to catch a train home. Jana had warned us during rehearsals to keep eyes on her and to not be distracted by the many people rushing by. As we performed, she smiled often. When we returned to the waiting room afterwards, she let us know that she was very pleased. An enthusiastic email from her on the following day confirmed this.

Our final gathering before the holiday break was on Monday, December 12, for the annual holiday potluck at our usual rehearsal site. I made a point of not taking field notes for this informal social event. Everyone enjoyed the food and conversations. Weekly rehearsals seldom allowed time for relaxation and casual conversation, so the two annual potluck events provided an important opportunity for all to get to know each other better. We had worked hard for three performances, and this was a time to celebrate together before taking a month-long break.

96 *Chapter Four*

CONTINUING THROUGH THE WINTER

After a winter holiday break of a few weeks, the chorus reconvened to continue rehearsing for more performances in winter and spring. The first rehearsal in January, scheduled for the 9th, was canceled because Jana's concert with her high school students on the 6th had been postponed to the 9th due to heavy snow. The following Monday was Martin Luther King Day; because it was a school holiday, there could be no rehearsal at the UFT site. What had been a four-week break turned into six.

Historic Women's March

The day after Trump's inauguration, millions of women worldwide participated in the historic Women's March. The center of the global event was Washington, DC, but New York City's estimated crowd, according to the mayor's office, was 400,000 participants.[28] I marched with about a dozen female and male members of the NYCLC and about the same number from the Brooklyn Women's Chorus, whose banner we followed. We wore our labor-chorus badges on our coats or winter hats. Barbara Bailey, who was still taking a break from the chorus rehearsals until February, was with us. Tom Karlson was with his teen-aged grandson. Karlson, who had written the poem for the 25th-anniversary concert, self-identified as "white and Caucasian," was age 74, and had been a chorus member for about six years.[29] He is a retired teacher of 30 years in New Jersey who had previously worked in construction of tunnels for commuter trains but quit after counting 17 deaths of co-workers in accidents. The crowd moved slowly in a stop-and-go pattern to the north toward Trump Tower. There were many colorful signs and spirited chants, and our two choruses added singing. Songs included "We Shall Not Be Moved,"[30] "Solidarity Forever,"[31] "Blowin' in the Wind,"[32] "We Shall Overcome,"[33] "If I Had a Hammer,"[34] and "This Little Light of Mine."[35] After a couple hours and before reaching the march's end point, I left to catch a train home. I was tired but felt inspired by the grand turnout.

Return to Rehearsals for More Performances

We finally had our first rehearsal of January on the 23rd, but a cold and windy rain kept many members home. The weather did not keep eight people from an audition before the rehearsal. Jana conducted the auditions without chorus members present. I was among several chorus members who arrived early, and we were pleased to see that some younger people were among the new prospective members. Due to the low turnout, the rehearsal did not last the full two hours. During announcements, Jana gave out her holiday cards with photos of her son at age three and a half, saying that she had meant to have them ready for the chorus before the holidays. Over the years, Jana had brought her son to a few chorus events, and he had become another member of the chorus "family," as so many liked to describe the community. This evening also included the first announcement for the Great Labor Arts Exchange (GLAE), which was scheduled for three days in late June at the Tommy Douglas Conference Center in Silver Spring, Maryland. Soprano Betty Reid made the announcement for this annual event, just as in prior years. The difference this year was the plan for a "choral convergence" of about a half dozen labor choruses in the US and Canada. This had happened only once at GLAE, in 2004, so this was going to be a special opportunity to bring groups together.

The weather was better on January 30, and there was nearly a normal turnout for rehearsal. I counted 44 members (13 sopranos, 15 altos, 8 tenors, and 8 basses). As we prepared to sing, Jana told us that the biggest factor of our improvement was looking up and singing more expressively. While rehearsing "Follow the Drinking Gourd," Jana gave basses instructions for marking their music.[36] One bass replied, "It's not my music," explaining that he was borrowing Georgia's copy while she looked on with her soprano-neighbor. Jana then, while smiling, exclaimed, "Then mark yours when you get home. UGHH!" She had only the basses sing a difficult passage for a while, and Tom Karlson at one point said out loud, "It's a little off." Jana, sighing and smiling, replied, "Thanks, Tom," which drew plenty of laughter. Announcements included three performances in March. Tenor Jesse Kasowitz mentioned that demonstrations at Ellen's Stardust Diner were continuing and that he had been there on the prior Saturday. The final song rehearsed was "Bread and Roses."[37] Jana stated, "Look up and hold notes!" She gave a reminder that this had always been an important song for us.

Immediately following the rehearsal on the 30th, there was a meeting for the Arts and Culture Committee. Jesse and I were welcomed as newly elected members from the tenor section. Jana led the discussion over which songs the chorus should sing for three March performances. She suggested starting with the list from the anniversary concert, and everyone agreed. We also picked a few songs that would work well for Women's History Month, which would be the theme of one the performances. I relayed song requests from a fellow tenor, and the committee had mixed reactions. The meeting lasted 10 or 15 minutes.

The rehearsal on February 6 started with happy and sad announcements. First, eight new members were welcomed. This was the largest new group that I had seen in my five and a half years with the chorus. The new members left the room to complete the information form and, if ready, to pay the annual dues. While they were out, there was a tribute to Ricky Eisenberg, a long-time bass member who had died on February 2 after a long illness. Tom Karlson spoke first and smiled when he said that, through visiting Ricky together with Jeff Vogel, his friendship with Jeff grew. Jeff also spoke, saying that Ricky had fought against death just like he had fought against injustices. It was also announced that Fran DeLairre, who was not lately with the chorus but was an original member, had also died within the last week. The new members returned, and the rehearsal began. Jana told them that it would be fine just to listen at first. She assured them that most members were not sight-readers and that they would probably be "putting their best foot forward," which drew some laughter. Before mid-rehearsal announcements, the new members introduced themselves. Board members and section leaders then introduced themselves to the new recruits.

As rehearsal began on the following Monday, Jana told new members that it would be fine not to sing for the March 4 concert. While we worked through the first few songs, Jana commented repeatedly that we sounded tired and sluggish: "Today just seems like the Monday of all Mondays!" During announcements, Barbara asked for a show of hands from anyone who could sing four songs at the wake for Fran DeLairre. I could not due to a schedule conflict. The rehearsal continued with some rough moments. Jana closed by saying, "You know which songs are the problem songs. Work on them. This was not our best rehearsal."

Because it was Presidents Day, there was no rehearsal on February 20. We continued our work on the 27th. Bobby announced at the start the board's decision that new members would not sing for the concert on the coming Saturday. Two new sopranos expressed disappointment, and then, after some discussion across the room, Bobby stated that any new member who felt ready could sing. Mimi Bluestone announced that she had information on a bus to Washington, DC, for the climate march in April. Jana started with a reminder that it was the last rehearsal before a performance. She decided that only sopranos and altos would sing the verses of "Deportee"[38] and that tenors and basses would join only for the last line of the chorus. There were announcements about two absent alto members, each suffering a broken arm from falling. Rehearsal continued with a quick run through every song on the list for Saturday. Jana's final words were encouraging: "Good! Practice, practice, practice! See you Saturday. Good rehearsal, guys!"

Three Performances in March

I was unable to join the chorus for its performance on March 4 at the People's Voice Café, a weekly coffee-house event in the large basement of a Unitarian

Universalist church in east Midtown. I was in Richmond, Virginia to present ideas for my research-in-progress at the Equity and Social Justice Conference, an annual event for progressive educators. The People's Voice concert was an annual event for the chorus, and I had fond memories of audiences with enthusiastic responses to our music there. I was disappointed to miss it.

Part of the rehearsal on March 6 was a discussion about the concert. Jana started rehearsal by saying, "Great job Saturday." Details came out later during announcements. The concert was on perhaps the coldest night of the entire winter. All seats were filled, and Bobby reported that it brought in $700 for the chorus. A young man, appearing to be in his twenties, introduced himself as a new tenor. He had been in the audience for the concert, and many chorus members were noticing that he was singing along to many of the songs. Jana gave him an audition immediately after the concert, and he was ready to join. He added in his introduction that he was working as an attorney representing Chinese restaurant workers, and Bobby replied that he could bring in food any time. Jana said again that she was pleased with everything about the concert before we continued with the rehearsal. A final announcement was that Velma Hill was the new featured member on the chorus's web site. After a couple more songs, Jana let everyone leave early except tenors and basses. She told us that we could leave early also if we did well, and Tom Karlson replied that he never wanted to leave when singing with Jana. We practiced "Ain't You Got a Right" first.[39] Jana told tenors to pronounce the "Tell" of "Tell the people" more clearly; it was sounding like "ell the people." We also practiced "Bread and Roses" before Jana let us go.[40]

March 13 was our final rehearsal before performances on the 15th and 24th. Jana announced that the March 20 rehearsal was canceled because her school's open-house had been rescheduled for that evening after a bad-weather cancellation. Barbara announced that Tom would read a poem during our performance on the 24th. He read it to everyone and received an energetic applause. We rehearsed all songs that would be included in the two coming performances. A snow storm was in the forecast for the next day, and Jana told us that we would perform on the 15th unless notified otherwise.

We did sing on the 15th at City Hall for the fourth annual Women's Herstory Month event there. The title of the current year's event was "Celebrating Women in the Labor Movement." Our arrival time was 4:00, and many of us were on time after traveling through a heavy snow because subway trains were not affected by the weather. Dennis was running late, though, and Jana started our rehearsal without him. She was disappointed in our sound. Dennis then arrived, and we sounded much better with his accompaniment. We performed at the end of the program, which honored 10 women and featured performances by Creative Outlet Dancers and UFT Storytellers. Hosting the event were NYC Council members Laurie A. Cumbo and Helen Rosenthal.

We were scheduled to sing three songs but ended up with two—"Bread and Roses,"[41] and "Ain't You Got a Right."[42] The audience gave us an enthusiastic applause after the bridge of the latter, and then again upon finishing the song. After we finished, Jana told us that she was very pleased with our sound. She had us line up for photos in the large and ornate room adjacent to the event's room, and she took a couple selfies with us in the background.

Our third and final performance in March was our participation in the 106th annual memorial of the Triangle Shirtwaist Factory fire of 1911, in which 146 garment workers—123 women and 23 men—lost their lives. Friday, March 24, was a cold, windy day, and it never warmed up to the level predicted in the forecast. About 30 chorus members convened in the late morning at the site where the historic marker appeared on a building just east of Washington Square Park. A stage was in the middle of the street, and we sang shortly after the start of the event. Since it was a weekday morning, Jana was teaching and was unable to join us. Tom started us with a reading of his poem about the fire. Barbara did the conducting for our singing while the wind kept trying to push her music off the music stand. We sang "Bread and Roses,"[43] "This Land is Your Land,"[44] "If I Had a Hammer,"[45] and "Rockin' Solidarity" before a crowd of about two hundred.[46] The descendants of the dead from the disaster held up shirts, each with the name of the family member who died. On stage after us was a bagpipe and drum group. As much as I wanted to stay, I left for my warm nearby office to escape the cold wind.

FINISHING THE YEAR IN SPRING

Three days after the Triangle Shirtwaist Factory memorial, the chorus gathered for another rehearsal. The next performance was a new one for the chorus. The Queens Museum was hosting an event to honor activist groups on April 9, and one of the organizers invited our participation. Before we started singing, Jana thanked Barbara for conducting at the Triangle Shirtwaist event and said that she heard it went well. After rehearsing a few songs, Jana dismissed everyone who would not be singing at the Queens event. All who stayed practiced "Do You Hear the People Sing."[47] A week later, on April 3, we rehearsed again—this time with an organizer of the event and a guest pianist who would accompany our singing in Queens. All who planned to sing for the event rehearsed again, and the rest of the members joined later for the rest of the evening. During announcements, a soprano let everyone know that an alto member was going to have surgery for uterine cancer on the coming Friday and asked for prayers or positive thoughts. Before we returned to singing, Jana announced that she felt like a champion because her 3-year-old son was finally going to preschool with underwear, not diapers. She said that it was a struggle because she is a Type-A personality. Someone replied that that is why he rebelled, which drew laughter.

On the afternoon of Sunday, April 9, I took two subway trains for nearly two hours to arrive at the Mets-Willets Point station between Citi Field and Flushing Meadows Corona Park in Queens. I waited there with a few other chorus members for a shuttle bus that would take us to Queens Museum. The 2:30 shuttle had not arrived by 2:45, and I invited others to join me for the 15-minute walk. I walked alone and found Tom sitting on a bench outside the museum. I used his cell phone to call Barbara, but I could not hear her voice or message over the traffic noise from Grand Central Parkway. Eventually, everyone made it to the museum either by taxi or a ride from a chorus member with a car. About 20 members lined up at the front of the stage in the grand lobby at the start of the ceremony. A solo singer performed first in a space partway up the stairs behind us. Then we heard the familiar piano line for "Do You Hear the People Sing" from our guest accompanist, and Jeff Vogel, who wrote lyrics for the second verse, performed his solo in his strong and clear bass voice.[48] We all came in on the chorus after each verse from Jeff. Afterwards, I went down to the floor to see a few more performances before my trip home. Performers included dancers, poets, and multi-media artists, and the common theme was activism for social justice.

The chorus skipped two Monday rehearsals due to Easter and Jana's travel to Korea for her brother's wedding. When we reconvened on April 24, Jana let us know that she was still jetlagged even though she had been home for a week. She reminded us that our next performance would be the following Monday for the Clara Lemlich Awards. We rehearsed all songs listed for that event. During announcements, we welcomed back an alto member who had been out for weeks with a broken arm. Another alto, Mariana Gastón, passed out post cards to send to Albany for promoting New York as a sanctuary state in response to the Trump Administration's threat toward escalating deportations of undocumented immigrants. Bobby passed out information on events for labor history month in May. There was also good news that two members were recovering well from surgeries. We finished rehearsal singing in mixed groups, meaning that sopranos, altos, tenors, and basses were interspersed. It was a new experience to sing next to others with parts that differed from my own. Jana stated that in mixed positions it becomes clear who is wrong; then she said that she was just kidding, and laughter filled the room.

May 1 is International Workers' Day, and that was the date of the chorus's return to the annual Clara Lemlich Awards, hosted by the organization Labor Arts at the Museum of the City of New York. This ceremony honored senior women who had made great contributions toward social justice. Barbara

Bailey had received a Lemlich Award in 2014 for her leadership in the chorus since becoming a co-founder, and alto Kathy Goldman had been honored in 2011, the first year of the award, for her work toward organizing with oppressed communities for food security and nutrition.[49] After arriving around 6:00, chorus members enjoyed time in conversations in front of the museum's entrance, where mini-gourmet sandwiches, wine and other beverages were served to all attendees. We later met with Jana in a basement room and then walked in order back outside to sing "This Land is Your Land"—the first verse and also our new verse penned by tenor Bob Harris, which the audience applauded enthusiastically.[50] We finished singing the chorus while walking inside to the rotunda for the ceremony. There were speeches from six new honorees. Invited guests also performed a poem, song, and rap. At the end we sang "Ain't You Got a Right,"[51] "Bread and Roses,"[52] and "Rockin' Solidarity."[53] Grand applause met us after each song. After the ceremony ended, I gladly accepted an offer from a fellow member for a ride across Central Park to the 1 train for home.

The Groundbreaking Final Performance

Only three rehearsals remained before our final performance of the year, which would be our first time singing for the commencement ceremony of SUNY Empire State College's Harry Van Arsdale Jr. Center for Labor Studies. The acting associate dean for the center invited our participation, and I joined with alto Barbara Lipski, a research librarian for the center, in working out the logistics with Barbara Bailey and Bobby. We were hoping that this would be the chorus's first of many performances for this annual event.

The rehearsal on May 8 was special because we started work on a new song. Its title was "Three Five-0," and the sheet music at the top gave the words "With a solid Reggae feel."[54] Mimi Bluestone, an alto, spoke to the chorus about the meaning of the title—350 parts per million being the limit for a safe level of carbon in the Earth's atmosphere. Jana explained that the selection of the song went through the steps of approval from the Arts and Culture Committee and the board. She had us read the words to the rhythm, and then we tried singing it for the first time. It would not be ready for performance until after the summer break, but Jana wanted us to have an early start. Bob Harris asked Jana, "Is it possible to get a rehearsal file [as a sound recording on the chorus's website]?" She asked in reply, "Is it possible you'll practice?" Jana took time to debrief our performance at the Clara Lemlich Awards. She said that our diction for the added verse of "This Land Is Your Land"[55] was good and that the audience understood it. She laughed, saying that she could not get us away from the sandwiches, and the chorus joined in laughter. She added that inside the museum our four groups were divided a bit but that we had worked in mixed position and sounded good. She also commented that "Ain't You Got a Right"[56] had become a "winner" for us. We finished rehearsal in mixed position with "Imagine."[57]

The next rehearsal was two weeks later, on May 22. I arrived early and met a visitor, a young man who was there to observe for his master's thesis on labor choruses. We exchanged cards and wished each other luck on our respective projects. Barbara then announced that Jana would miss the rehearsal due to back pain. Upon Barbara's invitation, the graduate student introduced himself and took a minute to tell everyone what he was doing with his study. Barbara then did the conducting in Jana's absence. While we sang "Deportee," Dennis worked with everyone on the rhythm.[58] When we finished "Ain't You Got a Right," Barbara told us that we sounded great.[59] We applauded her in return for her intrepid efforts to conduct. There were several announcements. Betty Reid was excited to say that 28 members were planning to attend the Great Labor Arts Exchange in June. I then took a moment to tell everyone that I would be moving to Albany over the summer, and I forlornly added, "I'll miss you all, and I'll miss the singing we do." Another announcement was from an alto who invited all to her upcoming performance with another chorus—the Stonewall Chorale, whose members were from the LGBTQ community. Another alto invited everyone to hear a performance with her other chorus called Wednesday Sings. Also, two performances of Jana's high school students were approaching, and, on Jana's behalf, all were invited to both. Barbara asked Dennis if he had anything else to say, and he replied to all, "You sounded good tonight." Rehearsal then was over, and several members came to me with kind words in response to my announcement. The graduate student announced to all an invitation to talk with him if interested. I then left to another room to interview Velma Hill.

The final rehearsal of the calendar year was on June 12, and I could not attend due to two days of meetings for work in Saratoga Springs. It was the only rehearsal that I missed for the year, and I was disappointed to be absent. I knew that I would have only one more chance to sing with the chorus, and that was for the final performance of the year.

On the late afternoon of June 16, the chorus convened at Columbia University's Lerner Hall for our breakthrough performance at the commencement ceremony of the Van Arsdale Center. Interim Associate Dean Sharon Szymanski and Van Arsdale staff helped to arrange the logistics with Jana, who started by lining us up on the small stage off to the side of the main stage. We were then in a waiting room with the faculty and distinguished guests. Jana did some warm-ups with us. Staff took us to the lobby where we waited more than a half hour. I counted 36 members. There were very few places to sit, and several members sat on a radiator by the front wall. We applauded the students as they entered the auditorium, and then a union group playing bagpipes and drums marched in to start the ceremony. After a few speeches, we were able to enter. We stood through two alumni speeches, and then Dr. Szymanski introduced the chorus. We sang "El Pueblo Unido,"[60] "Ain't You Got a Right,"[61] and "Rockin' Solidarity."[62] There were only three basses, but they sounded strong in the bridge of "Ain't You Got a Right." The audience responded with grand enthusiasm, especially to Denise's solos in "Rockin' Solidarity." We exited after singing, and Jana let us know that we did well as we waited for the waiting room to be unlocked. I thanked Barbara Lipski for having the idea of our performance at this event. She replied that it was Dr. Szymanski who first approached her with the idea.

There was still one final event to bring the chorus together—the year-end potluck celebration on the evening of Monday, June 19, at our usual rehearsal location. As I had done at the winter holiday potluck, I decided not the take field notes. A regular part of this annual celebration was presenting checks to Jana and Dennis for another year of hard work. I was truly surprised and touched when Bobby also took a moment to wish me well in my new home in Albany, and then a few more members also publicly gave me a warm farewell. I cannot remember exactly what I said. I thanked Jana and everyone for making me a better singer, and I said that I would take six years of great chorus memories with me. In Albany I would be much closer to my sister and her children, but I felt like I was leaving family with the chorus.

NOTES

1. Woody Guthrie, "Union Maid" (New York: Ludlow Music, Inc., 1961).
2. Ralph Chaplin, "Solidarity Forever" 1915.
3. Emma Lazarus (words) and Irving Berlin (music), "Give Me Your Tired, Your Poor" (London: Universal Music Publishing Ltd., 1949).
4. "Tina Sizwe," South Africa Zulu freedom song.
5. Peter Schlosser, arranger of traditional song "Johnny, I Hardly Knew Ya'," 2006.
6. Robert Solomon, "Peace by Piece" (New York: Transcontinental Music Publications, 2003).
7. Tom Karlson, "25 Years," New York City Labor Chorus, *25th Anniversary*, 2016, 34.
8. Jane Wilburn Sapp, words and music, "Ain't You Got a Right."
9. Solomon, "Peace by Piece."
10. Bobby Darin, "Simple Song of Freedom" (Nashville: Alley Music Corp., 1969).

11. Elizabeth Alexander, music to Zimbabwean proverb, "If You Can Walk You Can Dance" (St. Paul, MN: Seafarer Press, 2009).

12. John Purifoy, arranger, "Hallelujah Chorus," George Frideric Handel (New York: G. Schirmer, Inc., 2001). Words to "Life on Earth, So Amazing" by Jeff Vogel.

13. Pete Seeger (words and music), Paul Halley (arranger), "To My Old Brown Earth," (New York: Stormking Music, Inc., 1964).

14. James Oppenheim (words) and Mimi Farina (music), "Bread and Roses," 2004.

15. Ralph Chaplain (words) and David Welch (arrangement), "Rockin' Solidarity." Variation of Chaplain's "Solidarity Forever."

16. Guthrie, "Union Maid."

17. John L. Handcox, "We're Gonna Roll the Union On." Library of Congress credits Handcox as singer, and Charles Seeger and Sidney Robertson Cowell as "recordists," 1937, Washington, DC, https://www.loc.gov/item/afc9999005.6547/.

18. "We Shall Not Be Moved" is a traditional African American folk song.

19. Chaplin and Welch, "Rockin' Solidarity."

20. New York City Labor Chorus, 2019, http://www.nyclc.org/

21. United Federation of Teachers, "About the United Federation of Nurses/UFT," 2019, http://www.uft.org/chapters/federation-nurses/about

22. Chaplin and Welch, "Rockin' Solidarity."

23. Chaplin, "Solidarity Forever."

24. "We Shall Overcome" is a folk song with African American roots from the song "I Will Overcome."

25. Alfred Hayes (words) and Earl Robinson (music), "Joe Hill," 1936.

26. Guthrie, "Union Maid."

27. Ludwig van Beethoven, final movement of Ninth Symphony, 1824. "Hymn to Joy" adapted by Edward Hodges (1796-1867). Henry Van Dyke, 1907, alt. "Ode to Workers" adapted lyrics by Henry Van Dyke, Paul Robeson, and Jeff Vogel. Sources for this endnote are sheet music used by NYCLC and p. 13 of *25th Anniversary* concert journal.

28. Emma G. Fitzsimmons, "In Trump's Hometown, a Clear Message of Defiance from Women." New York Times, January 21, 2017, https://www.nytimes.com/2017/01/21/nyregion/womens-march-donald-trump-manhattan.html

29. Tom Karlson, interview by the author, February 27, 2017.

30. "We Shall Not Be Moved," traditional.

31. Chaplin, "Solidarity Forever."

32. Bob Dylan, "Blowin' in the Wind" (Warner Brothers, Inc., 1962; renewed 1990 by Special Rider Music).

33. "We Shall Overcome," traditional.

34. Pete Seeger and Lee Hays, "If I Had a Hammer," 1949.

35. "This Little Light of Mine," traditional African American folk song.

36. "Follow the Drinking Gourd," traditional African American folk song. Arrangement by Peter Schlosser, 2004.

37. Oppenheim and Farina, "Bread and Roses."

38. Woody Guthrie, "Deportee" (Woody Guthrie Publications, Inc. & TRO Ludlow Music, Inc. [BMI], 1961). Arrangement by Peter Schlosser.

39. Sapp, "Ain't You Got a Right."

40. Oppenheim and Farina, "Bread and Roses."

41. Ibid.

42. Sapp, "Ain't You Got a Right?"

43. Oppenheim and Farina, "Bread and Roses."

44. Woody Guthrie, "This Land Is Your Land" (Woody Guthrie Publications, Inc. & TRO Ludlow Music, Inc. [BMI], 1956).

45. Pete Seeger and Lee Hays, "If I Had a Hammer."

46. Chaplin and Welch, "Rockin' Solidarity."

47. Claude Michel Schönberg (music) and Herbert Kretzmer (lyrics), "Do You Hear the People Sing?," from the musical "Les Miserables" (original text by Alain Boublil and Jean-Marc Latel). Including adapted lyrics by Jeff Vogel.

48. Schönberg and Kretzmer, "Do You Hear the People Sing?"

49. Labor Arts, "I've Got Something to Say!" http://www.laborarts.org/lemlichawards/2017/

50. Guthrie, "This Land Is Your Land," additional verse by Bob Harris.

51. Sapp, "Ain't You Got a Right?"

52. Oppenheim and Farina, "Bread and Roses."

53. Chaplin and Welch, "Rockin' Solidarity."

54. Fred Small, "Three Five-0" (Pine Barrens Music [BMI], 2009). Arrangement by Jim Scott.

55. Guthrie, "This Land."

56. Sapp, "Ain't You Got a Right?"

57. John Lennon and Yoko Ono, "Imagine" (Lenono Music, 1971). Arrangement by Mac Huff (Lenono Music, 1991).

58. Guthrie, "Deportee."

59. Sapp, "Ain't You Got a Right?"

60. Sergio Ortega, "El Pueblo Unido." Arrangement by Peter Schlosser.

61. Sapp, "Ain't You Got a Right?"

62. Chaplin and Welch, "Rockin' Solidarity."

Chapter Five

Findings from Interviews

Interviewing for qualitative research is a science and an art. The science is in being prepared with a purposeful list of questions, and I brought the same list to each interview. The first few questions were about the person's background, including age and self-identification in terms of gender as well as race, ethnicity, and/or nationality. Also included in this opening part were questions about the person's past in upbringing, work, activism, and music. The next and central part of the interview was about the person's experiences with the chorus and thoughts about its mission and work. The final part brought closure with personal reflections and final commentary. My questions were quite open-ended, and I tried to facilitate the telling of stories and opening of rich testimony. I invited all chorus members—including the conductor and accompanist—to participate in an individual interview and/or a focus group. I started by holding most of the interviews in my college office in lower Manhattan, but I visited the homes of two interviewees upon their requests. Later, I found that it was more convenient for most members to arrive early for rehearsal and meet me then and there for the interview. The pre-rehearsal interviews took place in a small hall annex used for storing an extra piano. I finished with testimonies from 29 individuals during the 2016–2017 calendar year of the chorus; there were 85 listed on the roster, and a typical rehearsal had 45 to 50 in attendance. I later was able to add a phone interview with one of the co-founders who was never a singing member but was one of three women to bring the idea of the chorus to reality.

The art of the interview is in letting the communication become a dialog. Carspecken called the information obtained from an interview "dialogical data."[1] He noted that an interview is quite unlike any other communication in that the interviewee has intensely focused attention from the interviewer. He added that the interviewer needs to take the initial role of facilitator rather than peer, noting that debate and deeper discussions of theory can come later.[2] It was helpful that my focus group happened after most individual interviews had been completed. That was the right time to have participants engage with each other from differing perspectives.

When I conducted my data analysis of the interview transcripts, I identified ten themes. By merging some together, I narrowed them to six as follows: community; diversity; activism and education; music quality; remembering past members, leaders, and events; and current leadership. Of course, there are some overlaps among these six, but each has a unique place worthy of focused consideration. I will address each in this chapter while citing the interviews and focus group. I will not re-introduce members whom I introduced in previous chapters.

COMMUNITY

As I have noted in previous chapters, an organization does not last 25 years without having established a sustainable community. "Community" is a common word with many uses that often refer to superficial bonds or loose connections. In the case of the NYCLC, though, several members have made a heart-felt statement that the chorus is like a family. That is a strong statement, and I made that statement, too, in my concluding comment of the last chapter. I was with the chorus only six years, but it was quite difficult to leave.

When a new member sees the fruits of community in the group from a fresh perspective, that is an important source of confirming authentic community. When I interviewed Kathy Martino, she had been a member for only two years.[3] She was age 66 when interviewed, and she identified herself as "white and of Irish and Italian heritage." She was retired after working as a machine attendant for a company that made sugar packets for restaurants, and she had been a member of the International Brotherhood of Electrical Workers and the Longshoreman International at different times. She said that an important factor for her in staying in the chorus was that she was having fun: "It makes a difference to have a place where you're not like, 'oh my god, what do you do now?' And if you know what I mean, just sort of having a fun place to be." One of the four themes in the 25th-anniversary was joy, and joy does not exist without many moments of having fun. Martino found in the chorus a place where she did not have to explain herself to others, and she found a community that shared many fun moments.

Tom Karlson spoke of comradery.[4] After he asked me my age, he commented that it is a sign of comradery and trust to be 55 years old and able to ask group members personal questions in an interview. He made a valid point. I had had no idea that more than two dozen out of around 60 regular-attending members would want to participate in an interview with me and then continue after hearing questions that can be taken as personal. This surprisingly high turnout was a sign that many wanted to have a voice as part of a community. Tom went on to say further how he valued the affirmations of community: "And then the discussion page where I can put a poem down and people pat [me] on the ass. That's always nice, you know, to be appreciated. And then everybody is. . . . It's a. . . . You know real powerfully human never-ending song that happens every Monday that you can make it, that it's open. And then the performances that teach us to get up there and not be afraid and just you know. . . . Now we go up there and we just sing our asses off, you know." This working together toward a shared goal certainly is a community-building process.

I already have noted in Chapter 3 how Eugene Hamond and Jana Ballard used the word "family" to describe the sense of community that they had experienced with the chorus. Denise Jones had this to say: "Well, the chorus is like a family, so that when I got diagnosed with breast cancer, they always were there to support me. I had Susan who used to go with me to my chemo treatment. And Diana who fully supported me and chorus members that actually went through the whole process with me and supported me."[5] If ever there is a sign of community, it is when one member is in a time of need and others respond in love and kindness. I was not yet in the chorus when Denise overcame cancer, but I did see in my years in the chorus many times in which members showed support to fellow members who were in difficult times with health problems or with losing a loved one.

One final note on community is the value of traveling as a group. I have addressed the trips to Sweden, Wales, and Cuba in Chapter Three. There never was a trip during my six years in the chorus. I started shortly after the Cuba trip, and many members were still talking about the trip months later. The trips provided opportunities for members to get to know each other better, and they also helped to form bridges of solidarity with workers and singers from the visited country. I interviewed soprano Judy Kleinberg, who was not yet in the chorus for the first two trips but did go to Cuba.[6] Kleinberg, a retired school psychologist, was 72 at the time of the interview and identified herself as Jewish in ethnicity. She was excited to visit Cuba because she had grown up scared in the McCarthy era with parents who were communist and Jewish. During the stay in Cuba, she was enjoying the celebrations for the 50th anniversary of the defense against the Playa Girón (Bay of Pigs) invasion. On the second day in Havana, she tripped on a mattress in the hotel lobby and injured an ankle. A local nurse and then a doctor came to the hotel to attend to her. She ended up in a hospital for X-rays, which revealed no fractures but a bad sprain. The Cuban doctor applied a cast on her ankle. When the only available crutches were too short, he gave her a wheelchair for the remainder of the trip. All this came with no charge even though Judy did have her own insurance. Fellow members took turns pushing Judy in her chair for the rest of the trip. She said the following in conclusion: "Yeah, just it's a different world. Even though they're [Cuban people] so poor, just—and then singing with all these different choruses from the national chorus to these children's choruses, community choruses and everywhere you went, well, you've made a roadside stop and had a margarita and of course they played "Guantanamera" [a song in the NYCLC's repertoire] everywhere, everywhere, and it was great." Judy was beaming as she spoke; she was thrilled just to be able to talk about the experience. During my last couple years in the chorus, there was talk about a group in Japan wanting us to visit, but the cost and long flight deterred the NYCLC leadership from accepting.

Diversity

The NYCLC has a diverse membership in terms of race, ethnicity, gender, and age; however, there were statements among the interviews identifying needs for greater diversity in these areas. The chorus sings for the struggles of workers especially in New York City, but the diversities in chorus membership do not match the same in the city's working population. Members of color are underrepresented in the chorus, as are immigrants. A shortage of men results in tenor and bass sections that are quite smaller than soprano and alto. The limited age range emerged as a discussion point in many of the interviews.

Racial diversity has not been constant over the course of the chorus' first 25 years. Photos from earlier years clearly show a membership that is nearly half people of color. One of these is undated on the NYCLC website, showing members in the old uniform that included a long-sleeved white shirt with a red vest.[7] Another, with the uniform having a red jacket on the outside, is on the back cover of the CD of the chorus in 2000 titled "Workers Rise: Labor in the Spotlight."[8] The proportion of members of color was much lower by the time I joined in 2011.

I asked interviewees to identify themselves in terms of "race, ethnicity and/or nationality." Of the 29 chorus members volunteering to be interviewed (including the conductor and accompanist), five self-identified as "black" or "African American"; one as "African American" and "Afro-Caribbean"; one as "white Latina" and "Cuban"; and ten as Jewish (most clarifying as Jewish by culture or ethnicity). The rest used terms "white," "Caucasian," and/or those of specific European nations. One interviewee, who appeared to be white, used the word "human," which begs the question whether it is from privilege that a white person can say that while never knowing what people of color experience from racism.

Only a few interviewees discussed race openly. Inez West, a retired teacher at age 65 when interviewed, self-identified as "a black woman."[9] She had been in the chorus five years and mentioned her appreciation of the diversity in the music: "Well, I think the selections of songs are really, really good. There is a wide variety of multicultural. But the emphasis is on the chorus as a group. It's not so much the emphasis as soloists in the chorus and whatnot." She went on to say that she would like to see more solos. She did not say directly, but perhaps having more solos would bring out the diversity among talents in different genres of music in a more pronounced way. Bobby Greenberg noted the decline in diversity but held out hope: "We have always been very weak on Latinos. . . . now I think we have one. . . . We were very strong among African American women especially, and we're getting weaker. You know, just with natural attrition, but replacement is largely white. I was very happy last night [at rehearsal] that there are two African American women that joined the chorus."[10] Kathy Martino, when asked about the strengths and needs of the chorus, spoke to her perception of racial inequity: "And I think also perhaps diversifying a little bit, we're very white . . . I'm not sure what it is, whether it's—people are having more friends and inviting them in or what kind of—I don't know, people here are certainly not overtly racist, but a lot of times white people can be really unwarily racist mostly in how much space we take up."[11] Her point is an important one, addressing subconscious racism and the often unintended but real existence of microaggressions. The chorus is a group of politically progressive people, but a commitment to growth in diversity needs intentional efforts to guard against the subtle manifestations—whether in individuals or in groups—of attitudes or behaviors stemming from white supremacy, anti-Semitism, and/or xenophobia.

Gender is another area of diversity that did not receive much attention in interview testimonies. One of my background questions was "What gender pronoun do you prefer to use for yourself?" Nobody identified as lesbian, gay, bisexual, or transgender, but I did not ask about sexual orientation or the cis-gender/transgender spectrum specifically. Only one interviewee discussed sexual orientation.[12] Velma Hill stated, "I'm a member of a church AME group, but there's a lot of things within my church. I try to follow the rules as close as I can, but I don't always agree with everything that has been said because when it comes down to people that's gay, I don't think that's none of my business, I'm not in the bedroom with them." Velma explained further that she was driven by love and her faith to embrace differences in people and to see each individual as someone with much to give: "They all got something to offer me, they make me smile, they make me cry, and I'm very happy about it because to me it makes my life more fuller and God is still blessing me." Velma certainly walked her talk when it came to the biblical command of "love thy neighbor." I sat next to her several times in the tenor section, and she impressed me right away as very kind person with a big heart.

Issues of gender involved the low number of men as members and the extent to which the chorus upheld equity for women in the workplace and beyond. Among members interviewed, only eight of 29 were men. That may be proportionate to the overall membership—more than a three to one ratio, women to men. Recruiting and retaining male members seemed to be an ongoing challenge as I noted with the relatively low numbers of men in different counts in Chapter Two. Judy Kleinberg mentioned that she found the NYCLC through her singing in the Brooklyn Women's Chorus when three members of both groups let her know about the labor chorus.[13] She later left for the NYCLC, wanting to be in a group that included male voices. As I noted in Chapter Four, the NYCLC has honored women with great contributions in social justice by performing each year for several years at the Clara Lemlich Awards ceremony. The chorus has in its repertoire songs by and about women in the labor movement, serving to correct a history that often overlooks the many great accomplishments and contributions women have made.

A matter of diversity that did receive plenty of attention in interviews is age. As I noted in previous chapters, the chorus in recent years has had a membership ranging almost entirely of people either at or near retirement age. Long-time members were middle-aged in the 1990s, and nearly all newer members have ranged from middle age to retirement age. Many interviewees expressed feeling troubled by the pattern of an aging chorus without enough younger new members to sustain the organization far into the future.

Nine interviewees spoke of the importance of performing in schools to increase awareness of labor history and to possibly gain new chorus members among educators. I will cite three here. Betty Reid claimed that the chorus needed a contact person to help in connecting with schools: "We have not been able to bridge that gap to try to get into the schools because we haven't really had like an inside person . . . We have many teachers [in the chorus, mostly retired], but they don't have that as an inside to say that 'Oh, go to this public school today or this middle school tomorrow.'"[14] Barbara Bailey spoke of past performances in schools and the recent problem of school budgets in decline: "They cut school budgets, they cut who comes, who entertains. When we sang in the schools, the kids were fascinated, and we were well received . . . You used to be able to go to the school and use the school facility for meetings, and all that's cut out now. And it's a shame because it makes it difficult to get to the children who are really the foundation for the next generation."[15] Terry Weissman discussed the prospect of performing with youth choruses: "I really love when there can be like some intergenerational stuff . . . like to have some high school choirs come just be with us, invite them to rehearsal, have them sing along with us, learn a couple of songs together and then go to their school and sing together."[16] She added a note of frustration that she had these ideas but did not "know how to get them in the pipeline." While a significant number of members share the desire to perform in schools again, there remain the hurdles of low school budgets and a missing contact person. An additional challenge is that conductor Jana Ballard is a teacher in a secondary school, so she would not be able to conduct the chorus in a performance during school hours.

ACTIVISM AND EDUCATION

The NYCLC serves to educate the public on struggles for social justice, particularly in the labor movement, through its music. It is a concert chorus but also an activist organization that invites organizers to request its services at a "picket line, rally, meeting, or other event."[17] All interviewees talked about their personal experiences in activism within and beyond the chorus. Many had been active members or even leaders in a union, and some had additional stories of activism in social movements other than labor. All had found a home in the chorus as a community for expressing some degree of sympathy or solidarity with workers' struggles through song.

Accompanist Dennis Nelson connected his spiritual faith with social issues from an early age.[18] "So when I was a teenager, we had a youth group. Even though our primary focus was Christian contemporary music that was the message of the Gospel as we were really engaged in spreading by our music, but we also talked about social issues and our music also meant it." This experience set him on a path that led to the NYCLC. "I think the chorus kind of took me to another level in terms being directly involved in actual issues. Where I might have been before, interested in it, reading about it but only maybe indirectly involved but when I found the Chorus, the commonality of interest of the Chorus, its cause, I was very much in touch with it and felt really more invigorated directly through the plans of the Chorus." Nelson expressed in his concluding words more of how the chorus brought him satisfaction: "I will just say that myself that I had a great experience with the Chorus, I have always loved the idea of using music as a positive vehicle and not just playing for the sake of playing, and the Chorus has given me that opportunity and it is a great unity of people with great model for people." He added a final note about having enjoyed working with all three conductors of the chorus. The interview was my first opportunity to sit and talk with Dennis for more than just a passing minute, and I enjoyed hearing the testimony of the skillful accompanist whose music I had appreciated and admired week after week in rehearsals.

So many members had moving stories of their activism before joining the chorus, but those of Kathy Goldman were exceptional. As noted in Chapter Five, Goldman was a recipient of the Clara Lemlich Award in 2011, the first year of the annual award. She was 85 years old when I interviewed her, but she smiled and made a point of saying 85 and a half, noting that "when you get to this point you count everything you can get."[19] She replied, "I am a white woman," in response to my question concerning her self-identity for race, ethnicity, or nationality. Her father, a carpenter, and her mother, a writer, were radical leftists, and she said she was a "red-diaper baby." She was retired after a career in community organizing but was still working as a consultant on occasion. She became an activist as a young adult, going to Hungary in the World Youth Festival in 1949 in part to look for relatives among survivors of the Holocaust. Years later, when she had two children in the public schools, she became active in a movement for racial integration in New York City schools. By the mid-60s, after some triumphs and losses in the struggles for integration, Goldman emerged as a leader in efforts to bring nutritional food to the schools. She recalled the poor conditions:

> The only food programs that existed seems to fit school lunch, nothing more, and it was very minimal, there wasn't breakfast, there wasn't after school anything, there wasn't summer meals—all these programs did not exist. The food stamps didn't exist because at that point the government was giving out packages once a month of cheese that they bought out from farmers with dairies that couldn't sell. I mean, it is a stupid system that we have; honestly, you can't sell it so you give it away, but if you do that it keeps the price up which is why the people don't have in the first place [laughter].

Goldman spoke of organizing parents, especially mothers, and creating strategies together that brought change for better school nutrition. After those victories, there was momentum for further struggles against food poverty in neighborhoods affected by food deserts, large urban areas without affordable grocery stores. Further efforts in schools led to free breakfast for all students in 2003, and then free lunch for all was coming soon in 2017, after the time of the interview. Free lunch for all students, as Kathy explained, would eliminate the problem of students in poverty not eating in order to avoid the stigma from having peers see them as poor. She continues to mentor and inspire community organizers in New York City, and she is recognized as one of two co-founders of the organization Community Food Advocates.[20] Kathy talked also about the chorus, highlighting how she enjoyed the trips to Wales and Cuba. The NYCLC has brought together many people with amazing life stories, and I was grateful to have been able to hear and later read Kathy's inspiring testimony.

The newest members among interviewees were Lucy and Richard Zaslow, a couple who choose to be interviewed together.[21] They had been members a little under two years. Lucy, age 72, was a retired teacher in adult education, and Richard, 74, was retired as a social worker who worked in schools for the second half of his career. Both self-identified as white or Caucasian in response to my question on race, ethnicity, and/or nationality, but they added that they do not think about that often. Both added that they also identify as culturally Jewish. Both also grew up with the label "red diaper baby" due to their parents' politics. Lucy recalled that her activism started in high school while participating in a youth march for racial integration. She continued to be active in social causes in college but later was "pretty quiet" until meeting Richard and becoming active with him in the anti-nuclear movement and in the anti-war movement during the US War in Vietnam. Richard also started in activism while in high school, recalling a march organized by the War Resisters League to raise awareness of the dangers of nuclear war. He continued in college as an activist in the anti-war and civil rights movements. The two had met before college in a political youth camp in the late 50s, but they did not start dating until their college years. Both grew up with music in their homes. Lucy played oboe and even became a music major in college. Richard, especially, had an early start in music for activism, singing at age 13 in the Earl Robinson Children's Chorus in Brooklyn. Richard pointed out that Robinson had been music composer for "Ballad for Americans,"[22] "Joe Hill,"[23] and "The House I Live In."[24] While late in their careers, Lucy and Richard wanted to join the NYCLC but were too busy with work. When both were able to retire, they joined.

Both expressed a satisfaction with involvement in music and activism together. Richard added a small-world story: "At the camp we met at, but I think the year before Lucy was there, we put on a musical with 'Down in the Valley'. And both I and Terry Weisman, who's another [NYCLC] member, of course, but we were members of that cast." All three of us laughed. Lucy added that it was Terry who eventually invited them first to come to a concert by the NYCLC and then to join. Although Lucy was nervous about the audition, they both became members. Lucy expressed her enduring appreciation of combining music with activism: "For all those years, I listened to people singing to me, and I feel like this is paying it forward. It feels so good to be singing for other people, to be doing it. And so, yes, it's very much activism on my part and paying it forward." The enthusiasm that both had for the chorus was clear from start to finish of the interview. They had found the right fit for their activism and singing.

As noted in Chapter Three, there is some tension in the chorus regarding a perceived imbalance favoring concert performance over actions in the street. This came up in the focus group. Tom Karlson spoke of gathering a committee for activist events:

> We need a group of people . . . that are trying to figure out when the next strike, you know what strike is going on now and what picket line is going on and then have some sort of social media way of contacting all of us. It doesn't have to be that time [announcements] at the Monday meeting because sometimes people aren't even listening. I know you two [Barbara Bailey and Bobby Greenberg, president and vice president, respectively] were very eloquent, but sometimes your words are falling on deaf ears when the same question is asked four or five times. So we need to have that like a flying squad.[25]

Jesse Kasowitz later spoke of a need for wider participation in street-level actions:

> I love the concert performances. I like our willingness to go to street demonstrations if we had better participation with that. If we were the only singers now, there was one demonstration we went to at Ellen's Starlight Diner where they were singing as well, and that was fine, it almost didn't matter how many of us showed up. But if we were the only singers, I think we need to sing with a larger group. We lose the sound and it does disservice to the demonstrators if too few of us show up for these things.

Perhaps Tom and Jesse could be two among others who form a new committee. The Arts & Culture Committee would continue to recommend songs to the board for concerts while a new committee would organize those who are able and willing to sing at picket lines and other demonstrations on short notice. How many chorus members are enough for these events? Are there enough members interested in doing these actions on a regular basis?

QUALITY OF MUSIC

I addressed the NYCLC's quality of music in some depth in Chapter Two, but I can cite a few more interviews here. Many expressed their appreciation of Jana Ballard's leadership in bringing the chorus to a better sound. That improvement came also from a willingness by the chorus to work diligently with Jana week after week in rehearsals. I know that I felt a deep satisfaction in preparing carefully for a performance and then being part of a successful outcome. Although I was not in the chorus before Jana started, I can appreciate the contributions also from the two previous directors; Geoffrey Fairweather led the chorus to a quite successful start with his talents and charisma, and then Peter Schlosser helped keep the chorus together as an interim and then long-term director while leaving several fine song arrangements to the chorus. The chorus has been fortunate to have these three.

Ann Gael commented that the NYCLC had not reached a musical level that was challenging to her, but she appreciated that it was inclusive and open to singers of average ability: "I know that it [singing at highly advanced levels] is not really possible with our constituency, and we want, in the final analysis we want to keep the constituency that we have because there are all different kinds and levels and we don't want to have just wonderful singers and just be this angelic chorus. We want to represent the labor movement as well as speak to the labor movement and speak to the general public about labor."[26] I came to the chorus with experience in community bands with my trumpet but without any formal training in singing, and I know that my singing improved during my six years with the chorus. The chorus does require an audition and does not accept all who try, but there is a wide range of abilities among members.

One of the qualities of the music in the NYCLC is the diversity in genres and messages. As noted in Chapter Four, not all songs have a direct message for the labor movement or even for social justice in general. Barbara Schwimmer stated that she would love to have the chorus try a song by her favorite composer, Stephen Sondheim: "I guess it's unrelated to the music we're doing. I find I can identify with the words and feelings. He's darker. He goes inside, and I don't know, somehow it talks to me. I'll go to anything he does. Books that he wrote, and music, there's just something about what he says, and the music. Like I said, it just touches me."[27] I asked her whether she had ever thought to request a Sondheim song to the Arts & Culture Committee, and she replied that she would think about it. She mentioned that Lennon's and Ono's "Imagine" came the closest to capturing Sondheim's sound and that it had become her favorite in the chorus.[28]

Patricia Logan spoke of being nervous when the chorus was searching for Peter Schlosser's replacement, but she was quite pleased with the outcome: "When Jana came it was obvious right away pretty much that she was going to be the right fit for us. And that was wonderful, and it's been the growth that we experienced in the last few years, is just phenomenal, I'm very proud of it. I was always proud of being in it but now I mean I'm just so proud when I invite people to come to the concerts."[29] This pride has a way of boosting confidence and a desire to continue improving. Like Patricia and perhaps all chorus members, I invited friends and family members to our concerts, especially the fundraising gala concerts. I was glad when they accepted and elated afterwards when they genuinely expressed how much they enjoyed the music.

During the focus group, Georgia Wever spoke to the importance of connecting high-quality music with activism.[30] Wever, a retired welfare case worker at age 76 who self-identified as Caucasian, had been with the chorus for nearly 20 years. I find the need to quote her at length:

> I think the main thing that we've done well during my time with Chorus is we've improved our sound. People appreciate that very much. We sing to the choir a lot and we sing to lay people a lot. But they all want to hear good music, they want to hear good sound. At one time we sounded like a bunch of old people singing. We just had an old-voice sound, but that has improved a lot under Jana and I really appreciate that. Because I think we have a responsibility to bring our best to the labor movement and to the community organizations we sing for. That's the main improvement I've seen. The other thing is I think that we've taken some of the old songs and adding new words, topical words is really, really important. I think people appreciate that. They sit up, you know, they take notice all of a sudden, you know. And it's wonderful that we sing to people who really love us. The excitement of going to the nurses for instance, the nurse educators, and having that kind of thrill over every year, that kind of thrilling thing. And going to, well, being part of Occupy, that was kind of a thrill. There was so much excitement around Occupy and we were there too.

Georgia expressed clearly her reason for wanting the chorus to sing well. She wanted people in the labor movement to appreciate the music as well as the words. Also, bringing in new words to old songs was a creative way to connect traditional music with current topics. Bringing the best sound possible to the Occupy encampment at Zuccotti Park was a highlight for her to remember, and perhaps some Occupy activists as well will continue to remember the singing of NYCLC members there.

Several chorus members have contributed to new lyrics for old songs, and Jeff Vogel has been at the forefront of these efforts.[31] Vogel recalled his first occasion to bring new lyrics to a classic song:

> But [creating new lyrics] started at the very beginning. So, when we—Geoffrey Fairweather says, 'I think we should learn this song.' And he shows me 'Ballad for Americans', one of Paul Robeson's most famous works. So, I said I couldn't believe it. I was like, [Geoff], you know this song, because that was like—that was one of the songs that I loved hearing him [Robeson] sing when I was a kid. I said, 'Oh, wonderful! Let's do it.' So,—but it was written in 1939, so I said, 'I'm going to try to update it a little bit.' So, that was my first attempt with lyrics and I sent them to Pete Seeger for his [indiscernible] with my lyric revisions to see what he thought, and Odetta as well—Odetta actually had done a recording

of it [Robeson's version]. They both thought they were good, so that we wound up singing those lyrics, which were on the recordings [for the NYCLC's CD 'Workers Rise: Labor in the Spotlight].[32]

The University of Chicago published the complete lyrics to "Ballad for Americans" with Vogel's revisions within a collection of sources on Paul Robeson.[33] An example of Vogel's work outside of the chorus is in this poem, which became the lyrics to a song published on the website of Transport Workers Union Local 100 when a composer added music:

> SOUL OF THE CITY (by Jeff Vogel)
>
> If a city has a soul,
> You'll find New York's down under.
> Times Square's all glitter and gold,
> But our subway's got real soul.
>
> The tunnels echo with the sound,
> Of those that built the subway
> The third rail a reminder,
> Of those lost along the way.
>
> It takes teamwork quite unique,
> To keep the trains a runnin'.
> From trackman to conductor,
> They create a symphony,
> For people hurryin' by 24 and seven,
> This great ol' subway surely holds the key.
>
> The subway city is alive,
> In a way that's quite beguiling.
> Folks of all persuasions, movin' to and fro',
> To a rhythm and a beat of the subway's own creation,
> With haunting melodies from performers down below.
>
> So if you want to take a bite,
> Out of this here big old apple,
> Get down into the core that lies beneath your feet.
> It's the city's blood supply,
> Moving people by the millions,
> I know it's kind a' gritty,
> But it's also kind a' sweet.[34]

With efforts by Vogel and a few other chorus members, there are new words added to old songs and some new songs created to address the lives of workers in New York City along with other current issues ranging from climate change to mass incarceration to drone warfare. Adding new words to classic songs was a tradition in the labor movement dating back to at least Joe Hill and the IWW, and the NYCLC honors that tradition.

Several others in interviews noted their appreciation of the improving sound of the chorus, but those cited above and a couple others in Chapter Three, including Jana Ballard's testimony there, capture the range of perspectives well. I made efforts to find and interview non-chorus members who had heard the chorus perform multiple times over the years, but I was unable to make those connections due to a busy teaching schedule that limited my time for research. I ended up being delighted that as many as 29 chorus members participated in the interview and/or focus group, but the lack of testimonies from non-chorus members was an unfortunate limit. As I noted in Chapter Four, though, when the chorus debriefed the 25th-anniversary concert, some members shared how their invited guests had noticed great improvements in the quality of the chorus' sound. That was important feedback to hear, because we chorus members heard ourselves week after week, unaware of the gradual but steady improvement. It was truly rewarding to work with others in a shared goal and to accomplish what we had set out to do.

REMEMBERING PAST EVENTS, MEMBERS, AND LEADERS

Chapter Two covers a history of the NYCLC in its first 24 years with many citations among the interviews. One of my interview questions was "What would you like to share about your experience with the chorus?" I tried to leave it open for interviewees to focus on people and events in their own ways. Here I would like to add more from testimonies of long-time members about people and moments in different stages of the organization's life.

When recalling events, many members spoke of trips. Georgia Wever spoke of a travel committee that was once active in the chorus.[35] She joined the committee before the trip to Washington, DC, in 2004 for the Great Choral Convergence. By 2005, she became quite active in planning for the trip to Toronto:

> But I also remember getting very, very excited in organizing a tour of the chorus to the MAYfest Festival, which is a labor festival sponsored by the Toronto Labor Council in Canada, and we went up there and I organized everything, places to stay, where we would eat. I arranged first not only to sing at the festival, but also to see . . . Some of the people in the chorus went to a Seder in a progressive synagogue, and it was a labor Seder. So they had to sing, too, and they made us

their honored guests, and some people had no idea that there was that kind of Jewish community.

By the time of planning for the Wales trip in 2009, Georgia was chairing the travel committee. Accompanist Dennis Nelson spoke of the admiration that many in Wales had expressed for Paul Robeson: "I always remember in Wales singing in a building named after Paul Robeson. And just remembering what a hero he is considered there even though he is not as he is in this country as he should be remembered in this country."[36] Director Jana Ballad, right before describing the chorus as "like a family," spoke about the Cuba trip: "Cuba is always going to be a huge memory for me, because it was in 2011. I had only been with the choir for a year. So, I was still figuring a lot of stuff out about the chorus and then the trip itself was amazing. So, that's a huge memory."[37] The trips certainly helped the chorus to build community within its own ranks and with people from other parts of the world.

Some members spoke about memories from their earliest days in the chorus. Bob Harris, a retired teacher and guidance counselor, was 78 and identified himself as Caucasian, adding, "But I don't think about that, right?"[38] He remembered joining the chorus during the year of the centennial for Paul Robeson, which was 1998, and he shared his memories of his first event with the chorus: "The first time I ever performed, that was a memorable thing because in Brooklyn at the Taxi Drivers Organizing Committee and there must have been 20 Chorus members and there were about 20 people in the audience [laughter]. I remember the first time singing before an audience; it felt like a real high, it was a great lift. It was like I had been on marijuana or something like that, I never was interested in, but it was incredible." Nearly twenty years later, it was still easy to see and hear the enthusiasm that Harris brought to his singing in the tenor section. Going back farther in time, Betty Reid recalled her initial contacts with the chorus as one of the first members to join in its 1991 beginning.[39] She attended a recruitment event for union members and ended up being the only one from her union after a co-worker did not join her as planned. Barbara Bailey was there, and she invited Reid to attend a rehearsal for an audition the following week. Betty went to the rehearsal on a rainy night, and Geoffrey Fairweather, the conductor, was running late. When Geoffrey arrived, Barbara introduced him to Betty, who sat in the front row to sing with the others there. Betty recalled, "I sat down and he [Fairweather] was rehearsing and as we rehearsed, he said to me open the [indiscernible] wider you know, showed me how to expand to bring the voice out more, so I did and everything like that." Betty added that when the rehearsal ended, Barbara asked Geoffrey, "So Geoff, you didn't audition Betty?" He replied that he had auditioned her and that Betty was a soprano. Twenty-five years later, Betty was still singing soprano in the chorus and was the main organizer for gathering members to attend the Great Labor Arts Exchange in Maryland each year.

Some commented on missing fellow chorus members who had died. Chapters Two and Four have examples regarding deaths of original director Geoffrey Fairweather and members Percy McRae and Ricky Eisenberg. There is more to add here, and I wish that I could devote an entire chapter or article to memories of past members who left the chorus over the years due to health issues or death.

Upon the interview with Denise Jones coming to closure with my question asking whether she had any additional commentary, she replied, "No, I just had some pictures of some few chorus members that had passed, and I thought you might want to see them."[40] I replied, "Yeah, I would love to." She showed me photos of Percy McRae, called him "an outstanding singer," and mentioned the songs in which he sang solos. She also pointed out a woman named Edna without giving her last name. Then she added, "Chorus members that passed but they were really [pause]. Ginger [Pinkard]! Who recently passed." I replied, "Yeah, we've really felt her loss in the tenor section and the whole chorus." Denise added, "Very connected, to Ginger, always the travel, sometimes ride on Ginger's, we would travel together with Ginger's accessor-ride to the airport and she would make everybody crazy." While Denise spoke, she smiled from the fond memories that she held in her heart from these members who had been special to her. They were much more than peers; as she had noted in other parts of the interview, they were like family to her.

Velma Hill shared memories of Ginger Pinkard while talking about aging chorus members: "We really need some younger people because when we are now our 70s and 80s and we have had people to die—a lot. It's like we lost Ginger last year, and look how old Ginger was."[41] I said, "She was 90, I believe." Velma continued, "Yeah. And she was from the beginning. She was my first section leader. She was strict to me [*laughter*]. But she became a really, really good friend. And we used to do a lot of performance. We were all younger too. Then there were nights that I would spend the night with Ginger because during that time she was driving and then we would be able to make it to whatever we were performing early in the morning, 8:00 in the morning." The close friendship between Ginger and Velma was one of many special bonds between members after so many years singing together. Five days after the email announcement of Ginger's death to the chorus in June of 2016, about a couple dozen chorus members on a Saturday at noon gathered with Ginger's son at the apartment in the Bronx that he had shared with his mother. It was a sad time but also a celebration of her life, and we chorus members sang a couple of Ginger's favorite songs from the chorus repertoire.

Because Ginger was a fellow tenor, I was able to get to know her a bit from a few rehearsals when we happened to sit together. She was kind to me when I was a new member trying to figure out how to fit in.

A final subtopic from remembering the past is leadership, and Chapter Two has several citations from interviews on this. I will add more here. Many interviewees had plenty to say about any of the three directors they had known, and some also spoke of the board of directors.

All accounts among interviewees who were with the chorus before Geoffrey Fairweather's departure agreed that he was a fortunate find. NYCLC co-founder Laura Friedman spoke with great enthusiasm regarding the contributions by the original conductor:

> He really didn't have . . . a trade-unionist background; he was a very classically trained conductor. It was a great growing experience for him to work with us, and for us to work with this wonderfully classically trained musician from Jamaica who not only had a primary understanding of music but also brought that wonderful Jamaican life force to the chorus. He was an amazingly wonderful first conductor for us, and he's sorely missed to this day as you know he died.[42]

What Fairweather lacked in a labor background he more than made up in his musical abilities and leadership qualities. When the chorus was short in higher voices of the soprano and tenor sections, Fairweather encouraged those with mid-range voices to try the higher parts and gave them plenty of support. Bobby Greenberg stated that he was in that mid-range category but became a tenor with Fairweather's help and was still a tenor at the time of the interview.[43] That was an example of leading individuals to bring their best to the needs of the chorus.

As I noted in Chapter Three, Peter Schlosser came to the chorus without the intention of staying long term. Tragically, Fairweather became ill after leaving on sabbatical from the chorus in 2003 and died. Schlosser agreed to stay as director, and I found that interviewees had mixed recollections about him. He had a labor-music background and wrote some fine arrangements that the chorus continued to use after he left, but he lacked the charisma and leadership style that the chorus admired so much in Fairweather. Schlosser stayed with the chorus until 2009, and his legacy in the organization has a positive note in his skillful arrangements of several songs.

Before I move to the current era with Jana Ballard as director, I will return to the board of directors, which is at the top of the organization's leadership. Laura Friedman spoke about Pete Seeger's advice to her that the board of directors should never "get stale."[44] A stagnant board, according to Pete through Laura's recollection, "would kill the organization." Laura remained a board member from 1991 until 2004. She commented that there was some turnover among board members but not a great amount. She saw a need for balance between institutional memory from established leaders and fresh ideas from new leaders. If the board has a pattern of slow turnover as Friedman suggested, there must be a reason. Either newer members are unwilling to go up for election, or long-time members are not encouraging them enough to do so. My impression from my six years in the chorus was that it likely was a bit of both. I never asked to try for a leadership position until my final year in late 2016, when I expressed interest in joining the Arts & Culture Committee. I became a member when the representative of the tenor section wanted to step down and nobody opposed me for an election.

Leaders of the board for at least all six years of my membership were co-founder Barbara Bailey as president and Bobby Greenberg as vice president. I did not ask how far back they had served in these roles. Only one interviewee, who asked to go by a pseudonym, expressed concern that one person was holding too much power in decisions but did not say who that one person was.[45] If this concern had been raised by others, it would have become a difficult but necessary topic of the focus group, which occurred after almost all interviews. Greenberg summed up the change in leadership over time: "We come from three women who made all the decisions and then we move to a board that increasingly collectively made decisions."[46] He explained that this transition accelerated when Bobbie Rabinowitz left to live in California and then when Laura Friedman left the board upon spending much of her time in Italy. He added that neither of these two was a singing member of the chorus, that only Bailey was one among the co-founders. This set up Bailey with a great deal of responsibility to carry on as the only co-founder still with the chorus, but Greenberg made clear that she and he work well together, letting me know that he received an email from her right before the interview regarding a communication task with a union.

Among all interviewees who had been with the chorus longer than Jana Ballard, there was consensus that the organization was moving in the right direction since she had become director. The board put a great deal of effort into finding the best possible replacement for Schlosser, and they chose a music educator who, like Fairweather, did not have a background in labor activism but brought positive energy and a determination to bring out the best possible sound from the chorus. The entire chorus participated in the decision to hire Ballard, after each of four finalists took a turn conducting. The careful process produced a successful outcome.

PRESENT LEADERSHIP

As the chorus continued to improve its sound under Ballard's conducting, the board was working to improve its team leadership. Greenberg brought up in the interview that the board was working on becoming more transparent and democratic in its decision-making process.[47] I asked him whether the board welcomed non-board chorus members to attend board meetings. His reply was quite interesting:

> Technically, I guess they can; none do. I don't think anyone is comfortable, I don't think they would feel comfortable. And in fact, they might even be asked by someone on the board even though I don't think we have a rule. They'd say, 'What are you doing here? what do you want you know?' So it's not a–that's another area that we'd be very [pause], why not without a vote because, you know, we barely have enough time to get all things done, but certainly to listen and, yeah, that's a great idea. I'll bring it up next board meeting. Usually these ideas are initially shot down. We have a very, shouldn't say conservative grouping of the board, not politically conservative but in terms of organizational openness a little tight [or 'tied'?] chest, tight to the chest.

Greenberg added that one member was good at passing notes to the board whenever he wanted to raise a question or suggestion. I did not think to ask Bobby whether the board was asking for such notes from all members, perhaps in a suggestion box. I do not recall such solicitations during announcements within rehearsals.

I did not dig deeper to find reasons for non-board members not attending board meetings, which I believe were held monthly before a rehearsal or more often when necessary. I suspect that there could be a couple reasons. One is that members do not feel that they have time because the weekly commitment just to attend every two-hour rehearsal already is quite time-consuming, especially when you factor in the time it takes to travel in New York City from almost any point to 50 Broadway when one is unable to afford living anywhere near Downtown Manhattan. When I went to a rehearsal from my office in Manhattan west of SoHo, it was only twenty minutes total with the 1 train and some walking. When I went to or from my home in the northwest corner of the Bronx, it took 90 minutes, and I know that at least a few members living in Nassau County had a longer trip than mine. Another reason for members not attending board meetings could be confidence that their elected board members are representing them well enough with no need to have observers and outside participants in attendance. It could be a combination of these two factors, but I do not believe that apathy is the cause.

Barbara Bailey spoke of the difficult current times for labor and then of the goal that drives every board member:

> Of course, [workers] know that labor is in danger and their jobs and their lives are in danger from the present-day politics. . . . Every board member, every board meeting is aimed to figure out how we can break another ceiling, glass ceiling, to bring our message out to them. And to the fact that the chorus members have stayed with us. A lot of them stayed with us all this time to bring this message; this is encouraging that there is an understanding that we are necessary. We are necessary, and, as we appear at different programs, we always get such a standing ovation and such a pat on the back, thank you, thank you because a lot of, especially the old-timers, start thinking about during the Seeger days and during their days, and they realize we're missing something here.[48]

Bailey added that writers in the chorus like Jeff Vogel have worked to bring new lyrics to old songs in order to connect songs with contemporary issues. The board, in working with the recommendations from the Arts & Culture Committee, is committed to honoring the traditional songs while addressing current struggles within and beyond the labor movement.

Bailey's strong and enduring dedication to the NYCLC is apparent to all chorus members, and the broader labor movement has recognized her work with awards—in 2013 with a Joe Hill Award from the Labor Heritage Foundation at the Great Labor Arts Exchange, and in 2014 with a Clara Lemlich Award from Labor Arts. As noted in Chapter Five, Barbara reached a time after the 25th Anniversary Concert when she needed a break and took a hiatus from the chorus for a couple months. Chorus members expressed gratitude to her in rehearsals just before and after her hiatus. Having a highly effective leader in a co-founder and board president is a true blessing, but it also comes with a challenge.

Nell Lindstrom (pseudonym) spoke of her concern about longevity in leadership: "There are people who are on the board who have been on the board since the beginning. . . . It's kind of Barbara's baby. There used to be two others."[49] I asked, and Nell confirmed that she meant the two other founding mothers. She continued, "The founding mothers, every time I hear that phrase, I want to [pause]. But, I mean, it's a wonderful thing that they did, and it's a wonderful thing Barbara does because she really holds it together. What's going to happen when Barbara goes?" Any organization that has a highly effective leader at the top for a long time must reckon with this difficult question. Undoubtably, there is a collective wish in the chorus that Barbara will be able to continue as leader for a long time to come. It is also certain that the chorus of the far future will remember her with deep gratitude and will honor her for as long as the NYCLC exists.

The chorus benefitted immeasurably from the leadership roles of Barbara Bailey, Bobby Greenburg, and all who had served on the board. As I noted in depth in Chapters Two and Four, Jana Ballard's leadership as director and conductor since 2010 was bringing steady and remarkable improvement in the singing produced by the chorus. Also, since 2002, the music by accompanist Dennis Nelson had been a steady asset to the chorus. The leadership was in a stable and positive place in the 25th-anniversary year, but Ballard continued to push the chorus to make further improvements, even after the big anniversary concert in November. I will end this section with Jana's final words from the interview: "I really love working with this group, and I really enjoy the opportunity and I enjoy that the choir members have embraced my style and determination to improve the group. I just really enjoy it."[50]

CONCLUDING THOUGHTS ON INTERVIEWS

The calendar year from September to June went by incredibly fast for me. For five prior years, I kept coming to rehearsals and kept doing my best for performances because I loved the singing and loved just being with so many others who enjoyed our singing and who cared about the labor movement and social justice. Little by little, I was getting to know some others in the tenor section and some members with whom I shared subway rides after rehearsals. Conducting these interviews, though, put me in a different position of responsibility to facilitate a dialog that enabled the participant to relax, to remember, and to share what the chorus meant. It was an awesome responsibility from which I felt humbled and honored. My field notes from observations were a central part of collecting data for an ethnography, but the interview was the time for making a mind-to-mind and heart-to-heart connection with a fellow chorus member. At the end of the year, by June, I came away with 29 testimonies from the interviews and the focus group. Two years later, I can remember each face and the unique tones and inflections of many voices. This was not the first time that I conducted interviews for a research project, but I did feel a sense of the chorus being like a family and deeply appreciated the time and energy that each person brought. I learned more about the chorus, individuals, and myself from these interviews than I could ever fit into this chapter. I felt heartbroken when I conducted interviews later in the Spring, knowing that I would soon be leaving New York City and, therefore, leaving the chorus. I needed to be an impartial researcher, but at the same time I was a human being conducting a focused but open conversation with a fellow human being within a unique and very special organization.

NOTES

1. Phil Francis Carspecken, *Critical Ethnography in Educational Research: A Theoretical and Practical Guide* (New York: Routledge, 1996), 154.
2. Ibid., 155.
3. Kathy Martino, interview by the author, April 24, 2017.
4. Tom Karlson, interview by the author, February 27, 2017.
5. Denise Jones, interview by the author, October 11, 2016.
6. Judy Kleinberg, interview by the author, November 22, 2016.
7. New York City Labor Chorus, "Who We Are: History and Purpose," http://www.nyclc.org/whoweare.shtml.
8. New York City Labor Chorus, liner notes to CD titled *Worker's Rise: Labor in the Spotlight*, 2000.
9. Inez West, interview by the author, April 30, 2017.
10. Bobby Greenberg, interviewed by the author, February 7, 2017.
11. Kathy Martino, interview by the author.
12. Velma Hill, interview by the author, May 22, 2017.
13. Judy Kleinberg, interview by the author.
14. Betty Reid, interview by the author, June 5, 2017.
15. Barbara Bailey, interview by the author, March 6, 2017.
16. Terry Weissman, interview by the author, January 23, 2017.
17. New York City Labor Chorus, "News and Events," http://www.nyclc.org/newsandevents.shtml.
18. Dennis Nelson, interview with the author, March 27, 2017.
19. Kathy Goldman, interview with the author, June 5, 2017.
20. Community Food Advocates, "Our Team," 2018, https://www.communityfoodadvocatesnyc.org/about.
21. Lucy and Richard Zaslow, interview by the author, November 28, 2016.
22. Earl Robinson (music) and John LaTouche (words), "Ballad for Americans," 1940.
23. Earl Robinson (music) and Alfred Hayes (words), "Joe Hill," 1938, Bob Miller, Inc.
24. Earl Robinson (music) and Lewis Allan (words), "The House I Live In," 1943.
25. Tom Karlson, in focus group by the author, May 10, 2017.
26. Ann Gael, interview by the author, October 6, 2016.
27. Barbara Schwimmer, interview by the author, December 19, 2016.
28. John Lennon and Yoko Ono, "Imagine" (Lenono Music, 1971). Arrangement by Mac Huff (Lenono Music, 1991).
29. Patricia Logan, interview by the author, October 6, 2016.
30. Georgia Wever, in focus group by the author.
31. Jeff Vogel, interview by the author, January 25, 2017.
32. Robinson and LaTouche, "Ballad for Americans." Including adapted lyrics by Jeff Vogel.
33. Ibid., lyrics as published by the University of Chicago, http://www.cpsr.cs.uchicago.edu/robeson/links/NYlabor.ballad.lyrics.html.

34. Jeff Vogel, "Soul of the City." Used by permission. Combined with music by Joe Gutierrez for song featured on website of Transport Workers Union Local 100: http://www.twulocal100.org/story/nyc-artists-say-subways-are-soul-city.
35. Georgia Wever, interview by the author, October 24, 2016.
36. Dennis Nelson, interview by the author.
37. Jana Ballard, interview by the author, March 13, 2017.
38. Bob Harris, interview by the author, May 8, 2017.
39. Betty Reid, interview by the author.
40. Denise Jones, interview by the author.
41. Velma Hill, interview by the author.
42. Laura Friedman, interview by the author, October 10, 2018.
43. Bobby Greenberg, interview by the author.
44. Laura Friedman, interview by the author.
45. Marilyn Taylor (pseudonym), interview by the author.
46. Bobby Greenberg, interview by the author.
47. Ibid.
48. Barbara Bailey, interview by the author.
49. Nell Lindstrom (pseudonym), interview by the author.
50. Jana Ballard, interview by the author.

Chapter Six

Final Discussion and Conclusions

Bringing this book to closure is a time to look back on nearly four years of work. It is early Spring of 2019, and I began drafting an introduction in Fall of 2015 in preparation for the critical ethnography that I would conduct in the following year. As I collected and then analyzed data, it became clear to me that this work was becoming a critical *auto*ethnography by necessity. I needed to provide some degree of self-disclosure in order to make transparent my perspectives based on my life situations and experiences. This concluding chapter will return to why and how my project went in the direction of autoethnography. I will give more information about myself as an individual whose life experiences led me to the NYCLC and whose experiences in the chorus brought personal changes. I also will compose my conclusions about the chorus after having been a member for six years and having conducted this research project. I will end with my conclusions of how these experiences have changed me as a scholar, activist, and amateur musician.

THIS WORK AS CRITICAL AUTOETHNOGRAPHY

At some point on a spectrum of self-disclosure, an ethnography crosses a line and becomes an autoethnography. I was already a member of five years of the chorus before I collected data for a year, and I continued as a member and full participant in the work of the chorus while collecting data. I knew going into the study that I would need to let readers know a little of who I was as a chorus member and as the researcher conducting this study. As the introductory chapter shows, I did not set out to make the study an autoethnography. During my data analysis and then drafting of chapters, I often found the need to explain how my perspectives and biases needed to be in the open.

D. Soyini Madison addressed autoethnography in her work on critical ethnography.[1] She cited Reed-Danahay, who classified autoethnography as the study of one's own social group and oneself in mutual context[2] A critical autoethnography is one that addresses concerns about social injustices either explicitly or implicitly.[3] My work involved the study of a group to which I concurrently belonged as a member, but the autobiographical focus is not at the center. Still, I have tried to find a balance in which I provide all the self-disclosure necessary and only the self-disclosure necessary for a transparency that allows the light in and lets the reader see who I am in my experiences and limitations as the researcher in this study. The NYCLC remained the focus, but I kept a process in which I also looked inward for two reasons. One is to acknowledge to readers that I am a researcher who had a history with the chorus and, therefore, had to reckon with my own perspectives and biases in an honest and ethical manner. The other is to testify how the chorus has changed me as an individual. I did not stay with the chorus for five years prior to the study in order to prepare myself to study the group. I stayed because I found a personal connection with the group's purpose and ended up feeling valued as a member. Early in my fifth year with the chorus, I knew that I wanted to conduct the study.

This study is a work of critical autoethnography because I have aimed to end with two evaluations involving matters of change agency for social justice. One concerns how well the NYCLC lives up to its stated purpose: "bringing the message of workers' history and struggles for social and economic justice through song to people everywhere."[4] The other involves how I have changed as an activist, scholar, and teacher educator from my participation as a chorus member. The first of these two remains the primary focus, but I cannot deny that my years in the chorus and my work in this study have challenged me and have changed me. I am not the same activist that I was before joining the chorus, nor am I the same in my personal and professional life. I strive to grow in my journey as a critical educator, and my experiences with the chorus have helped me to expand my levels of awareness and commitment.

What Led Me to the NYCLC

As I noted in the introduction, I had a middle-class upbringing. How did I become interested enough in the labor movement and in singing to join the NYCLC? I did not have experience as a child or adolescent in either working-class living or a sustained membership in choral singing. I have three memories, though, from my young adulthood as an undergraduate student at Indiana University that stand out for me.

The first of these memories was during the summer after my freshman year, when my parents and two younger siblings were in the process of moving from a Cincinnati suburb to a Pittsburgh suburb following my father's promotion in a large corporation. He was able to help me get a summer job in a steel warehouse in a small industrial town outside of Pittsburgh, and the hourly wage of $5.50 was decent in 1981 for a college student turning nineteen. I worked a 40-hour week with one man whom I believe was around 60 years old and who once told me that he had never visited the big city of Pittsburgh only about 10 miles away. We worked with a machine that cut long metal bars into small rods, which dropped into a 55-gallon drum to be filled, sealed, and then carried away by forklift. It was monotonous work, and the warehouse was full of dust that turned my nasal mucous black. As I was saying goodbye to my working partner at the machine on my final day, he told me to not drop out of college. That summer experience did help persuade me to continue with my college education, but it also planted in me a new perspective that viewed laborers as hard-working people who struggled with difficult working conditions and low income.

The second memory was from the campus. After I had changed majors a couple times, I had a new major in public affairs with a need to select a specialization. I had taken one course in criminal justice that sparked my interest in prison reform, but I was also considering labor relations as a specialization. I attended an event for students in public affairs to meet with faculty representing different areas of study, and I spoke briefly with a man at the table for labor relations. He told me that, if I wanted to work for the interests of workers, I would "have to tell people where to go." I think he sensed quickly that I was not such a Type-A personality and that I would have to overcome my quiet nature. I ended up choosing criminal justice as my specialization and then working a few years later for a lawyer in charge of monitoring prison reforms in Texas. Before finishing with my undergraduate courses, though, I took an elective in labor history. I remember a conservative student accusing the instructor of bias during a class discussion, and the instructor replied that he could go to the business school if he wanted to hear another side of bias.

Finally, there was an experience in my undergraduate years that sparked in me a desire to keep singing. During my high school years, while attending a summer camp in an organization called Young Life, I experienced a conversion to a form of Christianity that was fundamentalist unlike my Presbyterian upbringing. In my sophomore year of college, I experienced yet another conversion through a campus ministry of the local Church of Christ, which claimed that other churches were "denominations" that were not following the ways of the New Testament. During my senior year, I left that church to seek my spiritual journey elsewhere, but I never forgot how the absence of musical instruments (due to their omission in the New Testament) helped me to develop an ear for becoming a better singer. I never sang with a group again until I joined the NYCLC, but over the many years before then I continued to enjoy singing while learning to play chords on guitar.

How I Left the Chorus

I am not writing about my six years of experience as a NYCLC member. That would be another full chapter. I do feel the need to explain, though, how I ended up leaving the chorus. It was not a matter of quitting the chorus but rather of leaving New York City. The high cost of living was the main factor driving me away. I could not afford to live anywhere near my office in Manhattan, and, even though nearly all my teaching was online, I did not like working all week from home. I had never planned on living and working in New York City, but circumstances took me there. My first job in teacher education was in the San Luis Valley of rural south-central Colorado at Adams State College (now University). After two years there, it became clear that my wife Liliana and I both wanted to live in a less isolated place. I began a job search during the Summer of 2008, when the Great Recession was just beginning to bring a tough market in academic jobs. When the offer came from SUNY Empire State College (ESC) for its location on Long Island, I accepted and started in Fall of 2009. ESC has locations all over the State of New York, and the graduate teacher-education program is in every major urban center from Long Island to Buffalo. After two years on Long Island, I was able to move to the New York City location and wasted no time preparing to audition for the NYCLC. As much as I loved singing with the chorus, I knew within a couple years that I would want a transfer to an upstate ESC location and made my request to college administration.

My transfer to Latham, north of Albany, became a reality when ESC needed me there more than in New York City. I received the confirmation of the transfer in late March of 2017, while I was still collecting data for the study during the NYCLC's 25th year. The move then happened when our apartment lease ended at the end of July. I knew that I could not refuse the opportunity to move north, but I also knew that it would be terribly difficult to leave the labor chorus. I would find new groups for singing and activism, but it would never be anything like the NYCLC. I'll return at the end of the chapter to reflect on how the chorus has changed me.

CONCLUSIONS ON THE CHORUS

My words of conclusion on the NYCLC come from a unique but limited perspective. I conducted the study as an active fellow member of the chorus with five years of experience in the group. I was not an insider, though, in the same way that the original members were. Taking nearly a year to write fieldnotes from observations and to conduct the interviews gave me a chance to learn about the organization in a deeper way, but I do not claim to have all the answers to questions that have or have not received attention among members and leaders. I offer my conclusions as a researcher and former member who appreciates that the organization is much larger and more complex than I can ever encompass in a single book like this. With this limited scope in mind, I will address each of the six themes raised in the previous chapter. I also must be clear that I am neither a political scientist nor a musicologist by profession. I am a former secondary teacher who is now a teacher and researcher in higher education in the field of education, working with mostly secondary pre-service and new teachers, especially those in social studies.

As I noted in the introductory chapter, my point of view on education draws largely from Paulo Freire's concept of problem posing.[5] Freire conceptualized problem posing in opposition to what he called "banking," which was instruction under the assumption that students should be passive recipients of knowledge. The NYCLC in its stated purpose is an educational organization, working to raise awareness of the struggles and gains of workers through song.[6] Elements of problem posing have worked to build and sustain the chorus, even though the name "Freire" and the phrase "problem posing" do not appear anywhere on the organization's website. The chorus succeeded in its early stages because there was a commitment to welcome rank-and-file members of unions and to involve them in the educational work in meaningful ways. It was not an organization of union executives making top-down decisions on what to sing and how. The three co-founders, with some help from Pete Seeger, created a space where workers could cultivate powerful expressions of the current labor movement with old and new music. To the extent that the board of directors has worked to serve the needs and goals of workers as communicated by workers themselves, the NYCLC has employed problem posing. To the extent that the organization has room to improve in this process, a careful reading of problem posing can help.

Community

Many chorus members commented on having a strong sense of community, and some claimed it was to the point of being like a family. In a family, though, one does not choose to become a member except for the choosing of one's mate. Several chorus members who chose to join in the first year, 1991, were still among the most active members 25 years later. During my six years as a member, I saw a few new members come and then disappear but also several who joined and stayed. Because the NYCLC is a large group of 85 listed members (based on a roster compiled in 2015) and 45 to 50 in attendance for each rehearsal, joining the group can feel a bit overwhelming at first. I gradually came to know a few of the tenors because I sat with them during rehearsals. As I stated in the introduction, after my first year, I left the NYCLC to try a community chorus much closer to home. After three months away, I gladly returned to the Labor Chorus and felt welcomed again. As much as the music and activism of the NYCLC mattered to me, it was the sense of community that kept me there until the time came for me to leave New York City.

Freire, in his introduction to problem posing, addressed important aspects of building community.[7] Problem posing finds trouble with top-down announcements in the absence of bottom-up communication. It seeks to involve students from the problems they experience in and with the world.[8] The "students" in the context of the NYCLC's educational work could be the working public in New York City who may or may not be unionized. The chorus can sing for workers who are organizing to start a union, or for a union that needs encouragement during a strike. Whatever the situation might be, the chorus leadership has choices in how to communicate with workers. Allowing the workers to express their specific needs and to participate in song selections would be in line with problem posing. Another interpretation could be that the "students" are the regular chorus members, and the "teachers" are the board members, including the director. In this case, problem posing involves democratic participation in selections of performances and songs. How are board members representing the members who elected them? The same question could go to the Arts & Culture Committee in their work to recommend songs for performances. Freire stated that humanization comes from a process of fellowship.[9] The two potluck celebrations held by the chorus each December and June are important times for members to eat and enjoy conversation without the demanding work of rehearsing. Freire also saw community in acts of solidarity, stating that nobody is fully human while preventing others from being so. This goes to the heart of the chorus' work, responding to social and economic injustices in the workplace with messages of solidarity in songs. The chorus will continue to have strong ties of community within and beyond its ranks if its commitment to workers' struggles and solidarity remain in focus while inviting democratic participation in its work.

Diversity

Workers of New York City are diverse in many ways. The NYCLC is a diverse group in terms of race, cultures, gender, and age, but some of the interviewed members addressed real concerns. My life experiences as a white, straight male with a Protestant, middle-class upbringing place me on the side of multiple privileges. By becoming a chorus member, though, I did help to bring up the low number of men. While looking to Freire and theorists of multicultural education, I will discuss my conclusions on issues of diversity in the chorus.

Freire stated that problem posing responds to domination with a struggle for liberation.[10] In defiance of banking instruction, problem posing encourages learners to ask "why" regarding social conditions of domination. The chorus has no explicit plan to have any dominant group in its ranks. There are concerns, though, about low numbers of people of color, people younger than middle age, and men. I did not ask the extent to which the leadership has explored why there are such imbalances. Asking why, though, is the beginning of inviting change through problem posing.

The recruitment of two women of color among eight new members in Spring of 2017 was promising. Why, though, did the chorus go from a large proportion of members of color in its earliest years to one much smaller? How can the chorus restore a membership with a proportion of members of color that comes closer to reflecting demographics of workers in New York City? There have been steps in recent years to address this gap. The chorus has performed at the church of accompanist Dennis Nelson and other black churches. Also, recent performances have included the singing of "Glory" in a hip-hop arrangement and with a young rapper performing.[11] I believe the chorus is doing well in terms of including in its repertoire many songs from African American traditions, and there are also songs from South Africa. The songs in the Spanish language are from Spain, Cuba, and Chile, but it would help to have selections from Dominican and Puerto Rican traditions in order to better reflect New York City's demographics. As noted in Chapter Five in the interview with Bobby Greenberg, the board has made a priority of recruiting more members of color.[12] Inviting all chorus members to share ideas toward this effort would bring about a more dynamic discussion on alternative strategies.

Cultural diversity is another matter that has some intersections with racial diversity. As a white person, I can never know what a person of color knows about racism. Also, as someone with a Protestant upbringing, I can never know what a Jewish person knows about anti-Semitism. All I can do is strive to grow in my journey of privilege awareness and of solidarity commitment in work for justice. The NYCLC has many members who identify themselves as culturally or ethnically Jewish, and New York City has a long history of Jewish immigrants who were active in the labor movement. Some of the songs in the chorus repertoire are from Jewish tradition. Also, among members of African descent in the chorus, there are some with Jamaican heritage. I found it surprising that I could not find any classic reggae in the NYCLC repertoire. There certainly are songs by Bob Marley, Jimmy Cliff, and more that would be powerful with their messages of struggle for social justice, and a search for choral arrangements would be worthwhile.

In educational theory and practice, there is plenty of literature for culturally responsive teaching and culturally relevant pedagogy. Gloria Ladson-Billings in 1992 was the first to use the phrase "culturally relevant" in education research. While writing about examples of education in African American communities, she defined "culturally relevant teaching" as "a pedagogy of opposition that recognizes and celebrates African-American culture. It is contrasted with an assimilationist approach to teaching that sees fitting students into the existing social and economic order as its primary responsibility."[13] The NYCLC can continue to honor this approach to its educational work by finding more music that represents the many cultures among workers in New York City and by offering to sing in support of any struggling community wherever such an act of solidarity would be welcomed.

Regarding gender equity, the chorus has a few songs that are written by women or about women in the labor movement. "If You Want a Better Life" features words and music by Peggy Seeger.[14] "Bread and Roses," as noted in Chapter Three, has words focusing on the struggles and contributions of women in the labor movement.[15] Also, added recently was "We Were There," composed by Beverly Grant, director of the Brooklyn Women's Chorus, to which some NYCLC members have also belonged.[16] There could be more. Among the songs in the repertoire that are directly from the labor movement, in addition to "If You Want a Better Life," only one other classic has words by a woman—"Which Side Are You On" by Florence Reece.[17] Other women who contributed important songs to the movement are Ella May Wiggins, Aunt Molly Jackson, and Hazel Dickens, just to name a few. These names should be more recognizable, and the chorus could sing some of their songs. Also, the practice of bringing in new lyrics to old songs can include words to honor the contemporary #MeToo movement, which upholds justice and equity for women in all settings, including the workplace.

Regarding gender representation among chorus members, the shortage of men has been constant since the earliest days. I do not have any suggestion on what the chorus can do about this. I have been a member of four community bands also, and each had the typical pattern in which the brass and percussion sections were mostly men while the woodwind sections, other than saxophones, were mostly women. Perhaps boys have been conditioned by narrow gender norms not to be singers as well as not to be flute or clarinet players. I loved singing in eighth grade choir and playing trumpet in grades four to nine. When the time came, though, to let go of either sports or music in order to have enough time for studies, I chose to leave music. Fortunately, into adulthood I kept my trumpet and practiced on occasions, and I continued to sing at least in the car, in the shower, and when learning guitar chords on my own.

Age was the aspect of diversity most discussed by members when interviewed. Many, perhaps most, NYCLC members were retired during my six years in the group. Some interviewees mentioned that they waited until retirement to join. Living and working in New York City leaves precious little time for leisure. Young adults and middle-aged people are busy with their working lives and families. Getting around the city on buses and subways is time-consuming but much more affordable than paying sky-high amounts for car insurance and parking. Still, there is another social-justice chorus in the city that has had success in attracting and keeping young adults. During the focus-group session, Georgia Wever spoke about the Stop Shopping Choir (SSC), which performs religious satire with progressive themes along with an actor whose stage name is Reverend Billy.[18] Georgia knew someone who had left the NYCLC to join the SSC. A couple others in the focus group were familiar with the SSC and discussed how they sang with innovative arrangements and a small band, and how many members had formal training in music or acting. Nobody disagreed when Georgia concluded that the NYCLC could learn from the SSC. I once saw Reverend Billy and the SSC perform at a small venue with a stage and a restaurant. Most choir members were young, and they had an innovative sound, mixing elements of gospel, jazz, R&B, and pop. As my wife and I left, some choir members were asking the exiting audience for donations to the choir. It is wonderful that New York City can have both the NYCLC and the SSC. Each group could learn from the other, and both might achieve greater age diversity as a result.

Another explanation for the scarcity of youths in the NYCLC is that young people of the present have no memory of a time when unions flourished in the US. The middle-aged adults who joined the Labor Chorus in the 90s could remember stronger unions before the Eighties. Now, in the time of the Trump Administration, there has been a wave of strikes among teachers, including those in "red" states like West Virginia and Oklahoma. If the NYCLC wants to educate youths on the labor movement and its music, then performing again in schools is a way to go. This idea came forth in several interviews. I do not know the extent to which the NYCLC board has communicated with the United Federation of Teachers, the union representing teachers in New York City's public schools, regarding prospects for performing in schools.

An issue of performing in a school during school hours is that Jana Ballard cannot conduct the chorus while she is working in her teaching job. The member of the alto section who conducted at the nurses' event, or someone else, would have to step into that role. The board would need to decide whether the benefits outweigh the limitations and risks.

In so many ways the NYCLC is a diverse group that still has work to do in order to become more diverse. A community has strength in diversity, including a diversity of ideas. In some ways the chorus needs to uphold traditions, and in other ways it needs to be open to change. If the chorus continues to thrive to its 50th year, it will be both similar and different to the chorus of today. Having both stability and flexibility is key. I am not trained as a specialist in organization development, but I, again, point to Freire's problem posing as an educational process that can work to keep the NYCLC on a path to growth within its mission.

Education and Activism

The entire life span of the NYCLC has been in an era of unions in an historically weakened position and still under attack. The chorus exists to employ music in bringing strength back to the labor movement. It has an educational and activist mission. For Freire, there was no distinction between education and activism. All education is political, and it either reinforces a status quo of oppression or serves a movement for liberation by *how* learning occurs as much as by *what* is in the curriculum. Reading the word and the world is the path to critical consciousness. To learn authentically means to be changed and to become an agent of change. Critical consciousness in problem posing begins when there is an intentional commitment to reflect on consciousness.[19]

Problem posing comes with a commitment by the teacher to reject the schooling tradition of banking whereby a supposedly all-knowing teacher fills passive students with knowledge.[20] The problem-posing teacher tears down the traditional teacher-student contradiction and constructs a learning environment of mutual inquiry in which students engage in dialog with each other and with the teacher. Again, the NYCLC can consider where it lies on the spectrum between banking and problem posing in two ways. How does the board work with the regular members of the chorus? How does the chorus work with the public? Is there top-down decision-making and "instruction," or is there a democratic and dialogical process of communicating and learning together. Can the board, the rank-and-file chorus members, non-chorus workers, and the public work together as critical co-investigators to name problems and discuss what to do about them? Can workers who are not in the chorus but know and care about the chorus become board members and bring an outside perspective?

Problem posing involves a circular, ongoing process of critical reflection and action. Freire stated that problem posing "strives for the *emergence* of consciousness and *critical intervention* in reality."[21] When the NYCLC performs a concert with an audience of hundreds or more than a thousand, it is producing a critical intervention in reality with the objective to inform and inspire the public toward greater work in the struggles of the labor movement. The effectiveness of such an intervention depends on the extent to which there has been an open and intentional process of critical reflection in preparation. Likewise, when several or more members of the chorus sing at a picket line, they engage in a critical intervention in reality. How do striking workers appreciate the addition of singing in their action of protest? How much more would they appreciate it if the chorus members were to invite them in advance to participate in the planning for the singing?

When problem posing is done well, according to Freire, "people develop their power to perceive critically *the way they exist* in the world *with which* and *in which* they find themselves; they come to see the world not as a static reality, but as a reality in process, in transformation."[22] The NYCLC has a place in reviving, re-imagining, and reconstructing the labor movement in New York City, in the US, and globally. It is engaged in this project of transformation with workers, inviting workers of New York City and beyond to be inspired by old and new songs. With the advent of the Internet, parts of NYCLC performances are available for viewing worldwide. The chorus has the means to influence other labor choruses and different activist organizations around the planet, and the chorus can learn from other labor choruses and other organizations at the same time. Power shared is power multiplied; a global movement depends on it.

The NYCLC has worked with songs across social movements, and this helps to build bridges of solidarity. It was a great disappointment to the indigenous-rights and climate-justice movements in 2016 when the AFL-CIO issued a position statement in favor of pipeline construction at Standing Rock, but the response by some unions in support of the indigenous peoples' protest was promising.[23] A song added to the chorus repertoire in 2017 is "Three Five-0," which warns of the dire climate consequences when the carbon content in the atmosphere passes 350 parts per million.[24] More recently, the chorus has begun rehearsing the song "Water Is Life," by Sara Thomsen in dedication to Standing Rock.[25] Adding these songs shows that the chorus is in solidarity with the climate-justice and indigenous-rights movements, including the water defenders at Standing Rock. As the Green New Deal emerges to challenge the false divide between labor interests and ecology, the NYCLC can continue to show that it stands with those who struggle for an environmentally sustainable world with workers' dignity. Similarly, the chorus can keep working on including added lyrics or songs that express solidarity with additional contemporary movements such as Black Lives Matter, #MeToo, and LGBTQ rights. Following the guidelines of problem posing, separate movements can find where their causes intersect and how they can join forces to demand and create change. The NYCLC can represent labor and the arts in these mutual efforts.

Quality of Music

Without a doubt, the quality of the singing in the NYCLC has improved greatly since 2010, when Jana Ballad began working as director. I have cited a few of the many interviews that supported this claim. I will discuss now two practices that help to shape this improvement—auditions and solos. Auditions restrict who is admitted as a member, and solo assignments determine who sings the most challenging parts of some songs.

Week after week, in Monday rehearsals the chorus has seen and felt Jana work incredibly hard to lead the group to its best possible sound. She uses rehearsal tapes of new songs done by section for home practice. During rehearsals, she provides instruction of how to improve sound by placement of lips and mouth and by using the breath, among other techniques. As my field notes show, it sometimes was quite time consuming to work with one section on correcting mistakes. Given Jana's determination to improve the chorus's singing, and the chorus's willingness to work diligently with her, it is understandable that a rigorous audition should set the bar at a level to keep struggling singers from joining. One does not need to have highly advanced singing skills to join the NYCLC, but there is a threshold of ability that is necessary. I was nervous when I auditioned, but I managed to do well enough with the scales that Jana led with her piano support and in my *a capella* singing of a few verses of "Joe Hill."[26] I know that my singing improved over time with the chorus under Jana's direction. Still, I had no idea how complex singing is until I took ten private lessons from a professional singer after I left New York City for Albany. Making a big leap in improvement requires a good deal of guided practice and disciplined commitment to regular independent practice, which I did with audio recordings of each session with the instructor. With this recent experience I came to appreciate much more the difficult work that Jana has done to raise the performance levels of so many individuals and four sections in a large chorus.

During my years with the chorus, I felt humbled and honored to be a soloist for a few performances of one song. At first, I did not audition for the solo because I was new to the chorus and felt that the time was not right. Eventually, I changed my mind and tried after a rehearsal with others auditioning. To my surprise, I was able to get the words out and hold the melody without too much trouble. I was quite exhausted afterwards, though, in my untrained vocal chords and upper respiratory system. When I received the email days later to all members announcing the selections for soloists, I was delighted to be named as one of two to share the tenor solos. I was one of the soloists for four performances in my first year, and I did have some difficulty twice with the first part in the baritone range but finished well with the tenor part.

Solos were not always supported by the chorus leadership. Rona Armillas shared her thoughts about Jana and solos: "She's [Jana is] amazing! She makes it so much fun, and she's so open that it's, it's a joy to be there. It really is, and there's no competition between people like for, if we have solos. We don't have a lot of solos, but the conductor we had before [Peter Schlosser] was like, absolutely no solos, we are not ever having solos, because he felt it was very contentious."[27] Rona added that Schlosser made one exception to allow Denise Jones to continue soloing for "Rockin' Solidarity."[28] Certainly, there has been competition for some solos, but Jana has worked at finding ways to assign solo parts—large or small—to all individuals with the ability and desire to do one. Some songs have involved multiple short solos, allowing members to share the parts and reducing the element of competition. When I returned to New York City in November of 2018 to be in the audience for a NYCLC concert, I was delighted to see and hear many members doing very well with all the solos in several songs. The evening ended, like so many performances, with a stunning series of solos by Denise in "Rockin' Solidarity." It was a joy to see and hear how the chorus and Denise energized each other for a riveting finale. I felt proud to have been a member of the chorus, and I wanted to be on the stage singing with them.

A final word on music quality regards creativity. Freire asserted that banking "inhibits creative power" while problem posing enables it.[29] The chorus has demonstrated creativity through its openness to different genres of music and through the work by some members to bring new lyrics to songs. Jana finding places in songs to allow solos is a creative practice, and Peter Schlosser made his own arrangements of songs. These are all important examples, but the process is key. How are all members encouraged and enabled to bring their song ideas to the Arts & Culture Committee? How can the chorus hold onto classic songs of the labor movement while also moving into new directions to attract a younger generation that loves hip-hop and danceable R&B? The chorus has taken important steps to bring in contemporary music, and these efforts will continue.

Remembering People and Events

The 25th-anniversary year was a special time to remember and celebrate, but every year is important for keeping institutional memory alive and well. Freire stated, "Problem-posing education affirms men and women as beings in the process of *becoming*—as unfinished, uncompleted beings in and with a likewise unfinished reality."[30] Preparing for the future requires continuous reflection on the present and past as well as a faith that the work makes a difference toward creating a better future world.

The chorus has kept records of its history. The program for the 25th-anniversary concert featured a two-page dedication with photos that show deceased members and words to honor them.[31] I could not find a similar tribute on the NYCLC website, but that could be a source for memory and inspiration, too, if some members have time to create such a page.[32] The website does have a list of performance events in the history of the chorus.[33] This has some differences from the list that appeared in the concert program.[34] These lists were my starting points before I dug deeper to find more information for Chapter Two. In the website there is also a written statement of the chorus's purpose, which mentions the repertoire showcasing "the great legacy of US labor music" and then gives a brief overview of key events in the organization's history.[35] Available for purchase on the website are recordings of three NYCLC concerts from 2007 and earlier; two are CDs, and the other is now available only in cassette.[36] Time will tell when the chorus is ready to make a new recording available to the public on CD, DVD, and/or MP3. Meanwhile, there are numerous videos on YouTube of single songs from live performances. If resources ever permit, it would be interesting to have a single CD or MP3 with live recordings from the previous releases along with new recordings of the current chorus. Keeping the history of any organization with more than a quarter century requires an ongoing commitment from the leadership and all members who are able and willing to help. The chorus has a rich history and a powerful legacy in becoming the first multi-union labor chorus in North America in contemporary times and in inspiring other cities to start labor choruses. Hopefully, the history will continue to be available for all to appreciate how the chorus started, grew, and has made important contributions to the labor movement.

Leadership

The fact that the chorus was not just surviving but thriving after 25 years is a testament to effective leadership. The NYCLC was fortunate in its beginnings to have a dedicated team of leaders that expanded from the three founding mothers to a board of directors, and Pete Seeger's recommendation to hire Geoffrey Fairweather as director was another source of great fortune. Some of the original chorus members from the first year were board members during the 25th year. The mission of the chorus has kept the organization in focus during three eras of different directors.

Freire's call to leaders in problem posing was to be revolutionary, which he equated to being dialogical, from the start.[37] The NYCLC revolutionized labor music in a sense. Singing was a common act of solidarity in the early and mature stages of the labor movement in the US; however, singing of labor songs faded along with union membership after attacks from McCarthyism of the early 50s and from Reagan's 80s. The NYCLC brought singing back to what remained of the movement. It could have had a much different start if the three founders had insisted on doing everything their way without having an elected board. Having an elected board does not guarantee, though, that board members are democratic, inviting dialog and influence from the members they represent. The NYCLC board remains an elected body, so they are accountable to members. Also, the chorus itself has made efforts to stay in dialog with the unions still found through New York City. Unions' support for the chorus is evident in the many advertisement spaces that they purchase in each journal among the fund-raising concerts. The chorus also receives some revenue through the concert journals from small businesses but never from a large corporation. In so many important ways, the chorus operates as a democratic organization in order to serve its purpose in the labor movement authentically.

By the end of its 25th year, there were many signs that the NYCLC was moving in positive directions. The fund-raising concert celebrating 25 years was a great success, the chorus and Jana were continuing to work diligently to improve the quality of the music that had already come so far, and recruitment of younger members and members of color was making progress. It was clear that the leadership was not complacent and that there was a push to take the chorus to new horizons. If there was any cause for caution, it would be the lack of newer members on the board. The list of board members in the concert journal reads like a "who's who" of original and long-time members.[38] As of this writing in April of 2019—two years after the 25th-anniversary year—the NYCLC's web page shows the exact same 12 members plus the addition of Dennis Nelson as accompanist.[39] As Pete Seeger told co-founder Laura Friedman, there is a need to rotate board membership in order to keep a leadership with fresh perspectives.[40] Veteran board members need to encourage newer chorus members to become candidates for election. Cultivating the leaders of the future is an investment in keeping the organization healthy for many years and decades to come.

My brief experience in the Arts & Culture Committee (ACC) affirmed for me that the chorus took democratic participation seriously. If I had remained in the chorus, some more experience with that committee would have been instructive toward a possible run for a board position. I recommend encouraging newer members to seek a place on the ACC. My service on that committee was only after the fundraising concert, so I did not experience the work at its busiest. Still, I see the ACC as a responsibility that can reveal whether one is ready to consider running for the board.

I know that I have limits in how I can bring advice to the chorus leadership. My general conclusion is that the NYCLC has a rich history and strong momentum currently in serving the labor movement in a unique and truly important way. Ongoing challenges will be increasing diversities in the membership and cultivating leadership in newer members. My only hope is that the chorus will continue to do what it must to bring music to the labor movement and additional movements for social justice in an authentic way for many decades to come, and I am optimistic. If I live to be 79 years old, I hope to be healthy enough to attend the celebration concert of 50 years of the NYCLC.

HOW THE CHORUS CHANGED ME

I joined the NYCLC in 2011, knowing that it would be an efficient way to combine my passions for singing and activism into participation in one group. I left in 2017, knowing that my experiences in the chorus had changed me in important ways—musically, politically, professionally, and personally. If I were more poetically inclined and musically abled, I would write a song about my six-year experience. Mere prose will have to suffice somehow.

Upon leaving New York City and the chorus, I knew that I would need to find a new home for singing. In the NYCLC my reason for singing grew from an interest to a need. There was something about singing with the group that nourished my soul in a completely new way. Some songs were easy to sing, and others challenged me. Learning so many songs so well was a great pleasure, and each new song was like making a new friend. Jana made the work of singing both a challenge and a fun adventure. Singing with the same group of people week after week brought me a sense of community filled with important work and positive energy. Since leaving New York City, I have been singing with the choir of a Unitarian Universalist congregation. I have enjoyed the singing and fellowship, but I can never stop missing the people and the singing of the NYCLC.

The chorus also changed the way I view myself as an activist. It has made me want to become a stronger fighter for social justice across movements. Social movements need the arts to give creative expressions to the struggles and hopes that people share, and music is an art form that can bring many people together in mutual participation. The more I learn of how music strengthened the labor and civil rights movements, the more I believe that it can rise to that level again in current movements, including Black Lives Matter, #MeToo,

LGBTQ equality, Climate Justice, Indigenous Rights, and Fight for Fifteen. After moving to Albany, I shared my idea with others to form a new singing group. As of this writing, the Justice Singers of the Capital Region has passed its one-year anniversary with seven committed members and a goal to double that number within the next couple years. I am one of two guitar accompanists, and we hope to add someone with percussion skills. We rehearse twice per month with a break in summer, and we have brought singing to a rally, two marches, and an organizing meeting so far. Our purpose is not to perform for an audience but rather to invite everyone present to sing with us. Any grassroots movement needs grassroots participation, and the spontaneous singing of a simple song or two can add life to any organizing or protest event. The group has some momentum toward growth, and it exists because the NYCLC inspired me to find others like myself who want and need to sing with others for social justice.

It might seem like a stretch, but my participation in the NYCLC also changed the way I view my professional work in teacher education. I work with new and pre-service social studies teachers. As a former secondary teacher inspired by Freire and so many more theorists and critical practitioners, I introduce graduate students to critical pedagogy and encourage them to continue seeking with others a path of education for social justice. The NYCLC was where I practiced what I was teaching. I now am inspired to bring into my courses more sources and activities that promote the arts and activism together in social studies. Youths need to learn that ordinary people like themselves are the seeds of any grassroots movement and that the arts can work to inspire people toward greater wisdom and renewed energy in a struggle for justice. Critical social studies educators can invite an organization like the NYCLC to perform in their school auditoriums, or they can invite the appropriate number of chorus members to perform in a single classroom. Music is not the only medium, of course. There could be a group of union members who perform plays about workplace issues, or another group might guide students in creating a mural to depict laborers who built their city's buildings and infrastructure. With the advent of the Green New Deal, there are endless possibilities to combine the themes of environmental sustainability, workers' rights, and additional struggles in educational explorations involving reflection and action. More than a Green New Deal, there is a need for a Rainbow New Deal that builds bridges to bring various progressive movements together. Thanks to the NYCLC, I have a renewed energy and broadened perspective to rethink how I structure my courses and conduct my teaching of them.

Finally, I know that the NYCLC changed me in my personal life. I have experienced the power of community to the point where I felt like a member of a family, and I do not use these words "community" and "family" lightly. My parents, siblings, and spouse are still the people whom I know best and who know me best. The chorus, though, was a community that I chose to join, and then I chose to stay when I knew that I was experiencing a true community. Early on, I knew that I loved singing with the group. After a couple years of getting to know some members, I knew that I cared about them and that they cared about me. In a society that tells everyone to stay busy always and to settle for connecting with countless "friends" through social media, I found a real place where there is real community with real people making real music for a real social movement. It was real, and nobody can ever take the memories of six years away from me. I am a changed person for having experienced the NYCLC, and I experienced my downs as well as ups with the group. I learned that, no matter how busy I am with my chosen career in higher education, I need to make time for singing with others and for joining with others in a cause that is greater than ourselves. We can imagine a better world, and we can sing about the past and present struggles with voices energized by the undying hope and the solidarity that we nourish and cherish.

NOTES

1. D. Soyini Madison, *Critical Ethnography: Method, Ethics, and Performance* (Los Angeles: Sage, 2012), 197.
2. Debra Reed-Danahay, *Auto/ethnography: Rewriting the Self and the Social* (New York: Berg, 1997).
3. Sherry Marx, Julie L. Pennington, and Heewon Chang, "Critical Autoethnography in Pursuit of Educational Equity: Introduction to the IJME Special Issue," *International Journal of Multicultural Education* 19, no. 1 (2017): 2.
4. New York City Labor Chorus, *Who We Are*, http://www.nyclc.org/whoweare.shtml.
5. Paulo Freire, *Pedagogy of the Oppressed* (New York: Continuum, 2000, 30th Anniversary Ed.), 79–86.
6. New York City Labor Chorus, *Who We Are*.
7. Freire, *Pedagogy*, 79.
8. Ibid., 81.
9. Ibid., 85.
10. Ibid., 86.
11. John Stephens, Lonnie Lynn, and Che Smith (words and music), "Glory," arrangement by Mark Brymer, 2015, John Legend Publishing, Reach Music Songs, Think Common Music and Think Quick Entertainment, Inc.
12. Bobby Greenberg, interview by the author, February 17, 2017.
13. Gloria Ladson-Billings, "Reading between the Lines and beyond the Pages: A Critically Relevant Approach to Literacy," *Theory into Practice* 31, no. 4 (1992), 314.

14. Peggy Seeger, "If You Want a Better Life," 1992.
15. James Oppenheim (words) and Mimi Fariña (music), "Bread and Roses," 2004.
16. Beverly Grant, composer, "We Were There," 1997.
17. Florence Reece, "Which Side Are You On," 1931, arrangement by Peter Schlosser.
18. Georgia Wever, focus group conducted by the author, May 10, 2017.
19. Freire, *Pedagogy*, 79.
20. Ibid., 79-80.
21. Ibid., 81. Emphasis in italics by Freire.
22. Ibid., 83. Emphasis in italics by Freire.
23. Jeremy Brecker and Labor Network for Sustainability, "Dakota Access Pipeline and the Future of American Labor," https://www.labor4sustainability.org/articles/dakota-access-pipeline-and-the-future-of-american-labor/.
24. Fred Small (words and music), "Three Five-0," choral arrangement by Jim Scott, 2009, Pine Barrens Music.
25. Sara Thomsen, "Water Is Life," 2016, https://echoesofpeace.org/water-is-life.
26. Alfred Hayes and Earl Robinson, "Joe Hill," 1938, Bob Miller, Inc.
27. Rona Armillas, interview by the author, February 7, 2017.
28. Ralph Chaplain (words) and David Welch (arrangement), "Rockin' Solidarity." Variation of Chaplain's "Solidarity Forever."
29. Freire, *Pedagogy*, 81.
30. Ibid., 84. Emphasis in italics by Freire.
31. New York City Labor Chorus, *25th Anniversary*, 2016, 18–19.
32. New York City Labor Chorus, www.nyclc.org
33. Ibid., *Past Performances*, http://www.nyclc.org/performances.shtml.
34. New York City Labor Chorus, *25th Anniversary*, 4–5.
35. New York City Labor Chorus, *Who We Are*.
36. Ibid., *CDs and More*, http://www.nyclc.org/cdsandmore.shtml.
37. Freire, *Pedagogy*, 86.
38. New York City Labor Chorus, 25th Anniversary, 11.
39. New York City Labor Chorus, *Who We Are*.
40. Laura Friedman, interview by the author, October 10, 2018.

Selected Bibliography

Adams, Tony F., Carolyn Ellis, and Stacy Holman Jones. *Autoethnography.* Oxford, UK: Oxford University Press, 2015.
Adelfred (YouTube username). "Almanac Singers—Roll the Union On." Song by John L. Handcox. Video recording. 2009. https://www.youtube.com/watch?v=v4YeDI4R9MA.
Adelfred. "06 New York City Labor Chorus—You Are Still Mine." Audio recording of NYC Labor Chorus at celebration for Pete Seeger's 90th birthday. May 10, 2009. Madison Square Garden, New York City. https://www.youtube.com/watch?v=b1yfnr1AL50&list=PLxLwkHVTgXCbIm_4wfP_fOsTrIny8J_rE&index=4.
Allen, William F., Charles P. Ware, and Lucy M. Garrison (eds.), *Slave Songs of the United States.* Chapel Hill: University of North Carolina Press, 2011; originally published in 1867 in New York by A. Simpson & Co.
Bakunin, Michael. *God and the State.* No date. Reprint, Project Gutenberg e-Book, 2011. http://www.gutenberg.org/files/36568/36568-h/36568-h.htm.
Barker, Thomas P. "Spatial Dialectics: Intimations of Freedom in Antebellum Slave Song." *Journal of Black Studies* 46, no. 4 (May 2015): 363–383.
Betancourt Martin, Carlos R. (filmmaker) and New York City Labor Chorus. *Solidarity: New York City Labor Chorus in Cuba, 2011.* DVD. Recorded April 17–24, 2011, in multiple locations in Cuba.
Boal, Augusto. *Theater of the Oppressed.* New York: Theater Communications Group, Inc., 1979.
Brown, William W. (ed.). *The Anti-Slavery Harp: A Collection of Songs for Anti-Slavery Meetings.* 1848. Reprint, e-book, Charlottesville, Virginia: University of Virginia. http://utc.iath.virginia.edu/abolitn/absowwbahp.html.
Carawan, Guy and Candie Carawan. *Ain't You Got a Right?: The People of St. Johns Island, South Carolina—Their Faces, Their Words, and Their Songs.* 1967. Reprint, Athens: University of Georgia Press, 1989.
Carspecken, Phil F. *Critical Ethnography in Educational Research: A Theoretical and Practical Guide.* New York: Routledge, 1996.

Carter, David A. "The Industrial Workers of the World and the Rhetoric of Song." *The Quarterly Journal of Speech* 66 (1980): 365–374.

Cohen, Ronald D. *Work and Sing: A History of Occupational and Labor Union Songs in the United States.* Crockett, CA: Carquinez Press, 2010.

CommonThreadChorus (YouTube username). "Common Thread May 2010 Common Thread Community Chorus of Toronto." Video recording of "Common Thread." https://www.youtube.com/watch?v=lOU0w17PRco.

Darden, Robert. *Nothing but Love in God's Water: Black Sacred Music from the Civil War to the Civil Rights Movement.* University Park: Pennsylvania State University Press, 2014.

Davis, Angela Y. *Blues Legacies and Black Feminism: Gertrude "Ma" Rainey, Bessie Smith, and Billie Holiday.* New York: Vintage Books, 1998.

de Schweinitz, Rebecca. *If We Could Change the World: Young People and America's Long Struggle for Racial Equality.* Chapel Hill: University of North Carolina Press, 2009.

Derrida, Jacques. *Positions.* London: Athone Press, 1981.

Dirges, Dan D. "Red Wing." Video recording. 2016. Song by Kerry Mills (music) and Thurland Chattaway (lyrics), 1907. https://www.youtube.com/watch?v=IA0v-GgTp2E.

Donaldson, Rachel C. *"I Hear America Singing": Folk Music and National Identity.* Philadelphia: Temple University Press, 2010.

Douglass, Frederick. *My Bondage and My Freedom.* 1855. Reprint, New Haven: Yale University Press, 2014.

Douglass, Frederick. *Narrative of the Life of Frederick Douglass: An American Slave: Written by Himself.* 1845. Reprint, Gutenberg Project, 2006. http://www.gutenberg.org/files/23/23-h/23-h.htm.

DuBois, W.E.B. *The Souls of Black Folk.* 1903. Reprint, New Haven: Yale University Press, 2015.

Dunn, Megan and James Walker, "Union Membership in the United States," Bureau of Labor Statistics, September 2016, https://www.bls.gov/spotlight/2016/union-membership-in-the-united-states/pdf/union-membership-in-the-united-states.pdf.

Emerson, Robert M., Rachel I. Fretz, and Linda L. Shaw. *Writing Ethnographic Fieldnotes.* Chicago: University of Chicago Press, 2011.

Eyerman, Ron and Andrew Jamison. *Music and Social Movements: Mobilizing Traditions in the Twentieth Century.* Cambridge, UK: Cambridge University Press, 1998.

Freire, Paulo. *Pedagogy of the Oppressed.* Translated by Myra Bergman Ramos. 1970. Reprint, New York: Continuum, 2000.

Goldman, Emma. *Living My Life: In Two Volumes.* 1931. Reprint, New York: Dover Publications, Inc., 1970.

Gramsci, Antonio. *Selections from the Prison Notebooks*. Translated and edited by Quintin Hoare and Geoffrey Nowell Smith. New York: International Publishers, 1971.

Green, Archie, David Roediger, Franklin Rosemont, and Salvatore Salerno (eds.). *The Big Red Songbook.* Oakland: PM Press, 2016.

Habermas, Jürgen. *The Theory of Communicative Action: Volume One: Reason and the Rationalization of Society.* Boston: Beacon.

Hampton, Henry (executive producer). *Eyes on the Prize: America's Civil Rights Movement 1954-1985.* 1994. Arlington, VA: Public Broadcasting Service. Documentary film.

Handy, W.C. *Father of the Blues: An Autobiography.* 1941. Reprint, New York: Da Capo, 1969.

Higgins, Lee. *Community Music: In Theory and in Practice.* Oxford: Oxford University Press, Inc., 2012.

Hobson, Janell. "Everybody's Protest Song: Music as Social Protest in the Performances of Marian Anderson and Billy Holliday." *Signs: Journal of Women and Culture in Society* 33, no. 2 (2008), 443–448.

Honey, Michael K. *Sharecropper's Troubadour: John L. Handcox, the Southern Tenant Farmers' Union, and the African American Song Tradition.* New York: Palgrave McMillan, 2013.

Horton, Kristina. *Martyr of Loray Mill: Ella May and the 1929 Textile Workers' Strike in Gastonia, North Carolina.* Jefferson, NC: McFarland, 2015.

Hurner, Sheryl. "Discursive Identity Formation of Suffrage Women: Reframing the 'Cult of True Womanhood' through Song." *Western Journal of Communication* 70, no. 3 (2006), 234–260.

Karpf, Juanita. "For their Musical Uplift: Emma Azalia Hackley and Voice Culture in African American Communities." *International Journal of Community Music* 4, no. 3 (2011), 237–256.

Katz, Daniel. *All Together Different: Yiddish Socialists, Garment Workers, and the Labor Roots of Multiculturalism.* New York: New York University Press, 2011.

Klein, Naomi. *The Shock Doctrine: The Rise and Fall of Disaster Capitalism.* New York: Picador, 2007.

Korstad, Robert R. *Civil Rights Unionism: Tobacco Workers and the Struggle for Democracy in the Mid-Twentieth-Century South.* Chapel Hill: University of North Carolina Press, 2003.

Kropotkin, Peter. *Mutual Aid: A Factor of Evolution.* 1902. Reprint, The Anarchist Library, https://theanarchistlibrary.org/library/petr-kropotkin-mutual-aid-a-factor-of-evolution.

Landau, Ely (producer). *King: A Filmed Record: Montgomery to Memphis.* 1970. New York: The Martin Luther King Film Project and Kino Classics. Documentary film.

Lennon, John and Yoko Ono. "Imagine," single from the LP *Imagine.* 1971. Apple. Produced by John Lennon, Yoko Ono, and Phil Spector.

Lighter, Jonathan. *The Best Anti-War Song Ever Written.* E. Windsor, NJ: Loomis House Press, 2012.

Litterio, Lisa M. "Bread and Roses Strike of 1912: Lawrence, Massachusetts, Immigrants Usher in a New Era of Unity, Labor Gains, and Women's Rights," *Labor's Heritage* 11, No. 3 (2001): 58–73.

Lomax, Alan. *The Land Where the Blues Began.* New York: Pantheon Books, 1993.

Lomax, Alan (compiler), Woody Guthrie (notes on songs), and Pete Seeger (music transcribed and edited). *Hard Hitting Songs for Hard-Hit People.* 1967, Reprint, Lincoln: University of Nebraska Press, 2012.

Lomax, John A. and Alan Lomax. *Folk Songs as Sung by Lead Belly.* New York: McMillan, 1936.

Lynch, Timothy P. *Strike Songs of the Depression.* Jackson: University Press of Mississippi, 2001.

Lynskey, Dorian. *33 Revolutions per Minute: A History of Protest Songs, from Billy Holiday to Green Day.* New York: HarperCollins Publishers, 2011.

Madison, D. Soyini. *Critical Ethnography: Method, Ethics, and Performance.* Los Angeles: Sage Publications, Inc., 2012.

Marx, Karl. *Capital: A Critique of Political Economy.* New York: Charles H. Kerr & Co., 1906.

Marx, Sherry, Julie L. Pennington, and Heewon Chang. "Critical Autoethnography in Pursuit of Educational Equity: Introduction to the IJME Special Issue." *International Journal of Multicultural Education* 19, no. 1 (2017), 1–6.

McClendon, Aaron D. "Sounds of Sympathy: William Wells Brown's 'Anti-Slavery Harp', Abolition, and the Culture of Early and Antebellum American Song." *African American Review* 47, no. 1 (2014), 83–100.

Moonala 123 (YouTube username). "NYC Labor Chorus." Video recording. 2016. "Simple Song of Freedom." Words and music by Bobby Darin. Additional words by Jeff Vogel. https://www.youtube.com/watch?v=UNmaGCt8mQE.

Moonala123. "NYC Labor Chorus 2016." Video recording. 2016. "Life on Earth, So Amazing." Music from Handel's Hallelujah Chorus. Words by Jeff Vogel. https://www.youtube.com/watch?v=21aheK48cdY.

New York City Labor Chorus. *Workers Rise: Labor in the Spotlight.* CD. 2000. Directed by Geoffrey Fairweather. Recorded at Mirror Image Studios, New York City.

Newman, Richard. *Go Down Moses: A Celebration of the African-American Spiritual.* New York: Roundtable Press, 1998.

Nicholson, Phillip Y. *Labor's Story in the United States.* Philadelphia: Temple University Press, 2004.

Parmar, Priya, Anthony J. Nocella II, Scott Robertson, and Martha Diaz (eds.), *Rebel Music: Resistance through Hip-Hop and Punk.* Charlotte: Information Age Publishing, Inc., 2015.

Reagon, Bernice Johnson. *If You Don't Go, Don't Hinder Me.* Lincoln: University of Nebraska Press, 2001.

Robeson, Paul. *Here I Stand.* 1958. Reprint, Boston: Beacon Press, 1988.

Rocker, Rudolf. *Anarcho-Syndicalism.* Translated by Ray E. Chase. 1938. Reprint, London: Pluto Press, 2015.

Roscigno, Vincent J. and William F. Danaher. *The Voice of Southern Labor: Radio, Music, and Textile Strikes, 1929-1934.* Minneapolis: University of Minnesota Press, 2004.

Rosemont, Franklin. *Joe Hill: The IWW and the Making of a Revolutionary Working-class Counterculture.* Oakland: PM Press, 2015.

Rosenthal, Rob and Richard Flacks. *Playing for Change: Music and Musicians in the Service of Social Movements*. New York: Taylor & Francis, 2011.

Ross, Robert. "Bread and Roses: Why the Legend Lives On." In *The Great Lawrence Textile Strike of 1912: New Scholarship on the Bread and Roses Strike*, edited by Robert Forrant, Jurg K. Siegenthaler, Charles Levenstein, and John Wooding, 219–230. Amityville, NY: Baywood Publishing Company, Inc., 2014.

Rudd, Roswell. *Trombone for Lovers*. Sunnyside Communications, Inc. CD. Produced by Ivan Rubenstein-Gillis. 2013. Features NYC Labor Chorus on tracks 15 and 17.

Santelli, Robert, Holly George, and Jim Brown (eds.). *American Roots Music*. New York: Harry N. Abrams, Inc., 2001.

Santiago, Claude (producer). *The Last Poets: Made in Amerikkka*. 2012. Lussas, France: AndanaFilms. Documentary film.

Seeger, Pete, *Pete Seeger in His Own Words*, with eds. Rob Rosenthal and Sam Rosenthal. Boulder, CO: Paradigm Publishers, 2012.

Shevok, Daniel J. "Reflections on Freirian Pedagogy in a Jazz Combo Lab." *Action, Criticism, and Theory for Music Education* 14, no. 2 (2015), 85–121.

Slater, Judith J., Stephen M. Fain, and Cesar Augusto Rossatto (eds.). *The Freirian Legacy: Educating for Social Justice*. New York: Peter Lang, 2002.

Smiley, Tavis. *Death of a King: The Real Story of Martin Luther King, Jr.'s Final Year*. New York: Little, Brown, and Co., 2014.

Street, Joe. *The Culture War in the Civil Rights Movement*. Gainesville: University Press of Florida, 2007.

Thomas, Jim. *Doing Critical Ethnography*. Newburgh Park, CA: Sage Publications, Inc., 1993.

Tick, Judith. *Ruth Crawford Seeger: A Composer's Search for American Music*. Oxford, UK: Oxford University Press, 1997.

Various artists. *The Great Choral Convergence: Live!* CD. Bobbie Rabinowitz (Producer) and Labor Heritage Foundation. Recorded live, June 19, 2004, Washington Ethical Society, Washington, DC.

Volk, Terese M. "Little Red Songbooks: Songs for the Labor Force of America." *Journal of Research in Music Education* 49, no. 1 (2001), 33–48.

Weissman, Dick. *Talkin' 'bout a Revolution: Music and Social Change in America*. New York: Backbeat Books, 2010.

The Workmen's Circle. https://circle.org/.

Yetman, Norman (ed.) *Voices from Slavery: 100 Authentic Slave Narratives*. 1970. Reprint, Mineola, NY: Dover Publications, Inc., 2000.

Zinn Education Project. https://www.zinnedproject.org/.

Index

Aaron Copeland School of Music, 53
abolishment of slavery, 22, 52
abolitionists, 16, 21
activism: civil rights, 34; education and, 113–16, 140–42; immigrants' rights, 68; Kathy Goldman and, 114–15; Tom Carlson on, 116
Actors' Equity Association (AEA), 86
Adams, Tony E., 10
African Americans; and CIO, 30; community choruses, 6; and Great Depression, 26; NYCLC performances for community of, 50; and race riots, 35; racism against, 31. *See also* slavery; slaves
African American women; all-female singing groups, 35; in ILGWU, 28; NYCLC members, 137
"afterglow," 87, 88
age diversity, lack of, 139
aging of chorus, 112
"Ain't You Got a Right," 68–69, 90, 100, 102, 103, 104
"Ain't You Got a Right to the Tree of Life," 69
air traffic controllers strike, 3, 41
Alexander, Elizabeth, 75
Ali, Muhammad, 47
alienation, 6–7

Allen, William Francis, 20–21
Allende, Salvador, 66
Almanac Singers, 6, 29, 31–32
"Amandla! A Revolution in Four-Part Harmony" (documentary), 67
American Communist Party, 27
American Federation of Labor (AFL), 24, 30, 141
American roots music, 21–22
anarchism, 7–8
anarcho-syndicalism, 7–8
Anderson, Marian, 31
"And You Are Still Mine," 76
Anthony, John D., 45
The Anti-Slavery Harp: A Collection of Songs for Anti-Slavery Meetings, 21
anti-war songs, 70, 71
apartheid demonstration, 2
archival research, 14
Armillas, Rona, 46, 143
arts, as enriching life, 1
Arts & Culture Committee (ACC), 88, 89; membership in, 97, 124, 145–46; song selection and, 65, 81, 102, 116, 117, 126, 136
A. Simpson & Company, 20
Aunt Molly Jackson, 27, 138
autoethnography, 9, 10, 131
autoworkers, 31

auto workers strike, 31
awards; Clara Lemlich, 59, 101–2, 112, 114, 126; Joe Hill, 126

Baez, Joan, 54, 79
Bailey, Barbara; and 25th-Anniversary Concert, 91; and 25th-Anniversary Concert rehearsals, 86, 87, 88–89; and 25th-anniversay year, 94, 95, 96, 100, 102; as award recipient, 101–2, 126

background of, 41–43, 50; as board president, 3, 14, 124, 125, 126–27; as Clara Lemlich recipient, 101–2; on performances in schools, 112–13; on singing in schools, 52; ; and wake of Fran DeLairre, 98
Bakunin, Michael, 7
"Ballad for Americans," 45, 47, 115, 118–19
Ballard, Jana, 3; and 25th-anniversary year, 93–94; and 25th-anniversary year auditions, 96; and 25th-anniversary year final performance, 103; and 25th-anniversary year rehearsals, 86–89, 96–98, 99, 100–101, 102–3; and 25th-Anniversay Concert, 90, 91; and 25th-Anniversay Gala Concert, 75–76

background of, 55–56; contributions to chorus, 116–17, 127; on Cuba trip, 121; issues with performing during school hours, 113, 140; music quality and, 142, 143; political activism experience, 56; sense of community with chorus, 56–57, 109
banking tradition in education, 5, 140, 143
Barnicle, Mary Elizabeth, 29, 31
"Battle Hymn of the Republic," 23, 24, 80
Beck, Andy, 74
Belafonte, Harry, 46, 47
Bennett, Reggie, 4

Berlin, Irving, 68
"The Big Fat Boss, and the Workers," 27
The Big Red Songbook, 25
biracial groups, 32
blackface minstrel shows, 22
Black History Month, 50
Black Lives Matter, 2, 142, 146
Black Panther Party, 34, 35
Black Power movement, 34–35
Black Pride movement, 35
"Blowin' in the Wind," 96
"Blow Your Trumpet, Gabriel," 20–21
blues, 21–22, 29–30
Bluestone, Mimi, 89, 102
Boal, Agosto, 5
board of directors of NYCLC, 3, 11, 86; approval of concert programs by, 65, 70, 81; findings on leadership of, 123–24; formation of, 43–44; need to rotate members, 145; non-members, absence at meetings, 125; recruitment of members of color, 137; traditional songs and, 126. *See also* leadership
"Bourgeois Blues," 31
"Bread and Roses," 25, 79–80, 97, 98, 100, 102, 138
Bread and Roses Conference, 44
Brooklyn Women's Chorus, 52, 96
Brookwood College, 26
Broonzy, Big Bill, 29–30
Brown, Elaine, 35
Brown, William Wells, 21
Bryan, Alfred, 25
Butts, Calvin, 53–54

cannery workers, 31
capitalism, 6–7, 35, 79
Carawan, Candie, 69
Carawan, Guy, 69
Carl, Johnnie, 72
Carspecken, Phil F., 14–15, 107–8
"Casey Jones, the Union Scab," 24
"Celebrating American Labor Songs of the 1930s," 48

Central Park Summerstage, 45
Chaplin, Ralph, 24, 80
Chase, Murray, 78
Chattaway, Thurland, 78
"Chief Aderholt," 27
child labor, 81
Chile, songs from, 137
"Chinaman, Laundryman," 28
Chinese Revolution, 28
Civil Rights Act (1964), 35
Civil Rights movement, role of singing in, 34–35
civil rights unionism, 32
Civil Works Administration, 29
Clara Lemlich Award, 59, 101–2, 112, 114, 126
class consciousness, 6–7
classical music, 24, 73
classic songs, adding new lyrics to, 2, 24, 118–20, 126, 138, 143
classism, 9, 34–35
Cliff, Jimmy, 138
climate-justice movement, 2, 98, 141, 147
coal miners strike, 27
Cold War, 32–33
Comer, Ethel, 24
commodity fetishism, 7
Commonwealth Labor College, 26
"Common Thread," 74, 87
Common Thread Community Chorus of Toronto, 74
Communication Workers of America (CWA), 41, 50
Community Food Advocates, 115
comradery, 108–9
Congress of Industrial Organizations (CIO), 30–31, 32
content analyses, 14
Cooper Union, 45, 53–54
"Cotton Mill Colic," 27
country music, influence of slave songs on, 21–22
Crawford, Ruth. *See* Seeger, Ruth Crawford

Creative Outlet Dancers, 99
critical consciousness, 4, 5, 140
critical ethnography, defining, 9, 132
critical ethnography study; background of present study, 131–32; changes experienced by researcher, 146–48; data analysis, 14–15; ethical guidelines for, 10–12; how researcher left NYLC, 134; researcher experiences leading to NYLC, 132–34; validity, 14–15
critical ethnography study, conclusions on chorus, 135–46
community, sense of, 135–36; diversity, 137–40; education and activism, 140–42; leadership, 144–46; music quality, 142–43; remembering people and events, 143–44
critical ethnography study, data collection, 12–14; content analyses, 14; fieldnotes, 12–13, 15; focus group, 14, 15; interviews, 13–14, 15
critical pedagogy, 4–6
critical race theory, 9
critical theory, 8
Cuba: songs from, 137; trip to, 57–58, 109–10, 115, 121
cultural democracy, 6
cultural diversity, 137–38
Cumbo, Laurie A., 99

Danahar, William F., 26
Darin, Bobby, 70–71
data analysis, 14–15
data collection
content analyses, 14; fieldnotes, 12–13, 15; focus group, 14, 15; interviews, 13–14, 15. *See also* critical ethnography study
Daughters of the American Revolution, 31
Davis, Guy, 46
Davis, Ossie, 45, 47
Davis, Thulani, 54

DC Labor Chorus, 52
deconstruction, 6
Dee, Ruby, 45, 47, 53
DeLairre, Fran, 98
democracy, cultural, 6
Democratic Party National Convention, 44
democratic socialism, 81
"Deportee," 103
Depression. *See* Great Depression
deregulation, 7, 34
Derrida, Jacques, 6
dialogical data, 107
Dickens, Hazel, 138
diversity: conclusions on, 137–40; cultural, 137–38; in genres and messages of chorus, 117; as interview theme, 110–13; racial, 137–38
Dixon Brothers, 27
Doing Critical Ethnography (Thomas), 9
Donaldson, Rachel Clare, 28
Douglass, Frederick, 19, 21
"Down in the Valley," 115
"Do You Hear the People Sing," 100, 101
Du Bois, W. E. B., 22
dustbowl, 26

Earl Robinson Children's Chorus, 115
early labor movement, 1865–1928, 22–26
economic liberalism, 7
education; activism and, 113–16, 140–42; banking tradition in, 5, 140, 143; culturally relevant, 138; as human right, 81; as oppressive or liberating, 2, 4; problem posing, 140–41, 143–44
Ehert, Walter, 78
Eisenberg, Ricky, 68, 98, 122
Ella May (Wiggins), 27, 60, 138
Ellen's Stardust Diner, 92, 94, 116
Ellis, Carolyn, 10

"El Pueblo Unido" (The People United), 66, 104
"Emancipation Hymn of the West Indian Negroes," 21
Emerson, Laura Payne, 24
Emerson, Robert M., 12–13
Emma's Revolution, 74
Empire State College (ESC), 134
ethics, in ethnography, 10–12
ethnography, present study, 8–15. *See also* critical ethnography
evaluative/normative realm, 14, 15
Everton Bailey & the Instrumental Sounds of Praise, 90
Eyes on the Prize: America's Civil Rights Movement (documentary), 34

Fairweather, Geoffrey, 121; accomplishments as musician, 45; contributions to chorus, 52, 117, 123; death of, 50, 122; limited experience with activism, 56; and rehearsals, 121–22; remembrances of, 42–43
Farina, Mimi, 79
fascism, 31–32
Father of the Blues, 22
Federation of Nurses, 92–93
Feldon, Barbara, 54
"Female Suffrage," 25
feminism, defining, 9
feminist anarchism, 7
fieldnotes, 12–13, 15
Fight for Fifteen, 147
"Finlandia," 72
First Anniversary Celebration of the New South Africa, 45
First Red Scare, 28
Fisk Jubilee Singers, 22, 28
Fisk University, 22
focus groups, 14, 15, 118, 124
folk music, influence of slave songs on, 21–22
folk revivalist movement, 28–29
"Follow the Drinking Gourd," 97
Foner, Henry, 45, 46

Foner, Moe, 44
Food, Tobacco, Agricultural and Allied Workers of America, 32
Frankfort School, 8
Freedmen's Bureau, 22
"Freedom Songs," 32
Freire, Paulo, 2, 4–5, 135–37, 141, 143–45
Fretz, Rachel I., 12–13
Friedman, Laura, 41, 42, 51, 123–24, 145
Fruit of Labor Singing Ensemble, 52
"Fugitives' Triumph," 21

Gael, Ann, 43, 47–48, 94, 117
Gala Centennial Salute: Paul Robeson: Ol' Man River, 47
Garrison, Lucy McKim, 20
Gastón, Mariana, 57–58, 101
gender diversity, 110, 111–12
gender equity, 138–39
General Motors, 31
General Textile Strike (1934), 27
Georgia Sea Island Singers, 35
Ghana, 10
"Give Me Your Tired, Your Poor," 68, 87
"Glory," 137
Glover, Danny, 47
"Go Down, Moses," 22
"Going to Roll the Union On," 92
Goldberg, Whoppi, 47
Goldman, Emma, 7, 81
Goldman, Kathy, 102, 114–15
"Goodnight Irene," 33
gospel music, 21–22, 70
GQ, 58
Gramsci, Antonio, 7
Grant, Beverly, 138
Great Choral Convergence, 51–52
Great Depression, 26–31
Great Evenings in the Great Hall series, 53–54
Great Labor Arts Exchange (GLAE), 36, 60, 97, 103, 126
Great Migration, 23
Great Recession, 7, 134
Great War. *See* World War One
Greenberg, Bobby: and 25th-anniversary year rehearsals, 94–95, 98, 99, 102; background of, 47; as board vice president, 86, 87, 88–89; on diversity, 111; on Fairweather, 56; on Geoffrey Fairweather, 123; on lack of community, 49–50; on Schlosser, 55; on trips to Wales, 54; as vice president of board of directors, 124, 125, 127, 137
Green New Deal, 141, 147
"Guantanamera," 110
Guthrie, Woody, 26, 29, 30, 77; centennial of birth of, 78; joins military, 32; "This Land Is Your Land," 78; "Union Maid," 29, 78–79, 86, 92

Habermas, Jürgen, 14
Hackley, Emma Azalia
Halley, Paul, 76
Hamill, Pete, 54
Hamond, Eugene, 56, 109
Handcox, John L., 30–31, 66
Handy, W. C., 22
Harden, Tim, 71
Hard-Hitting Songs for Hard-Hit People, 29
Harkness, Georgia, 72
Harris, Bob, 93, 102, 121
Harry Van Arsdale Jr. Center for Labor Studies, 102
Hayes, Alfred, 24
Haywood, Carl, 66
hegemony, 7
Hendricks, Jefferson, 46
Henry, John, 77–78
Higgins, Lee, 6
Highlander College, 26
Highlander Folk School; biracial organizing and singing at, 32; and Civil Rights movement, 34

Hill, Joe (Joel Hägglund), 23–24, 46, 120
Hill, Velma, 46, 50, 88, 89, 99, 111–12, 122
hip-hop, 21–22, 35, 137
Hodges, Edward, 73
"Hold the Fort," 23, 31
Holliday, Billie, 31
Horton, Myles, 32
Horton, Zilphia, 33
"The House I Live In," 115
"How Can I Keep from Singing?", 74
Hudson River Sloop Clearwater, 54
Huff, Mac, 71
Humphries, Pat, 45, 74
Hurner, Sheryl, 25
Hurston, Zora Neale, 29
hymns, 20, 24, 34, 72, 74, 93

"I Am an Abolitionist," 21
"I Didn't Raise My Boy to Be a Soldier," 25
"If I Had a Hammer," 96, 100
"If You Can Walk You Can Dance," 74–75, 81, 91
"If You Want a Better Life," 138
"Imagine," 1–2, 71–72, 103, 117
immigrants; and labor songs, 23–24; undocumented, 101
Impact Repertory Theatre, 53
indigenous meanings, 13
indigenous rights, 141, 147
industrialization, 23
"The Industrial Workers of the World," 24
Industrial Workers of the World (IWW), 23–25; *Little Red Songbook* of, 24–25, 26, 80
"The Internationale," 28
International Ladies' Garment Workers' Union (ILGWU), 28
International Workers' Day, 101–2
interview findings, 107–27; activism and education theme in, 113–16; background to interviews, 107–8; community theme in, 108–13; conclusions, 127; current leadership theme in, 125–27; music quality theme in, 116–20; remembering past events, 120–22; remembering past leaders, 123–24; remembering past members, 122
interviews, 13–14, 15. *See also* critical ethnography study
IWW. *See* Industrial Workers of the World

Jackson, Molly. *See* Aunt Molly Jackson
Jara, Victor, 67
jazz, 21–22, 29
Jews, 49–50, 88, 137–38
Jim Crow, 32
"Joe Hill," 4, 24
Joe Hill 100 Road Show Tour, 25
Joe Hill Award, 126
"John Brown's Body," 23
"Johnny, I Hardly Knew 'Ya'", 70, 87
Johnson, Eustace, 44, 45, 51, 57
Jones, Bessie, 35
Jones, Denise; background of, 43, 50; on chorus as community, 109; on Cuba trip, 58; memories of deceased members, 122; on Peter Schlosser, 55; as soloist, 44, 80, 91, 92, 93, 104, 143
Jones, Marjorie, 20
Jones, Stacy Holman, 10
"Joyful, Joyful, We Adore Thee," 73
Justice Singers, 147

Karlson, Tom, 97, 98, 99; on activism, 116; background of, 96; on comradery, 108–9; poem of, 89–90
Karpf, Juanita, 6
Kasowitz, Jesse, 54, 97, 116
Katz, Daniel, 28
Kazan, Lainie, 49
Keats, John, 73, 75
King, Charlie, 51

King, Coretta Scott, 66
King, Martin Luther, Jr., 34–35, 52, 65
King: A Filmed Record: Montgomery to Memphis (documentary), 34
Kleinberg, Judy, 109–10, 112
Korstad, Robert R., 32
Kramer, Steve, 90, 91
Kropotkin, Peter, 7

Labor Arts, 126
labor colleges, 25–26
Labor Heritage Foundation, 36, 126
labor movement, early, 1865-1928, 22–26
labor songs, history of in workplace, 19–36; by abolitionists, 21; during Cold War, 32–33; in contemporary era of unions in decline, 33–36; during early labor movement, 1965–1928, 22–26; during Great Depression, 26–31; during McCarthyism, 32–33; by slaves, 19–22; during World War II, 31–32
Labor Songs Dedicated to the Knights of Labor, 23
labor strikes; air traffic controllers, 3, 41; auto workers, 31; coal miners, 27; metal workers, 77; miners, 77; shirtwaist strike of 1909, 25; textile workers, 26–27, 79
labor unions; air traffic controllers, 41; American Federation of Labor (AFL), 24; auto workers, 31; cannery workers, 31; communication workers, 41, 50; decline of, 33–36; and discrimination, 24; first major, 23; industrial workers, 23–24; Knights of Labor, 23, 24
ladies' garment workers, 28; membership decline, 33–34; and multiculturalism, 28; nurses, 59, 92–93; racism in, 30, 35; service employees, 90; sexism in, 30, 35; teachers, 59, 86; tenant farmers, 30–31; tobacco workers, 32; transportation workers, 95
Ladson-Billings, Gloria, 138
Lampell, Millard, 53
Last Poets, 35
The Last Poets: Made in Amerikkka (documentary), 35
Latin American songs, 66–67
"Lay the Lily Low," 27
Lazarus, Emma, 68
leadership, 125–27, 144–46. *See also* board of directors of NYCLC
Ledbetter, Hubbie (Lead Belly), 30, 31, 33
Ledbetter, Martha, 31
Left Coast Labour Chorus, 80
Lennon, John, 1–2, 69, 71–72, 117
"Let Us Speak Our Minds if We Die for It," 25
LGBTQ community, 9, 147
"Life on Earth, So Amazing," 75–76, 91
Lincoln Bicentennial Gala Concert, 53
Lindstrom, Nell (pseudonym), 126
Lipski, Barbara, 102, 104
Little Red Songbook, 24–25, 26, 80
Logan, Patricia, 43, 52–53, 117
Lomax, Alan, 29–30, 77
Lomax, John, 29, 30
"Lonesome Train," 53
"Lucy Neal," 21
The Lumpen, 35
Luthuli, Albert, 67
lynching, 31

macro-level social theory, 15
Madison, D. Soyini, 10, 132
Mann, George, 55
"Marching on to Victory," 25
Margolin, Julius, 55
Mark, Karl, 6–7
Marley, Bob, 138
Martin, Carlos Rafael Betancourt, 58
Martino, Kathy, 108, 111
Matthews, Dave, 54
McCarn, Dave, 27

McCarthy, Joseph, 33
McCarthyism, 32–33, 47
McCartney, Paul, 71
McGee, Brownie, 31
McLaughlin, Brian, 51
McRae, Percy, 47–48, 122
Meerpol, Alan, 31
metal workers strike, 77
#MeToo movement, 138, 147
"Mill Mother's Lament," 27
Mills, Kerry, 78
miner's strike, 27
"Miss Liberty" (musical comedy)
Moller, Vera, 24–25
Montgomery bus boycott, 34, 66
Moore, Fannie, 20
movements. *See* social movements
Murphy Institute for Worker Education and Labor Studies, 86
Museum of the City of New York, 101
"Music as a Weapon in the Class Struggle," 27–28
music education, Freirian pedagogy in, 5–6
music quality, 142–43
mutual aid, 7

National Association for the Advancement of Colored People (NAACP), 32
National Association of Negro Musicians, 6
National Folk Festival (NFF), 28
National Geographic, 53
National Labor Relations Act (Wagner Act; 1935), 30
National Labor Relations Board, 30
Native Americans, 78–79
"Negro Folk Songs as Sung by Lead Belly," 30
Nelson, Cary, 46
Nelson, Dennis, 59, 73; and 25th-Anniversary Gala Concert, 80, 90, 91; background of, 50; on music and social issues, 113–14; on Paul Robeson, 121; as piano accompanist, 3, 44, 51, 67, 80, 127; rehearsals during 25-anniversary year, 86–87, 99, 103; as soloist, 73
neoliberalism, 7, 34, 35
"The New Colossus," 68
New Deal, 28
New Era School, 66
new song *(nueva canción)* movement
Nineteenth Amendment, 25
"The Ninety and Nine," 24
Nobel and Holy Order of the Knights of Labor, 23, 24
"Nobody in the World Is Better than Us"
normative/evaluative realm, 14, 15
nuclear disarmament, 57
nuclear war, 115
nueva canción (new song) movement, 66–67
NYCLC (New York City Labor Chorus), 1; Appreciation Day, 91; Arts & Culture Committee, 65, 81, 87, 97, 102, 116; benefit concerts of, 44–46, 47–48, 52, 53, 54, 58–59; board of directors of, 43–44, 65; conductors (*See* Ballard, Jana; Fairweather, Geoffrey; Schlosser, Peter); Cuba trip, 57–58, 109–10, 114, 121; death of members, 85, 98, 122–23; debut performance of, 44; diversity of membership of, 3–4, 8, 49–50; elementary/secondary school performances, 52–53; as family, 127, 135–36; founding mothers (*See* Bailey, Barbara; Friedman, Laura; Rabinowitz, Bobbie); founding of, 3, 35, 41–42; fundraising concerts of, 3, 54; maturing chorus, 50–55; nonconcert events, 48; out-of-country concerts, 46; Paul Robeson centennial, 46–47; performances in historical buildings, 48–49; record keeping, 144; Sweden trip, 46; Triangle Fire commemorations,

57; Wales trip, 54, 57, 58, 87, 121; website, 144
NYCLC 25th-Anniversary Gala Concert, 65–81; conclusions concerning song set, 80–81; joy theme of, 73–75, 108; peace theme of, 69–70; struggle theme of, 65–69; twenty-five years theme of, 76–80
NYCLC 25th-anniversary year, 85–104; "afterglow," 87, 88; annual holiday concert and party, 95; concert, 89–91; end-of-year (Spring) performances, 101–2; final performance, 102–4; historic Women's March, 96; Labor Day parade, 85–86; March performances, 98–100; new members, 97–98; performance for nurses, 92–93; rehearsals, 86–89, 93–95, 96–98; singing for striking workers, 92; year-end celebration, 104

"O, Pity the Slave Mother," 21
Obama, Barak, 68
objective realm, 14–15
Occupy Wall Street, 7, 94, 118
"Ode to Workers," 73
Odetta, 118–19
"Oh Freedom," 30, 66
Old Crow Medicine Show, 78
"Old Kentucky Home," 21
Ono, Yoko, 71, 117
Oppenheim, James, 79
Ortega, Sergio, 66
"Our Battle Song," 23

"Peace by Piece," 69–70, 87–88, 90
Pedagogy of the Oppressed (Freire), 4–5
People's Songs, 32
People's Voice Café, 59, 98–99
Peress, Maurice, 53
Piantadosi, Al, 25
Pierre Deguyter Club, 28
Pinkard, Ginger, 43, 122–23

Pinochet, Agosto, 66
Plessy vs. Ferguson (1896), 23
Plunkett, Mary Ann, 54
political economy theories, 6–8
Pontarddulais Chorus, 54
Popular Front, 31–32
potluck celebrations, 95, 104, 136
"The Preacher and the Slave," 24
prisoners, 30
privatization, 7, 34
problem posing education, 140–41, 143–44
Professional Air Traffic Controllers Organization (PATCO), 41
Project Gutenberg, 21
protest songs; anti-war, 70, 71; during Great Depression, 27; during World War One, 25
punk, 35
Purifoy, John, 75

Queens College Chorus and Orchestra, 48
Queens Museum, 100–101
queer theory, 9
Quilapayún, 67

Rabinowitz, Bobbie, 41, 42, 51–52, 124
race riots, 35
racial diversity, 110–10, 137–38
racism; in AFL, 30; against African Americans, 31; blackface minstrel shows, 22; in craft unions, 35; in Jim Crow South, 32
radio, 26–27
Rainbow Coalition Conference, 45
Rainbow New Deal, 147
Reagan, Ronald, 3, 41
Reagon, Bernice Johnson, 35
recession (2008), 7, 134
Red Scare, 25, 28, 33
"Red Wing," 78–79
Reece, Florence, 27, 77, 138
Reece, Sam, 77
Reed-Danahay, Debra, 132

Reid, Betty, 43, 50, 57, 88, 97, 103, 112, 121
"The Relentless Walk," 4
religion-state alliances, 7
Republicans, and Southern Strategy, 35
restaurants, racism at, 31
Reverend Billy, 139
Ringwald, Roy, 68
Riverside Food Pantry, 53
Riverside Inspirational Choir, 53
R. J. Reynolds, 32
Robeson, Paul, 33, 46–47, 73, 118–19, 121
Robinson, Earl, 24, 53, 115
Rocker, Rudolf, 7–8
"Rockin' Solidarity," 80, 91, 92, 93, 94, 100, 102, 104, 143
rock music, influence of slave songs on, 21–22
"Roll the Union On," 31
Roosevelt, F. D. R., 26
Roscigno, Vincent J., 26
Rosenthal, Helen, 99
Rudd, Roswell, 4, 59

Sacco and Vanzetti, 28
Sanders, Bernie, 81, 86
San Francisco Bay Area Labor Heritage Rockin' Solidarity Chorus, 52
Sapp, Jane Wilburn, 68
Sarandon, Susan, 46
Sayles, John, 44
Schlosser, Peter; arrangement of songs by, 51, 66–67, 70, 74, 77, 123; chorus members opinions of, 55; contributions to chorus, 117; as interim conductor, 50–51; solo performers and, 143
school nutrition, 114–15
schools, performances in, 112–13
Schwimmer, Barbara, 58, 117
Seattle Labor Chorus, 52
Second Red Scare, 25
Seeger, Charles, 27–28
Seeger, Peggy, 138

Seeger, Pete, 118; and 25th-Anniversary Gala Concert, 74, 77; background of, 27–28; on board of directors, 123, 145; joins military, 32; ninetieth birthday celebration, 54, 76; and NYCLC, 32, 44, 45, 46, 47, 54; recommends Fairweather as conductor, 42–43; "To My Old Brown Earth," 76, 91; tribute to, 59; Woody Guthrie and, 29, 30
Seeger, Ruth Crawford, 27–28
segregation, legal in US South, 23
self-disclosure in present study, 131, 132
Service Employees International Union, 90
sexism, 30, 35
Shaw, Linda L., 12–13
Shevok, Daniel, 5–6
shirtwaist strike of 1909, 25
Sibelius, Jean, 72
"Si Me Quieres Escribit" (If You Want to Write to Me), 46
"Simple Song of Freedom," 70–71, 90
"Sing Along with Pete Seeger," 44
Sing Out! (journal), 33
Siyahamba, 46
slavery, abolishment of, 22, 52
slaves, history of singing for justice, 19–21
Slave Songs of the United States (Allen, Ward, & Garrison), 20–21
Smith, Rose Elizabeth, 24
SNCC Freedom Singers, 35
social class consciousness, 6–7
socialism, 81
social movements; anti-war, 34–35; Black Power, 34–35; Black Pride, 35; civil rights, 34–35; climate-justice, 2, 98, 141, 147; Fight for Fifteen, 147; indigenous rights, 141, 147; LGBTQ equality, 147; new song *(nueva canción),* 66; role of music in, 2; women's, 35
solidarity, 141–42

"Solidarity Forever," 24, 80, 86, 96
Solomon, Robbie, 69
Sondheim, Stephen, 117
"Song of Peace," 72
"Songs of Struggle and Protest: A Paul Robeson Centennial Anniversary Concert," 47
"Soul of the City," 119
The Souls of Black Folk (Du Bois), 22
South Africa, 2, 45, 67, 137
Southern Strategy, 35
Southern Tenant Farmers' Union (STFU), 30–31
South Wales Onllwyn Male Voice Choir, 47
Soviet Union, 32–33
Spanish Civil War, 33, 45–46
Spanish language songs, 137
spirituals, 22–23, 30
Springsteen, Bruce, 54
Squercieati, Marina, 54
Standing Rock, 141
"Stand Up, Ye Workers," 24
"Steal Away," 22
Stone, Lloyd, 72
Stonewall Chorale, 103
Stop Shopping Choir (SSC), 139
"Strange Fruit," 31
Strathairn, David, 54
Street, Joe, 35
strikes. *See* labor strikes
Student Non-violent Coordinating Committee (SNCC), 35
subjective realm, 14
"The Suffrage Flag," 25
suffrage movement songs, 25
Sussman, William, 46
Sweden trip, 46
Sweet Honey in the Rock, 35
"Swing Low Sweet Chariot," 22
Szymanksi, Sharon, 103, 104

Taft-Hartley Act (1947)
"Take Care," 44
Tallmadge, Emily, 23
Tallmadge, James, 23
Taylor, Marilyn (pseudonym), 48
tenant farmers union, 30–31
Terkel, Studs, 44
Terry, Sonny, 31
textile workers strike, 26–27, 29
theater of the oppressed, 5
"There is Power in a Union," 24
The Town Hall, 48–49
Thirteenth Amendment, 22
"This Land Is Your Land," 78, 100, 102
"This Little Light of Mine," 96
"This Old Hammer," 77–78
Thokoza, 45
Thomas, Jim, 9
Thomsen, Sara, 141
"Three Five-0", 102, 141
Thuli Dumakude, 45
Tick, Judith, 27–28
Tikkun Daily blog, 75
"Tina Sizwe" (The Brown Nation), 67, 87
Tin Pan Alley, 22
tobacco workers, 32
"Toiling on Life's Pilgrim Pathway," 27
"To My Old Brown Earth," 76, 91
Toronto, trip to, 120–21
transparency in present study, 131, 132
Transportation Workers Union, 95
traveling as a group, value of, 109–10
Triangle Fire Remembrance Coalition, 54
Triangle Shirtwaist Factory fire, 57, 100
Trump, Donald, 68, 89, 96
Truth, Sojourner, 35
truth claims, 14
Tubman, Harriet, 22, 35
Tucci, Maria, 54
"Two Little Strikers," 27

UFT Storytellers, 99
"Uncle Ned," 21
Union Caravan, 66
"Union Maid," 29, 78–79, 86, 92
unions. *See* labor unions

United Automobile Workers Union, 31
United Federation of Teachers (UFT), 59, 86
US Civil War, 70

validity, 14–15
Van Dyke, Henry, 73
Veterans of the Abraham Lincoln Brigade (VALB), 45
Vietnam War, 34, 71, 115
Vogel, Jeffrey; and 25th-Anniversary Gala Concert, 68, 71, 73, 74, 75, 88; and 25th-anniversary year, 92, 94, 101; background of, 43–44, 47; on Pete Seeger, 54; and Ricky Eisenberg tribute, 98; and writing new lyrics for old songs, 118–19, 126
voice culture, 6
Volk, Terese, 26
Voting Rights Act (1965), 35

Wagner Act (National Labor Relations Act; 1935), 30
Wales trip, 54, 57, 58, 87, 121
Ward, Charles Pickard, 20
war resistance, 71
War Resisters League, 115
war veterans, 70
Washington Ethical Society, 51–52
"Water Is Life," 141
Waterson, Sam, 53
"Weave Room Blues," 27
Weavers, 33
Weissman, Terri, 56, 94, 113, 115
Welch, Dave, 80
"We Made Good Wobs Out There," 24–25
"We Shall Not Be Moved," 31, 86, 92, 96
"We Shall Overcome," 32, 94, 96
West, Inez, 11, 50
"We the Africans," 67
Wever, Georgia, 94, 95, 118, 120–21, 139

"We Were There," 138
"When Johnny Comes Marching Home," 70
"Which Side Are You On?," 27, 77, 138
White, Josh, 31
Wiggins, Ella May (Mae), 27, 60, 138
Wilmeth, Kelly, 49
Wobblies. *See* Industrial Workers of the World (IWW)
Wolff, Milton, 46
women; all-female singing groups, 35, 45; Brooklyn Women's Chorus, 52; immigrant, in ILGWU, 28; #MeToo movement, 138, 147; songwriters during Great Depression, 27; suffrage movement songs, 25; voting rights, 25
women in labor unions; in CIO, 30; and discrimination, 24; songwriters in IWW, 24–25
Women's Emergency Brigade, 31
Women's Herstory Month, 99
Women's History Month, 97
Women's March, 96
women's movement, 35
Workers' Music League, 27
"Workers Rise: Labor in the Spotlight," 110, 119
Workmen's Circle, 49
Work People's College, 26
Works Progress Administration, 29
World War One, 23, 25
World War Two labor songs, 31–32

Yetman, Norman R., 19–20
"Yiddish in America," 49

Zanca, Debbie, 48
Zaslow, Lucy, 115–16
Zaslow, Richard, 115
"zipper" song, 66
Zuccotti Park, 94, 118

About the Author

Mark Abendroth at home in Albany, NY, with the mandolin that his maternal grandmother, Lorna Froberg, played.
Photo by Liliana Nova Abendroth, the author's wife.

Mark Abendroth first became engaged in social movements as a graduate student in the mid-1980s, when the global anti-apartheid movement applied pressure toward ending South Africa's racist regime. He is Associate Professor of Education at SUNY Empire State College. He is author of *Rebel Literacy: Cuba's National Literacy Campaign and Critical Global Citizenship* (2009) and several journal articles. He also co-edited *Understanding Neoliberal Rule in K–12 Schools* and *Understanding Neoliberal Rule in Higher Education* (both 2015).

www.ingramcontent.com/pod-product-compliance
Lightning Source LLC
Chambersburg PA
CBHW052046300426
44117CB00012B/2003